D0223233

Organizational Culture in Action

SECOND EDITION

To Keith, Matthew, and Laura, who gave the time and space to do the work and the love and support to make it worthwhile, and to my mother Harriette Laird, who is my perpetual role model and encourager.

To Angela, Eli, and Abigail, who gave the smiles, hugs, and laughter to remind me what matters most, and to my parents Ferne and Lawrence Driskill, who are always in the back of my mind as models of love and perseverance.

Organizational Culture in Action
A Cultural Analysis Workbook

SECOND EDITION

Gerald W. Driskill
University of Arkansas at Little Rock

Angela Laird Brenton
University of Arkansas at Little Rock

Los Angeles | London | New Delhi
Singapore | Washington DC

Copyright © 2011 by SAGE Publications, Inc.

All rights reserved. No part of this book may be reproduced or utilized in any form or by any means, electronic or mechanical, including photocopying, recording, or by any information storage and retrieval system, without permission in writing from the publisher.

For information:

SAGE Publications, Inc.
2455 Teller Road
Thousand Oaks, California 91320
E-mail: order@sagepub.com

SAGE Publications Ltd.
1 Oliver's Yard
55 City Road
London EC1Y 1SP
United Kingdom

SAGE Publications India Pvt. Ltd.
B 1/I 1 Mohan Cooperative Industrial Area
Mathura Road, New Delhi 110 044
India

SAGE Publications Asia-Pacific Pte. Ltd.
33 Pekin Street #02-01
Far East Square
Singapore 048763

Printed in the United States of America

Library of Congress Cataloging-in-Publication Data

Driskill, Gerald W.
Organizational culture in action : a cultural analysis workbook / Gerald W. Driskill, Angela Laird Brenton.—Second ed.
    p. cm.
Rev. ed. of: Organizational culture in action : a cultural analysis workbook. 2005.
Includes bibliographical references and index.
ISBN 978-1-4129-8108-8 (pbk.)
    1. Organizational behavior. I. Brenton, Angela Laird. II. Title.

HD58.7.D77 2011
302.3'5—dc22   2010022479

This book is printed on acid-free paper.

10 11 12 13 14   10 9 8 7 6 5 4 3 2 1

Acquisitions Editor:	Todd R. Armstrong
Editorial Assistant:	Nathan Davidson
Production Editor:	Libby Larson
Copy Editor:	Kristin Bergstad
Typesetter:	C&M Digitals (P) Ltd.
Proofreader:	Sally Jaskold
Indexer:	Ellen Slavitz
Cover Designer:	Glenn Vogel
Marketing Manager:	Helen Salmon

Contents

Part III. Cultural Data Collection and Interpretation

Part IV. Cultural Analysis Application

Preface

In 1984, Angela Brenton, PhD, introduced a course on Organizational Culture to the graduate students in the Masters of Interpersonal and Organizational Communication at the University of Arkansas at Little Rock. Her students came from a wide array of organizations (high tech to medical to industry) and positions in those organizations (management to Human Resources Development [HRD] to entry-level employees). This same array of students continued to participate in the Organizational Culture course when Gerald Driskill, PhD, began to teach the course in 1994. Over time, our approach to working with these students resulted in this application-focused workbook.

The workbook is a hands-on approach to learning to "read" organizational cultures and using that cultural knowledge in symbolic management, training, organizational change, building effective teams, supporting diversity, and unleashing creativity. It also serves as an introduction to qualitative research methods, introducing students to field observation, interviewing, qualitative surveys, content analysis, and other methods of textual analysis.

Students have consistently commented on the practical and powerful nature of the approach outlined in this workbook for their professional lives. We have developed this text as an applied workbook to supplement and apply organizational theory. It answers the two central questions we always hear from our students: "How can I understand the intangible culture that is so important to working in an organization?" and "How can I use this cultural information once I understand it?"

We are convinced that the application of this text could help new managers shorten their learning curves and avoid costly mistakes, while understanding the power of strategic symbolic managerial performances in creating identification and values. It could help the new MBA to choose a company consistent with her values rather than realizing after 6 months she "just doesn't fit here." It will reinforce to the training and development director the importance of storytelling in organizational socialization. It will equip those seeking organizational change to understand ways in which change must happen through the culture to be effective.

We believe the value of this workbook can be seen by viewing life in organizations through the lens of a drama metaphor. We discuss more in Chapter 1 about why a drama metaphor is particularly appropriate in studying organizational culture, and we use the dramatic framework throughout the text as an organizing frame. There are a number of practical implications for organization members and leaders from the drama metaphor. To create an effective performance, actors must determine appropriate and effective ways to perform their roles. To craft an effective performance, the actor must explore within himself or herself as well as exploring the script and the character through various means. The "organizational drama" may leave a new organization member with many questions about why certain things are done, what certain actions mean, or why certain actors gain power while others do not. The answers to these questions are often found "backstage" in unarticulated organizational values and norms. The study of organizational culture provides the backstage experience needed to understand appropriate and effective organizational performances.

In a similar vein, to become a director or cultural leader, you must go beyond an understanding of a given actor's role or script. To produce an effective performance, not only must directors bring the troupe together as a team, but they must also be aware of previous performances and various options for interpreting the play. Organizational leaders face the same challenges of understanding the role of history and heroes in shaping the current organization, of understanding how members interpret actions and statements, and of understanding the interpretations of the same event drawn by members of organizational subcultures. Understanding culture is critical for the organizational leader.

We each participate in multiple organizations, and that participation demands the art and skill of interpretation and presentation, of making sense of what is going on around us and then determining what messages we need to construct in response. We want you to complete this workbook with an increased awareness of the value of cultural concepts. Yet we also want you to be able to transform theories into practice. To reach these goals, we have integrated a variety of activities for application. Neither of us uses all of the suggested activities; we encourage you to select activities based on your needs and interests.

Acknowledgments

Those who made this workbook a reality easily come to mind. For any names we omitted, we accept the blame and ask your forgiveness.

- Our students, who have journeyed with us in learning about culture, refining methods for teaching it, and sharing with us ways they have applied what they learned in their organizations

- Alumni of our course, Lyle Steward, Amy Amy, Pat Sweeden, and Patricia Hawkins-Sweeden for their frequent guest appearances in the course.

- Thanks to the faculty and students who have provided a wide array of cultural analysis example papers to be found on the companion website.

- Applause to graduate program alumni who provided feedback that shaped the first edition of this workbook: Debbie West, Robert Mock, Michelle Young, Pat Sweeden, Patricia Hawkins-Sweeden (another strange coincidence—a married couple who are both now named Pat Sweeden), Jane Martin, Sherrie Sandor, Cheryl Johnston, Elaine Wooten, Martha Lowry, Tracy Pleasants, Wanda Culbreath, Hope Coleman, Brenda Winston, Lisa Rawn, and Michael Strobel; and to other course alumni who gave additional ideas for the second edition: Brenda Burks, Mary Stramel-Busby, Belinda Dix, Stacey Golleher, Tracy Guilbeau, Harper Grubbs, Jennifer Lewis, James Mathis, Rashad Moss, Elizabeth Philpott, Andrew Pyle, Adena White-Strickland, Rhonda Troillett, and Albert Whitney.

- Current and emeritus faculty in the Speech Communication Department who motivate us to aim for excellence in the scholarship of teaching: Mike Hemphill, Linda Pledger, Carol Thompson, Rob Ulmer, Kristin McIntyre, Julien Mirivel, Avinash Thombre, Alan Ward, Jerry Butler, John Gray, and Ralph Eubanks.

- Reviewers of various drafts who encouraged us to develop this project: John Gribas, Phil Clampitt, John Meyer, Linda Putnam, and Holly J. Payne.

- Writers and colleagues who have shaped and enriched our thinking with their contributions to the study of interpretive approaches to organizational communication: Chuck Bantz, Lee Bolman, George Cheney, Charles Conrad, Terry Deal, Stan Deetz, Eric Eisenberg, Buddy Goodall, Allan Kennedy, Joann Keyton, Bob McPhee, Joann Martin, Nick O'Donnell-Trujillo, Mike Pacanowsky, Gerald Pepper, Barnett and Kim Pearce, Linda Putnam, M. Scott Poole, Patti Riley, Linda Smircich, Beverly Sypher, and Karl Weick.

- To our common mentor, colleague, and friend for his support during our KU days and beyond, Cal Downs.

- To you, the colleague, student, and/or practitioner, for what you will contribute to your organizations and to the dialogue over improving life in organizations.

PART I

Cultural Analysis Planning

1 Introduction

Setting the Stage

> *All the world's a stage, And all the men and women merely players: They have their exits and their entrances; And one man in his time plays many parts.*
>
> —Shakespeare, 1564–1616, *As You Like It,*
> Burchell (Ed.), 1954, p. 42

Objectives:

- Reflect on the pervasiveness of organizations in our lives
- State the goal of cultural analysis
- Apply guides for selecting an organization for analysis

Stage Terms:

- Organizational culture
- Cultural analysis
- Organization
- Organizational performance

Cradle to Grave

When we ask students to name and describe an organization, they often first think of a workplace they have been a part of as an adult. However, by focusing on workplaces, we miss the great variety of organizations that shape and define us throughout our lives. Our first experiences in organizations were like many of yours: Bright lights and masked strangers welcomed us into a hospital birthing room. Since that time, we have lived, breathed, laughed and cried, worked or consulted with, and dreamed and been bored in a wide array of organizations including business offices, advertising agencies, nonprofits, universities, prisons, and day cares. Some of them have inspired us, and some of them have broken our hearts. All of them create expectations and perceptions that follow us all the rest of our lives. Beyond the myriad examples of tragic and comic tales we could each tell from our experiences as employees, we also have countless stories from our experiences as customers, volunteers, and patients. The point is clear—we cannot escape an inextricable connection with organizations. Yet we easily take for granted the impact of organizations, the very stages on which we live out our lives. We know when to show up, we know when something goes wrong with a piece of equipment or a relationship, but we rarely see the big picture of how all the various aspects of the stage impact us. The purpose of this workbook is to equip us to create more competent organizational performances. Such performances are grounded in learning the way our communication shapes and is shaped by the culture of the organization and national culture as well.

> *Organizations are places that carry us from cradle to grave by shaping our sense of identity, role, and meaning in life.*

In the years that have passed since the startling birth experience, we have come to believe that organizations are no more and no less than a significant stage for human drama. Our research on cultures in hospitals, engineering firms, churches, banks, airlines, phone companies, schools, and day care centers and our service experiences in hospitals, multinationals, and nursing homes have all underscored our conviction that organizations are far more than the places where we work and make money. They are places that carry us from "the cradle to the grave" by shaping our sense of identity, role, and meaning in life.

Thus, while our motivation to study organizations began with a pragmatic sense that our livelihoods depended on being able to work in organizations, a deeper, more fundamental concern has emerged. We want to improve our ability to shape and direct organizations in ways that are more humane. We believe such an effort to be fundamental to practitioners, scholars, teachers, and students, but more importantly as participants in the human drama. The goal of this workbook, therefore, is not simply to teach you how to conduct a cultural analysis, but it has implications for your role as a change agent within an organization and within your community. In short, the workbook is designed to help you by heightened awareness to do better what you do almost every day—make decisions about the best ways to lead and communicate in your organization(s). The quality of such decisions is enhanced through engaging in the process of conducting a cultural analysis.

FAQs on Cultural Analysis

This chapter sets the stage for conducting a cultural analysis by clarifying the approach we take in this workbook. While the remaining chapters provide greater depth on the "how to" of understanding and improving organizational performances, our goal here is to respond to seven common questions about the major approach and features of this workbook. As you review our responses to these questions you should gain a clearer sense of the process of cultural analysis, as well as criteria to consider in selecting an organization.

1. What Do You Mean by Organizational Culture?

We provide several definitions in Chapter 3. Our favorite is from Geertz (1973), that culture consists of the webs of significance that we have spun for ourselves. His definition highlights that culture consists of meaning and that it is constructed and interactive. Each organization has a unique way of doing things. Just as each national culture or civilization has its own unique language, artifacts, values, celebrations, heroes, history, and norms, each organization is unique in these same ways. At a deeper level, organization members create and/or are indoctrinated into unique beliefs and assumptions that form the basis for acting together. Some beliefs and assumptions may operate at a conscious level. Basic assumptions such as those about human nature and human relations are more likely to operate at the unconscious level. For example, I might just assume that supervisors make decisions and employees carry them out without ever consciously questioning that assumption. In contrast, when actors understand and identify with the history, norms, and values of a group, they can become a true ensemble cast by coordinating their actions more effectively with others'. They can also understand the symbolic significance of events and actions in a more thorough way and identify the many subcultures that together form and shape the overall organizational culture. This practical knowledge can then aid us in being ethical and responsible in the way we shape these cultures in our interactions with others.

2. Just What Do You Mean by a Cultural Analysis?

Just as anthropologists immerse themselves in a foreign culture to understand it, students of organizational culture use many of the same methods to understand an organization's culture. For example, they systematically observe artifacts and interactions, analyze written documents, participate in rites and rituals, and interview culture members about the meanings they attach to organizational objects and events. Interestingly, actors use many of the same techniques of observation, interviewing, and analyzing scripts in the process of crafting a credible and compelling performance on the stage or in film.

We define a cultural analysis *as a process of capturing the unique qualities of an organization as revealed in values, history, stories, and other elements created through interactions that have significance for organizational effectiveness and the personal development of members.* One way to gain clarity about the organizational cultural analysis process is to use analogies: to make connections between the familiar and the unfamiliar, the known to the unknown. One organizational culture class participant said that the cultural analysis process was like the *Wheel of Fortune* television game. In that game, participants have to fill in the missing letters of a phrase based on a clue from the moderator. If participants guess too early and get it wrong, they are penalized by losing a turn. And of course, if they guess too late, they risk losing to other contestants willing to take a risk. The challenge is to have enough information about the word puzzle to make a credible interpretation. In the same way, if you attempt a definitive interpretation of a culture too early in the process, you may pay the price of misunderstanding the culture. We also recognize that, at some point, you have enough data for a realistic (although not perfect) cultural interpretation, and you need to move ahead to application. We agree with the need to balance thoroughness with timely application, and you will learn in this workbook a process of cultural analysis that emphasizes careful reflection on cultural data combined with application. We have identified two different analogies as a way to clarify the process and to encourage you to move systematically through the five cultural analysis steps outlined in this workbook.

Gerald's Analogy: Paint My Numbers

We have a painting in our home of a wolf. The dark eyes and menacing face peer out from behind the white bark of aspens. The painting was our son, Eli's, first time to paint by numbers. Not true art you might say. Imagine, however, if Eli did not have a color and number code. He would have to determine colors that seemed best together. He would need to create a convincing palette that made the wolf come to life.

A cultural analysis is like painting with numbers and colors without the code for three reasons. First, the cultural analysis process does not begin with a blank canvas. The paint by numbers box comes with a canvas with lines and numbers on it; the colors are in the box. In the same way, organizations come with a barrage of colors and numbers. In Chapter 4 we label these colors as elements of culture (e.g., values, stories, rituals). You do not have to create these cultural elements; you do have to identify them. You will have to find a corresponding, convincing match for the color with a number in the culture. In short, you will be called on to create a credible interpretation.

Second, the analysis process requires an awareness of how your background and assumptions color the process. Eli has seen pictures of wolves (and a few at the zoo). He has ideas of acceptable hues. In the same way, we begin the process with experiences that literally *color* the process. Thus, no two analyses are going to be the same. Yet for the picture to be convincing to those who view it, one must discern how previous experiences influence the interpretation process. We discuss in Chapter 5 the process of *bracketing,* which involves recognizing our reactions and responses that color our interpretation.

Finally, the analysis process influences the researcher and the organization. Eli completes a paint by numbers and in the process, he is more aware of one way wolves may appear in nature. His painting also influences others who view it. In a similar way, the cultural analysis process influences our experience with life in organizations. You will attend to communication in ways that will be new to you. Our hope is you will become more adept and responsible in your communication based on this analysis. Furthermore, the questions you ask during interviews and the report you provide the organization will prompt reflection on and possible changes in communication practices. The potential impact of your analysis indicates the importance of maintaining high ethical standards in the process.

Angi's Analogy: The Jigsaw Puzzle

The cultural analysis is similar to putting together a complex jigsaw puzzle without having a picture on the box to guide your efforts. The point of this analogy is to understand the tensions between seeing parts versus the whole and to appreciate the impact the process has on the person doing the analysis. This metaphor applies in several ways:

First, it is often difficult to get a sense of the big picture when you are looking at individual pieces. Only after you have assembled a number of segments can you start to get an idea of the picture the puzzle will create.

Second, it takes both dark and bright pieces in most cases to assemble a complete puzzle. I recently read a story of a young girl who secretly stole pieces of a puzzle her family was assembling and hid them under the sofa cushion because they were so ugly. In frustration, her family began to despair of ever being able to put the puzzle together because so many pieces were missing. Only when the girl provided the dark pieces could the entire picture be revealed. Sometimes in our cultural analysis it is tempting to linger on the positive stories and upbeat images. They rarely form the complete picture. Sometimes you must provide the dark elements to understand the complete culture. Critical theorists such as Mumby (1993), Deetz (1991), and Deetz, Tracy, and Simpson (2000) have encouraged this phase of analysis.

Finally, the process of putting together the puzzle is often as important as the finished product. The mental exercise of seeing connections, of developing creativity, and of growing in patience and discipline will develop the puzzle builder even if the particular puzzle is not an interesting one. Chapter 8 guides you through this process of interpretation of cultural data.

Unlike puzzles, which have a set order and only one way for all of the parts to fit together, cultural analysis is a complex and interpretive pursuit. Four different people sitting around a table would see the picture from different perspectives and develop similar but varying pictures, and each of those constructions would have degrees of validity and usefulness for understanding the organization.

3. What Is an Organization?

Keyton (2005) defines *"an organization"* as a "dynamic system of organizational members, influenced by external stakeholders, who communicate within and across organizational structures in a purposeful and ordered way to achieve a superordinate goal" (p. 10). While we concur with Keyton's focus on "dynamic systems," our approach in this book takes a social constructivist perspective (Pearce, 2007). We view organizations as continually constructed and reconstructed through interactions. In other words, communication is not just something we do to one another, but our interactions are at the heart of the organizing process (Weick, 1979). This focus on communication as an organizing process suggests that while organizational members have "superordinate goals," the process of cultural analysis reveals the paradoxical, unintentional, and sometimes contradictory nature of these goals.

There are a wide variety of organizations, from churches, families, and civic, social, and nonprofit groups to government agencies and corporations. Today's organization is especially diverse, with virtual organizations, outsourcing, and multinational hybrids. The boundaries and membership of organizations are not always as cut and dried as they may appear. For example, who counts as a member of a professional sports team? Only the athletes, cheerleaders, and coaches? Team physicians who may be members of a medical practice but travel with the team on weekends? What about the die-hard fans who come to every game and may have a 50-year history of following a team? A significant decision you will face is who "counts" as an organization member and where you want to draw your boundaries of the organization. There is no single correct answer to how you define an organization. For some purposes, a researcher might want to define an organization more narrowly by focusing primarily on employees, while for other purposes an expanded view that includes organizational stakeholders might be more appropriate. In short, organizations are multilayered and multifaceted, consisting of individuals and groups with both common and competing interests.

4. What Is the End Goal of the Process?

Comments from practitioners who have applied this cultural analysis process provide examples of how they have used the cultural insights.

- I now have the ability to see situations from different frames.

- I got my last job because the interviewer was intrigued by my answers about organizational culture and how quickly I could "read" the organization.

- I have improved my ability to apply theory to the real world.

- I saved myself a lot of time and energy by deciding during an interview process that I didn't fit the culture. Even though the salary was great, I would have become frustrated quickly.

- I have gained a better understanding of my organization and the steps involved in a cultural analysis.

- Seeing how I impact an organization. It was a little upsetting to see how I could have made more of a positive difference. I wish I had known last fall what I know now.

- I have learned that in any organization, change must start with me.

Although you may not make one of these statements, we are confident that anyone completing this process will learn how to conduct a cultural analysis. You will also be taken through an application section that allows you to develop links between your analysis and organizational effectiveness, diversity, change management, symbolic leadership, and ethics. We included these application chapters because many students ask how they can use their new cultural insights in practical ways. We are convinced that culture gives a new and distinct lens through which to view organizational processes such as change, leadership, and the encouragement of diversity. We are confident that as a result of this workbook, you can become a more competent and assured actor in your organization, better able to understand and question basic organizational assumptions and practices.

5. Why Use a Dramatic Metaphor in This Text?

Viewing organizational life through the lens of dramatism has a long history, from Aristotle to Kenneth Burke (1972) and Erving Goffman (1959, 1974) to more contemporary writers. Boje, Luhman, and Cunliffe (2003) point out that writers have used the theater metaphor in two broad ways in describing organizations: those describing organizations as "like theater" (Goffman) and those who treat organizations as being theater (Burke). We see value in understanding organizations through a drama/theater lens, whether through Goffman's metaphor or Burke's literal approach.

Organizational life can be illuminated by examining it through the lens of theater. Organization members are actors who coordinate their actions in performances—some tightly scripted and traditional; others, improvised and informal. Like dramatic genres, organizational performances sometimes can be categorized by themes or archetypes. Some organizations are highly controlled with the emphasis on directors or stars, while others are ensemble casts. Some organizational performances by leaders have employees as intended audiences, while other performances involve all organizational members with consumers or policy makers as audience.

Pacanowsky and O'Donnell-Trujillo (1983) write about organizational communication as performance and say that organizational performances have four characteristics: they are interactive, contextual, episodic, and improvisational. Some performances are episodic on an interpersonal level—with two employees enacting an episode to determine power or credibility in their relationship. Others are larger organizational performances with a company trying to recover credibility after a crisis or mistake. As you conduct a cultural analysis, you will be challenged to listen in on performances. For instance, you might hear an employee story (episode) about what one coworker said to another (interactive) about recent layoffs (contextual) as they discuss the various ways organizational members are responding (improvisational) to management mandates.

Rehearsal 1.1 Applying the Drama Metaphor

Purpose: Identify the value and limits of the theater metaphor.

1. What value do you see in using the theater/drama metaphor to reflect on organizational life and communication?

    _____

    _____

2. What limits or possible cautions should we consider in using this metaphor?

    _____

    _____

6. What Is in This Workbook?

The workbook is organized around *five major steps* for conducting a cultural analysis. These steps are reviewed in the next chapter and provide the skeleton for this text. You will be taken through background material on the concept of culture before covering the basics of data collection, interpretation, and application. The major chapters share in common the following features:

- *Stage Terms:* At the start of each chapter we list important terms and concepts covered in the chapter. The reader may want to pay special attention to definitions and explanations of these terms contained in the chapter.

- *Connections:* In sections labeled "Connections" we assist the reader in making connections between theories and constructs and organizational practice by extended examples.

- *Rehearsals:* A variety of case studies and other activities are designed for hands-on experience with concepts. We incorporated activities that we have found enriching for workshop participants and students. You will find these activities in Rehearsal boxes in the workbook as well, at the ends of most chapters.

Each of the chapters builds toward a final project of analyzing an organizational culture in depth. You may want to analyze your own organization to understand its culture more fully, or you may want to practice your skills by choosing an organization of which you are not a member, or only a tangential part. Each choice has advantages and disadvantages.

7. How Do I Select an Organization for a Cultural Analysis?

There are a variety of factors to consider in selecting an organization. First and foremost, much depends on your goals for a cultural analysis. Use the following Rehearsal to determine your goals:

Rehearsal 1.2 Determining Your Purposes
for a Cultural Analysis

Purpose: Reflect on and identify possible purposes of the analysis you will conduct.

Check any of the following purposes that describe your reasons for conducting an organizational cultural analysis:

_____ Learn cultural analysis skills for work as a consultant

_____ Gain insight into another type of organization for career development

_____ Develop insight as a new employee to move up in your organization

_____ Learn to use cultural data to be a more effective leader in your own organization

_____ Identify ways to serve community organizations through knowledge of their respective cultures

_____ Learn about a different culture in an organization similar to your own to compare and contrast

_____ Other reason: _____

Your answers to these questions should influence your decision to do an analysis or audit as an "insider," a person who works for the organization you analyze, or as an "outsider," one who comes to the organization as a stranger. To facilitate your decision, we have outlined the pros and cons associated with each role.

As you reflect on your goals in light of the relative advantages and disadvantages of insider/outsider roles, realize that that these options may be viewed more as a continuum. Your relative knowledge and experience with an organization should be weighed. For example, in your own workplace, you may be new to the organization and/or industry, thus your knowledge of the culture and ability to work with the culture are far different from that of someone with extensive knowledge or experience. On the other hand, outside of the workplace, you may be a relative insider as a volunteer for the Arthritis Foundation or a church organization. You may also be somewhat of an insider due to weekly visits to a favorite restaurant or health club. Farther down the continuum toward being an outsider, you may never have worked for GM, but you have worked for another major auto company, and thus know something of the basic aspects of this industry. You may have read widely about a given industry, but have yet to visit an actual site. And then there are organizations that are completely alien to your world—you have heard of high-tech companies but have not read about, visited, or studied one.

The key to examining the pros and cons of the "insider" versus "outsider" perspective is more complex, and perhaps your decision ultimately comes down to your immediate and/or long-range goals for developing this skill set. We have found value, as have our students and workshop participants, in engaging in a cultural analysis with goals ranging from "becoming a consultant," to "learning the ropes as a newcomer," to "enhancing the way one serves in the community." Regardless of your decision, the steps we outline will guide you in gaining valuable experience in conducting an analysis.

Other considerations (in addition to outsider/insider) might guide your choice of organization as well. What contacts do you have that might provide access to an organization to analyze? What organizations might provide especially interesting sites to study for your personal or professional development? Organizations are particularly interesting sites at some stages, such as start-up of new organizations at which culture is being formed, or major organizational transitions such as downsizing or leadership changes at which culture is being modified.

You should have confidence in proposing a cultural analysis to a potential organization. The report you will provide is professional and has significant value to the organization. If we were doing such a study for an organization, it might cost them several thousand dollars.

Rehearsal 1.3 Identifying an Organization

Purpose: Identify organizations that you might make the focus of an analysis.

Steps:

1. Review the pluses and minuses of being an insider versus an outsider in the cultural analysis process in Table 1.1.

2. Consider an organization you might serve as an outsider/consultant and then list the top three reasons it would be advantageous to the organization for you to serve in this role.

   Organization:

   _____

   _____

   _____

3. Consider an organization you might serve as an insider and then list the top three reasons it would be advantageous to the organization for you to serve in this role.

   Organization:

   _____

   _____

   _____

Table 1.1

As an Insider in the Organization	
Advantages	*Disadvantages*
Ease of access	Lack of perceived freedom for analysis
Personal communication insights	Bias due to being enmeshed in the culture;
Potential value to your own organization	start with hidden assumptions
Time—ease of data collection	Too familiar, thus "see less," ask fewer questions
	People do not explain things to you the same way they would to an outsider as an outsider to the organization
Advantages	*Disadvantages*
Insights for career development	May misinterpret some cultural data
Skills for "newcomer" socialization	Access to the organization
Less familiar, thus "see more"	Time outside of job to collect data
See the more obvious layers of the culture	

Connections: The Value of Reflection and Critical Insight

This workbook will have the greatest value to readers willing to shift from going through the motions of acting on stage without reflection and critical cultural insight to full engagement in the production. Competent leadership in organizations involves going backstage; that is, active reflection on the cultural forces that shape communication practices and the way our communication practices shape culture. The steps previewed in the next chapter reflect a process that we all participate in each day. For instance, we decide what and how and when to communicate in our organizations; we decide what changes in organizational practices we can and/or should encourage or discourage; and we determine what changes we believe we are empowered or powerless to introduce. Perhaps most critical of all, we make decisions whether to reflect on our communication or remain somewhat unconscious of our influence in an organization. In all, we share in common the fact that our communication behavior is based on interpretive processes that we take for granted.

These day-in and day-out taken-for-granted interpretive processes are based on our informal "data collection" about our organizations (e.g., norms, what is allowed, what is expected, how to communicate, whom to communicate with). Based on our interpretations of these data, we act and react. Before reading this workbook, you may never have considered yourself someone who collected and used cultural data or thought of yourself as an actor on an organizational stage. However, you may have heard a story about a recent firing and wondered if all the details were true. You may have read a staff development workbook and been left wondering why no one seemed to follow the suggestions on career paths in the organization. Or you may have heard during a performance evaluation that no one else was having trouble with clients like "you are," and found yourself wondering about the norm: "Am I really that bad?" When faced with the mysteries or uncertainties embedded in these types of questions, we may become more aware of unspoken or unwritten rules and values in an organization.

This workbook assumes that we can always improve the quality of the data we collect and the accuracy of our interpretations, as well as our organizational communication performances in response to these data. As you move through this workbook, we hope you will be reminded of what we observe each time we cover this material in the classroom, in a training, or consultation—how and why we communicate in our organizations matters. To extend Shakespeare's well-worn analogy, our challenge is to be on the stage not merely as players or actors but also as co-directors and producers of the communication practices in our organizations.

> *We can always improve both the quality of the data we collect as well as our communication performances in response to these data.*

Summary

- An organizational culture involves the unique ways of doing things in an organization that are best captured by such elements of culture as the history, norms, and values of a group.

- A cultural analysis involves improving on methods we use each day in our organizations—we observe, ask questions for understanding, and read various documents such as newsletters. In the process of analysis we not only gain insight about the organization but may also improve our capacity for effective communication.

- How we define an organization is based on the boundaries of the membership. You will need to make a decision in the organization you analyze about who is considered a member, which may entail a narrow (employees, management) or a broad (customers, stakeholders, etc.) definition.

- The end goal of the process is to learn how to conduct a cultural analysis and make application of this analysis to critical aspects of organizational life such as ethics, change, and diversity.

- This workbook will help you understand the concept of culture as well as the basics of data collection, interpretation, and application. Pay attention to the key organizing features of the book: *Stage Terms*, to introduce relevant theories and concepts; *Connections*, to aid your understanding of concepts; and *Rehearsals*, both within the chapters and at the end of chapters to aid you in application.

- You should have a clear sense of how to select an organization for a cultural analysis based on the pros and cons of being an insider versus an outsider.

Rehearsal 1.4 Method Acting and Getting Real

Purpose: Reflect on your expectations concerning the process of conducting a cultural analysis in order to identify beliefs that may help or hinder your progress.

Overview: Method acting is a term that captures a major approach to training actors (Vineberg, 1991). At the core of this method is active observation of the real and genuine emotion (or mining the real experiences of the actor or actress). Strasberg (1987), the major proponent of this method in the United States,

(Continued)

(Continued)

notes that the procedures for developing an actor's capacity are "equally, if not more, necessary for the layman" (p. 201). This activity is designed to apply method acting concepts to your own work in the cultural analysis process. In short, the more you are real with your own reactions and emotions concerning the process, the more you will be able to overcome hurdles to making it a valuable experience.

Steps:

1. Briefly list two or three of your own initial reactions to this first chapter. What was clear? Unclear? What appeared promising for your own application? What emotions, if any, did this chapter evoke in you?

   _____

   _____

   _____

2. Have you had a previous positive experience with cultural analysis in which you gained insight into what "made an organization tick" or how to be more effective in an organization? What happened? What was your reaction?

   _____

   _____

   _____

3. Have you had a previous negative or confusing experience with cultural analysis? Perhaps you discovered information about an organization that was disappointing. Or perhaps you were baffled by why something happened in an organization. What happened? What was your reaction?

   _____

   _____

   _____

4. What will need to happen for you to have a positive, fulfilling experience in learning about conducting a cultural analysis? In particular, what concerns do you have? Questions?

   _____

   _____

   _____

2

The Significance
of the Stage

Most anyone entering an unfamiliar work setting knows the feeling of being an outsider. . . . Real wisdom in such situations means recognizing that the unspoken is more powerful than what can be conveyed through speaking. One gradually gains a sense of the feel, the smell, the personality of a workplace, a way of working, or a kind of work—though it may be difficult to translate all of this into words that an outsider could grasp.

—Louis, "Perspectives on Organizational Culture," 1985, p. 27

Objectives:

- Appreciate the value of a cultural analysis
- Explain the theories of social constructivism and structuration as a foundation for a cultural analysis
- Learn the five major steps in the cultural analysis process

Stage Terms:

- Construct
- Culture
- Structuration
- Social constructionism

The Tales We Could Tell

We all have stories about a wide array of experiences in organizations. These tales reveal the good, the bad, and the ugly about life in organizations. These stories prompt laughter and tears, meaning and confusion, love and hate, hope and fear. We have all been told and listened to stories mirroring these ranges of experiences. From mundane frustrations over time schedules, to anguish in dealing with a difficult boss, coworker, employee, and/or customer, to fears over a change, one theme common in organizational stories relates to the challenges placed on our communication abilities.

In order to gain a new perspective on our experiences in organizations, to shed light on the good, bad, and ugly found in our stories, we developed this workbook. In this chapter we introduce our personal hopes for you in this process, some history on the study of organizational culture, the value of cultural analysis, and the major steps in the process.

Any Hope of Change?

Unfortunately, theory is not always translated in a way that will assist us with the range of difficulties listed above. It is not uncommon to hear the following complaint against theory: *I don't see how this theory helps my life now!* In the midst of reading, reflecting, and theorizing about organizational communication, we have been asked fair and challenging questions like the following:

- Is all of this work of analysis really worth it?
- How can I apply the cultural information I'm learning?
- Can a cultural analysis really help me bring change to my organization?
- Given the ingrained nature of communication habits, is it realistic to expect change in myself or in the organization?

Our reply to such questions continues to be the same: If we were to say no, then we would see the need to give up not only on the teaching enterprise but on the human experience as well. As educators and as human beings, we hold an optimistic view of the human condition: that we are all capable of change and growth. As far as personal changes go, we have had the good fortune and blessing of witnessing changes not only in our communication behavior but also in others as a result of courses and workshops that use the learning approach presented here. However, for this workbook to work, for any development in our communication abilities to happen, we have to be willing to play 100%. Organizational change is also possible. Many change efforts fail because they are undertaken without sufficient knowledge of the nature or importance of organizational culture. We note throughout the text that knowledge of culture is essential for significant organizational change.

While we *affirm that change is possible*, it is often difficult and uncomfortable. We have developed habitual ways of acting and reacting. Changing ingrained habits in any area, whether it is nail biting, reactions in conflict, a golf slice or tennis serve, is not easy. Often in the change process we get worse before we get better because the new behavior seems unnatural. Our old response was unconscious, and in contrast we must think constantly about the new behavior. Only in time does the new behavior fade into the comfortable, the taken-for-granted. Strasberg (1987) comments on the basic premise of method acting—that to create a performance that seems natural and unpracticed takes many hours of practice and preparation. He writes, "The preparation of every art must be conscious—you must know how and what you are going to do. Don't trust your inspiration. . . . Then being trained in the method do it to the best of your ability. Conscious preparation, unconscious result" (p. 79). So while this workbook will provide the tools for change, ultimately we realize that it takes a longer period for the new behaviors and habits of interpreting and developing messages, and for organizational change strategies, to take root. The significance of the construct called "organizational culture" is that it can aid in this change process.

We also provide a number of other applications of cultural knowledge in addition to change—symbolic leadership, diversity, ethics, and organizational effectiveness. We believe that cultural knowledge can help you choose the right job, can help you become socialized in an organization, and can help you as a leader in understanding the motivations and values of your employees.

A Bit of History

We recognize that *culture* is a *construct*—a term or concept used to explain events or various phenomena. A construct is "a theoretical creation that is based on observation, but cannot be observed directly or indirectly" (Babbie, 2001, p. 21). Culture, like other constructs (e.g., personality, intelligence, motivation, climate, attitude), has value if it helps us make sense of our world. Thus, as we discuss this construct, it is important to understand that the term has its own story to tell. A brief history of this construct also suggests the enduring value of the study of culture to organizational life.

Culture became a buzzword in the late 1970s and the 1980s. Popular books, such as Deal and Kennedy's (1982) *Corporate Cultures: The Rites and Rituals of Corporate Life* and Schein's (1992) *Organizational Culture and Leadership* introduced the general public to the concept. About the same time, Pacanowsky and O'Donnell-Trujillo (1982) introduced communication scholars to the concept of organizational culture, although the notion of interpretive studies had emerged in the social sciences in the 1970s. Their basic premise was that organizations needed to be studied as cultures of interest for their own sake: as places where we "gossip, joke, knife one another, initiate romantic involvements, cue new employees to ways of doing the least amount of work that still avoids hassles from a supervisor, talk sports, arrange picnics" (p. 116). Pacanowsky and O'Donnell-Trujillo (1983) recognized the explicit link between cultural competence and the metaphor of acting in their article "Organizational Communication as Cultural Performance."

Over time, a variety of approaches to studying organizational culture emerged. We discuss these approaches in the next chapter. In brief, some organizational consultants see culture as a variable that can be manipulated in organizations to achieve more positive outcomes, and they talk about pragmatic uses of cultural information. Researchers who operate from a more interpretive framework question whether culture can be manipulated and are more interested in in-depth studies of how culture is created, maintained, and changed through social interaction. Still others, known as critical theorists, contend that the use of cultural data can become a tool focused solely on serving managerial interests. They believe a cultural analysis should focus on hidden, taken-for-granted, and potentially abusive uses of power (Deetz, 1991). Whether you take one of these contrasting approaches or a middle position, such as the one we advocate, cultural knowledge has important implications.

Descriptive studies of organizations capture insights into communication practices that might otherwise go unnoticed. For example, Mary Helen Brown (1990) described a typology of stories told by employees to socialize new employees in a nursing home. That typology might be used in future studies to determine the effectiveness of various narrative techniques in socialization. More recently Meares, Oetzel, Torres, Derkacs, and Ginossar (2004) examined employee stories of mistreatment in the workplace and illuminated how some voices were privileged over others. Their study provided implications for organizational strategies to treat all employees with respect and dignity. In addition, the researchers suggest strategies for employees to "gain voice" to resist unjust treatment.

Furthermore, a cultural analysis may provide insight into communication patterns that have proved frustrating. Most of us, for example, could tell stories of dealing with a management dictate that makes little sense. We may feel trapped by a culture and constrained in our communication choices. As Scott Adams (1996), the creator of the *Dilbert* cartoon, illustrates, a business plan has two steps: (a) "gather information" and (b) "ignore it" (p. 162). While we may find humor in frustrated *Dilbert* characters dealing with meaningless business plans, none of us likes to be in those roles. The power of analyzing a culture is that new options might emerge that had not been seen. For instance, employees might find that a cultural ritual had been so ingrained and unconscious that it had blinded them to more effective ways to interact.

Rehearsal 2.1 Creativity and Constraint

Purpose: Discern how communication behaviors involve both novel or creative responses to inherent tensions as well as more stable or constrained responses.

1. Describe a taken-for-granted practice in your organization.

2. How was/is this practice created through interaction?

3. How does it constrain future interaction?

Example: In most classrooms, teachers are in an authoritarian role. They direct interaction in the classroom setting, and the students (for the most part) sit passively at attention and obey directions given by the instructor. This pattern of authority is created through interaction. Each class that the teacher and students have enacted over their educational careers has reinforced the authoritarian role of the teacher and the submissive role of students to the point that most students would not think of violating the expectations or enacting a different kind of role. This pattern, present in varying degrees depending on larger national culture norms, constrains more egalitarian roles in the classroom. Many students would resist behavior by a teacher asking them to take a more active role in setting their own educational goals and taking responsibility for their own learning. Conversely, certain questions or more assertive student behavior is often constrained by patterns of teacher authority.

In summary, culture, as a construct, continues to appear in the popular and research literature (Eisenberg & Riley, 2001; Frost, Moore, Louis, Lundberg, & Martin, 1985; Goodpaster, 2007; Kotter & Heskett, 1992; Stohl, 2001; Toor & Ofori, 2009). The continued use of this construct suggests that it is not merely a fad. Culture appears to be something almost every organizational member recognizes as important. Our goal is to refine our understanding of this construct so that we can best use it in the conduct of an organizational cultural analysis. Two overlapping theories help us build a bridge between theory and practice.

Introducing
Two Practical
Theories

We sometimes have our students write down their definition of *communication*. As we process these definitions, we discuss how we all hold implicit theories about communication (Edwards & Shepherd, 2004). We share two theories in this section to illuminate the communication processes that shape the organizational cultures you will be studying.

Structuration

A theory called "structuration" helps explain the grassroots nature of culture, how members shape culture, and also how culture constrains their actions (Giddens, 1979). Structuration assumes that both choice and constraint are simultaneously present in our communicative behaviors. A review of structuration theory illustrates the practical nature of this theory in the context of studying the culture of an organization (Poole, Seibold, & McPhee, 1986).

The term *structuration* implies that we are constrained by structures (i.e., social norms, organizational decision-making hierarchies) but that we participate in maintaining, changing, and defending these structures in an ongoing process (Poole, 1992; Poole et al., 1986). For example, according to this theory, each time I decide to follow a management directive, although I may feel constrained by the directive, my willing submission to the directive adds to the power of such directives in the future. We also have the choice to disobey the directive, which may result in a revolution within the system (or being fired!). Kirby and Krone (2002), for instance, argue that employees in a federal organization communicated about work–family policies in ways that created expectations (structures) that made employees hesitant to act on available policies. Structures are thus reproduced through our collective action because their constraint on our actions is often not at the level of our consciousness.

For another example, consider a church organization. Do members continually question how to celebrate a ritual, such as communion, or how to select leaders or conduct worship? If you are like most of us, you simply take such structures for granted as the way things are done. In some denominations, however, these very processes are challenged at some point, such as when ordination of women was first proposed in some churches. This point of change is the time when the unconscious structure moves to conscious questioning, and a time when a new structuration process, over the years, may create a new taken-for-granted reality. In other words, as humans, we actively participate in creating and re-creating the determinative power of our communication structures.

The process of structuration is part of what we seek to understand in the study of culture. We study how organization members create values, norms, and metaphors, as well as the binding force or power of culture once it is developed. We also consider the process of cultural change at periods in which members challenge existing ideas.

Social Constructionism

This process of structuration is related to the second theorectic frame that informs our work. Social constructionism assumes that our interactions with one another create our most basic understandings of life (Berger & Luckmann, 1966). Put differently, families, groups, organizations, and cultures are created by people in conversation (Pearce, 2007). This theory places the significance of our communication behaviors in the foreground. For instance, creative risks in an organization are more likely to occur in the context of members telling stories about being rewarded for such risks. Creative risk as a value in the organization is derived from the power of members talking to one another. Stephens and Davis (2009) studied how interaction in meetings creates norms about use of electronic devices and multitasking during meetings. Even though the issue may never be discussed explicitly, interaction patterns build expectations about how employees will use smart phones or other electronic devices during meetings.

Unethical or potentially harmful organizational practices can be viewed from this perspective as well. You may have faced situations in which you felt that an organizational culture and relationship with management dictated your decisions. Such constraint may be a problem if you believe the decisions might be unethical or harmful to the company. From a social constructionist perspective, if you follow the dictates, you are reinforcing these negative cultural patterns. A recent example is the risk-taking behavior of Wall Street firms that created bundled security products in the last decade, leading to a global recession. Individuals throughout the financial sector both consciously and unconsciously created this pattern. What is the nature of the culture not just of a single firm, but of a financial sector that created such high expectations for earnings and rewarded extreme risk-taking that resulted in such an outcome? How did the government regulatory structure contribute to this industry culture? Until we understand these deeper social construction dynamics, simplistic solutions of limiting executive compensation will have little effect on preventing similar crises in the future. The analysis process can provide insights into such fundamental questions. Answers to these questions underscore the benefits of studying culture.

Lyon (2008) provides answers to some of these questions. He studied communication patterns at Enron and concluded that language use and communication styles in the culture created social capital for individuals who talked about the "new economy," engaged in combative communication tactics, and possessed a nonindustry brand of "smartness." The culture led to these behaviors being interpreted more positively within the company than they subsequently were judged by objective outsiders. These behaviors were viewed by outsiders as keys to the company's collapse.

Connections: Benefits of Studying Organization Culture

The structuration and social construction processes imply the importance of paying closer attention to culture. The study of culture focuses on symbolic processes that facilitate shared meaning (Morgan, 1986). Because "cultures are communicative creations, they emerge and are sustained by the communicative acts of all employees, not just the conscious persuasive strategies of upper management" (Conrad & Poole, 1998, p. 116). This relationship between communication and culture suggests multiple benefits of a cultural analysis. As you review this list, we encourage you in Rehearsal 2.2 to capture these and/or other benefits most relevant to your organization. A cultural analysis can

- Provide a picture of major beliefs and values in the organization that influence communication practices and therefore help determine the kinds of communication skills needed in the organization
- Prompt reflection on the relationship between national and organizational communication patterns and norms
- Help organizational members see communication practices that go unnoticed, such as important rituals and routines or ways power is exercised for ethical/unethical purposes

- Create insight for new job orientation and job promotion practices

- Empower organization members in integrating ethics and values more deeply into organizational structures and practices rather than treating them as superficial training programs that have little effect

- Assist employees in determining cultural/value fit as they consider employment or service opportunities

- Improve the change management process by uncovering cultural strengths and potential problem areas

Rehearsal 2.2 The Value of a Cultural Analysis

Purpose: Identify what you believe would be the primary values of an analysis for your organization.

Steps:

1. Review the bulleted points above.

2. Write down the language you would use to capture *two potential values* of an analysis of your own organization or of the organization you are considering as a focus for an analysis.

_____

_____

_____

_____

_____

_____

_____

3. You might consider possible problems you currently perceive in the organization and describe how a cultural analysis would help you better identify solutions to these problems. Or you might reflect on current changes being considered or implemented and ways a cultural analysis would help in the process of change management.

_____

_____

_____

_____

_____

_____

_____

Cultural Analysis in Practice

This workbook introduces a five-step process for conducting a cultural analysis. When you have learned the process, you will have a set of tools for understanding the communication norms, the resources for and obstacles to introducing change, as well as insights for developing your own leadership communication practices. The five major steps are as follows:

* Articulate the value of the culture metaphor
* Define major cultural elements
* Use multiple data collection methods
* Synthesize and interpret cultural data
* Identify applications

1. *Articulate the value of the culture metaphor.* The concept of culture needs to be understood beyond the popular business literature on improving corporate culture. Understanding the richness of this concept will help us clearly articulate the value of a cultural analysis for organizations and for ourselves.

2. *Define major cultural elements.* We review research on and examples of elements such as stories, rules, and heroes. The importance of being aware of these elements is that each one provides a different vantage point on the often hidden aspects of organizational life. Too often an analysis will focus on one element to the exclusion of others.

3. *Use multiple data collection methods to understand the elements of culture.* We demonstrate the importance of using multiple methods as we focus on observations and systematic analysis of organizational texts to gain a rich data set. Surveys and interviews will also be introduced as alternative, but more obtrusive methods, for both insiders and outsiders. "Obtrusive" means how obvious the research method is to organizational members, thus how likely to alter their behavior.

4. *Synthesize and interpret cultural data.* You will be challenged to draft an interpretation of an organization. The notion of an interpretation is important in that a culture analysis does not claim to be an objective and neutral video recording. Instead, the analogy we use is that of a dramatic performance, like a play. Two directors may take the same play and stage two very different productions based on different interpretations of the written word. Indeed, the assumption with a cultural analysis is that an objective and neutral cultural recording is impossible. Instead, the individual (or team) works to provide a meaningful, valuable, and valid interpretation.

5. *Identify applications.* Like any good dramatic interpretation and presentation, an effective cultural analysis should inspire new insights. Again, because this process is not linear, these insights may occur before you have worded your final interpretation. In the final section of the text, you will be challenged to reflect on various application arenas including organizational effectiveness, diversity, change management, symbolic leadership, and ethics.

Summary

The following key ideas were introduced:

* Change in our own as well as organizational communication behaviors is enhanced by knowledge of culture.

* A *construct* is a term or a concept used to explain events or various phenomena—as a construct, culture was popularized in the 1970s and early 1980s.

* As a theory, *structuration* refers to the idea that we are constrained by structures (i.e., social norms, decision-making hierarchies, etc.) and that we participate in maintaining, changing, and defining these structures in an ongoing process.

- Social constructionism refers to the idea that our social worlds, such as families, organizations, and national cultures, are created through interactions.

- Seven major benefits of studying organizational culture include the following:

  1. Provide a picture of major beliefs and values in the organization that influence communication practices and therefore help determine the kinds of communication skills needed in the organization

  2. Prompt reflection on the relationship between national and organizational communication patterns and norms

  3. Help organizational members see communication practices that go unnoticed, such as important rituals and routines or ways power is exercised for ethical/unethical purposes

  4. Create insight for new job orientation and job promotion practices

  5. Empower organization members in integrating ethics and values more deeply into organizational structures and practices rather than treating them as superficial training programs that have little effect

  6. Assist employees in determining cultural/value fit as they consider employment or service opportunities

  7. Improve the change management process by uncovering cultural strengths and potential problem areas

- The five analysis steps include:

  1. Articulate the value of the culture metaphor

  2. Define major cultural elements

  3. Use multiple data collection methods

  4. Synthesize and interpret cultural data

  5. Identify applications

Rehearsal 2.3 The Value of a Culture Analysis

Purpose: Develop a convincing newsletter style article that conveys the value of conducting a cultural analysis.

Overview: Depending on your role as an insider or an outsider as well as on your relationship with the organization you analyze, you might find it helpful to take a step beyond the brainstorming activity on describing the value of a cultural analysis. We encourage you to take initiative and actually write an article that would argue for the merits of a cultural analysis. Such an article would have the pragmatic benefit of introducing your organization to the concept of cultural analysis.

Whether you propose to study your own organization, or you make a request to study a different organization, you will need to provide an explanation and rationale for the cultural analysis process. Why should a company want to do it? What benefits could they expect? This Rehearsal might yield information surprising to you. Furthermore, it might yield information of value for publication in a company newsletter.

(Continued)

(Continued)

Steps:

1. Read a research article (i.e., on the topic of organizational culture). As a research article it should be in an academic journal as opposed to a popular press magazine. It should include review of research literature, methods of analysis, and results. A research journal, if recent, will sometimes contain information about organizational culture studies that have not been picked up in the popular press.

2. Determine from the article two or three specific benefits of understanding the culture of an organization. You may want to add additional benefits discussed in Chapter 2 or that you identified in your brainstorming activity.

3. Summarize these values of the cultural analysis process in a one- to two-page (length will ultimately be determined by your organization/publication outlet) article that uses language that would be welcomed by members of your organization.

4. Use a format that would be appealing, like a newsletter style (e.g., catchy title, headers, bulleted points, relevant examples from your organization and the article).

PART II

Cultural Analysis Basics

3

Step One— Understanding the Concept of Culture

Constructing the Set

* **Articulate the value of the culture metaphor**

Define major cultural elements

Use multiple data collection methods

Synthesize and interpret cultural data

Identify applications

Man is an animal suspended in webs of significance he himself has spun, I take culture to be those webs.

—Geertz, *The Interpretation of Cultures*, 1973, p. 5

Objectives:

- Explain the concept of culture
- Differentiate between the different images and metaphors for understanding organizations
- Recall the three "levels" of organizational culture
- Deduce that most organizations do not have a single commonly understood "culture"
- Discuss the approach to defining culture used in this workbook

Stage Terms:

- Culture as a variable
- Levels of culture
- Culture as a root metaphor
- Metaphor

Good News, Bad News

To enhance our performances on the stage, we have to be clear about what play we are performing. The set construction will be determined not only by the play but also by the director's interpretation of the work. In short, in order to construct the set, we need to define the term *culture*. The good news is that culture can be defined. The bad news is that different ways of defining the term can sometimes lead to confusion. The examples below are just a few of these differing takes on the term *culture*.

- Culture is the way things are done in the organization (Deal & Kennedy, 1982, 2000).
- Culture is "a basic pattern of assumptions . . . that has worked well enough to be considered valid, therefore, to be taught to new members as the correct way to perceive, think, and feel in relation to these problems" (Schein, 1992, p. 9).
- "Culture is a system of shared symbols" (Geertz, 1973).
- "Organizational culture is the set(s) of artifacts, values, and assumptions that emerge from the interactions of organizational members" (Keyton, 2005).

The differences in definitions reflect important assumptions about what to study when analyzing culture. Each definition may produce different but useful views of organizational culture. Popular literature on organizational culture may not make the differences clear, and consultants and managers may not realize the importance of these differences. For example, if culture is just one more facet of an organization, then it may be changed as easily as a strategic plan or office layout. If culture is something an organization is, then it may be harder to change and should be considered in all other decision making within the organization.

The Concept of Culture

Smircich (1983) provides a good beginning place for defining culture by raising the key question concerning organizations and culture: Does the organization have a culture or is it a culture? According to Smircich, there are two major ways culture has been studied in organizations: as a variable and as a root metaphor. Most current research and consultation on cultures take one of these approaches or a combination of both. These two approaches indicate the richness and diversity of ways to study culture. Understanding these approaches will aid you when you pick up other books or articles on the topic of organizational culture in that you will better understand their focus. Furthermore, these differing approaches provide a backdrop for the approach we take in this workbook. After outlining major approaches to studying culture, we introduce our blended approach that foregrounds the role of qualitative research used to capture cultural elements, themes, and definitions that have practical significance for the organization you study.

Culture as a Variable

The culture-as-a-variable approach focuses on causality. Culture is thought to be able to predict and thus cause certain outcomes. You might view culture as variable "X" (values, norms, etc.) that is influencing variable "Y" (e.g., productivity). This relationship, as you might imagine, is complex due to the fact that culture is not an easily defined variable. For example, try to answer the question, *What makes a culture "good" or "strong"?* and you will find that the answers are not easily placed in a formula. Based on the variable approach, a manager who does not have a clear understanding of the complexity of the culture variable might say something like: "If we could just get our culture stronger, our productivity would go up." The challenge or potential problems arise when this same manager attempts to strengthen the culture without a clear sense of what is to be strengthened and how culture influences productivity. Are values to be changed or strengthened? History to be heightened? Setting to be enhanced? This approach also begs the larger question about whether it is possible for management to change culture, or whether culture is a deeper phenomenon that emerges out of the interaction of employees over long periods of time. Pepper (2008) offers the interesting example of PLH Technologies, an organization that spent millions to build a new corporate headquarters that would reinforce and display an organizational culture of openness, modernity, and fun. The new structure with its open floor plan, walking tracks, picnic areas, and glass walls was perceived and used by employees much differently from the executives' plan. It actually inhibited open communication and was seen as counter to organization values.

In the above example, the complexity of the variable of culture is evident. Within the variable approach, however, there are two lines of inquiry: internal variable and external variable. The variable approach may focus on internal variables thought to influence culture. In this instance, organizations are viewed as producing culture as evidenced in such cultural artifacts as rituals, heroes, and norms. Consultants and researchers are therefore interested in exploring aspects of culture (e.g., leadership values, norms, structures) that predict organizational survival and effectiveness (Collins, 2001; Deal & Kennedy, 1982; Peters & Waterman, 1982).

The variable approach is also evidenced in comparative or cross-cultural management research that takes into account culture as an external variable. As an external variable, culture is seen as a map for navigating differences across organizations and differences in national cultures. This approach tends to focus on ways to tap into national cultural differences to improve productivity or competitiveness (Moran, Harris, & Moran, 2007; Ouchi, 1981). For example, Mexican organizations have been compared with U.S.-based organizations in their orientation to time and relationships (Condon, 1997). In this comparison, the variable of national culture is used to explain why, for example, Mexicans tend to give priority to talk surrounding relationships whereas the U.S. norm is to have a greater task focus. Hofstede (2003), in a similar vein, has done extensive research on five underlying value assumptions that differentiate workers in one national culture from another. He considers these value assumptions as a "software of the mind" and thus central to exploring communication behaviors (Hofstede & Hofstede, 2004). A web-based resource has been developed that provides country scores from over 50 countries and 3 regions (Hofstede, n.d.). For example, cross-cultural comparisons depict the U.S. culture as highly individualistic in comparison to countries in South America and in the East. Given the widespread recognition of international economic interdependence, the importance of understanding national cultural influences will only increase. In fact, "nearly two-thirds of all U.S. companies conduct business internationally" (Eisenberg, Goodall, & Trethewey, 2010, p. 8).

Understanding the influence of national culture on organizational culture is an important, and often overlooked, aspect of organizational culture analysis. For instance, more recently, research has explored value dimensions to explain the U.S. role in the 2008 global financial crisis (Hofstede, 2009). This research will be discussed further in Chapter 11 where you will explore cultural data in light of ethics an communication. There is no doubt that many of the deepest unconscious assumptions we bring to our work life are often rooted in our cultural socialization. As Figure 3.1 summarizes, some researchers have

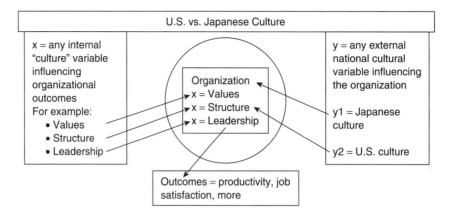

Figure 3.1   The Variable Approach to Culture

focused on cross-cultural organizational studies. The approach to cultural analysis that we take in this text, however, involves delving into the unique patterns of an organization. In organizational cultural analysis we seek to describe the patterns of assumptions, beliefs, practices, and artifacts that make an organization unique.

Root Metaphor

This second major approach to the study of culture focuses on understanding how organizational members create cultures and how the culture affects the members who are a part of it. It is more about culture as process than as product or variable. The core idea of this approach is that culture is something an organization "is" versus culture as something an organization "has." Thus, for example, if someone were researching or consulting with a Wall Street investment firm, consultants using the variable approach might determine how cultural practices led to organizational problems and seek to modify those practices. In contrast, a scholar or consultant operating from a root metaphor concept of culture might attempt to develop a deeper understanding about how cultural values and assumptions led to some of the surface practices. The goal would be deeper understanding of the influence of culture, not necessarily modification. Yet as you might infer from this example, both see the pragmatic value of understanding culture.

There are three major research traditions within the root metaphor approach. Researchers in these traditions formulate or focus on different aspects of culture.

1. *Culture as shared cognition.* In this tradition, the beliefs or assumptions of the members of the culture are the focus on the inquiry (Harris, 1979; Schall, 1983). Researchers examine how employees think and what patterns of logic are shared among organization members. Researchers, for example, might describe assumptive differences between members of the same organization who come from different national cultures (Auer-Rizzi & Berry, 2000; Driskill & Downs, 1995).

2. *Culture as systems of shared symbols.* This research places a focus on the actual language, nonverbals, and other organizational symbols (Eisenberg & Riley, 2001; Geertz, 1973; Smircich, 1983). A consultant or researcher using this approach might observe and record interaction patterns to understand and describe the way members use language to manage conflicts or build friendships (Jameson, 2001).

3. *Culture as the expression of unconscious processes.* This focus involves an exploration of the way symbols reflect underlying beliefs and assumptions of the members. Such research might explore the deeper unconscious meaning of a common metaphor used in the organization or on the underlying archetype that predominates the lives of the members (Jung, 1964; Levi-Strauss, 1967). For instance, Forbes (2002) explores the way women's discourse reveals dominant masculine values.

A visual depiction of these approaches captures the contrast (Figures 3.1 and 3.2). The internal variable approach assumes that culture is one element of an organization that can be studied and used to make predictions about organizational effectiveness. In the same vein, the external variable approach addresses culture as a force outside the organization, such as the norms of the larger national culture (e.g., Japanese vs. U.S. culture). In contrast, the root metaphor approach assumes that the organization is the culture and therefore, depending on how culture is defined, various aspects of the culture may be explored.

Organization
(management,
effectiveness,
structure,
values,
communication,
etc.)
=
Culture

Figure 3.2   The Root Metaphor Approach to Culture

Connections: Definitions, Levels, Metaphors, and Our Approach

These contrasting approaches to the study of culture suggest four practical connections. *First, definitions matter.* Definitions guide analysis. Definitions determine what we pay attention to or ignore. Therefore, it is important to keep several questions in mind before you embark on an analysis. You need to determine the following:

1. How will you define culture? *For example:*
   - As a variable? Internal? External?
   - As root metaphor?
   - Shared beliefs? Shared symbols? Unconscious processes?

2. How will the results be used? For example:
   - Change the culture?
   - Adapt to the current culture?
   - Determine ethical or unethical practices?
   - Assist multinationals via cross-cultural comparisons?
   - Identify effective and ineffective communication action/patterns?
   - Make unconscious processes part of our consciousness?

These basic questions, if bypassed, can lead to misunderstandings and frustrations. For example, you might be convinced of the root metaphor approach to culture and create a descriptive picture of the current culture, only to be confronted with a disappointed organizational leader who gave you access to the organization with the understanding that you would be giving recommendations on creating a more productive organizational culture. Or you might embark on a culture-as-variable approach only to find that cultural change is harder to achieve than you anticipated without deep employee involvement and sufficient time.

Rehearsal 3.1 How Do You Define Culture?

Purpose: Identify commonly held definitions of culture as well as your own definition.

One way to keep theoretic and definitional discussions from being meaningless is to engage in writing your own definition. Based on the review of perspectives above, answer the following questions:

1. What definition of *culture* do you believe to be most commonly held in your own organization?

   _____

   _____

   _____

   _____

2. How do you define the term *culture?*

   _____

   _____

   _____

   _____

Second, to understand culture, the reader should realize that not only are there varying definitions of culture, but also that culture can be viewed as having different levels. Schein (1992) describes organizational culture as consisting of three levels:

- Artifacts and creations such as technology, art, and behavior patterns (what we describe in this text as elements of culture)
- Values held collectively by the group
- Basic assumptions held by group members concerning relationship to the environment; the nature of reality, time, and space; the nature of human nature and activity; and the nature of human relationships

Schein explains that the deepest levels of culture, basic assumptions, operate at the preconscious level and affect our behavior without our critical awareness. We are more aware of our values, and can observe our artifacts and process, but often we do not understand their connections to our values and assumptions.

To illustrate Schein's levels, you might observe an organizational ritual in a factory of workers clocking in and out as they begin and end their workday. To fully understand the cultural meaning of that behavior, it would be necessary to dig deeper into values and assumptions. The time accountability might be based on assumptions about time, the inability to trust the honesty of workers, and accountability of employees to supervisors.

A third way to understand cultures, in addition to definitions and levels, is through metaphors. Morgan (1997) presents a multitude of images as a way to understand and capture our experience in organizations. These images range from common metaphors such as systems or cultures to less common images, such as prisons. Bolman and Deal (2008) take a similar approach but focus on four specific metaphors or frames for viewing organizations. Each frame (structural, political, human resource, and symbolic) represents a way of viewing organizations. For example, the structural frame focuses on organizational charts, work processes, and role definitions. Managers operating within this frame will tend more readily to see organizational problems and possible solutions in terms of role uncertainty versus role clarity. The political frame focuses on the use of power in the organizations and how interactions are structured to maintain or challenge power. The human resource frame directs attention to the training and motivation of employees. The symbolic frame is similar to what we present in this workbook as culture and views the organization as enactment of theater through symbols, stories, and performances that create meaning for employees.

Rehearsal 3.2 Playing With Metaphors

Purpose: Reflect on insights gained from identifying metaphors in an organization.

1. What metaphor would you use to describe your organization?

    _____

    _____

    _____

    _____

2. What are implications, both positive and negative, of this metaphor?

    _____

    _____

    _____

    _____

The value of reflecting on images or metaphors should be clear: Metaphors capture the assumptions we hold about ways to think and communicate about problems and solutions in organizations.

They may also be one way to get at the unconscious level of assumptions that Schein describes as the deeper layers of culture. Metaphors correspondingly provide clues to alternative ways to think about how we manage our communication behavior. For example, an image of an organization as a prison captures the reality of certain political restraints in an organization. Members of an organization or unit in such an organization might say things like, "I feel trapped here" or, "We don't hear much besides where to move next, never why." Such comments reflect the constraints members of this culture see in their organization. Leaders seeking to work with employees operating with this image of the organization may run into difficulty if they try to deny these perceptions. Saying "You have no reason to feel trapped" would do little to change things. Instead, the challenge for leaders and employees in this situation would be to explore the aspects of the culture that are influencing these perceptions (e.g., history, norms, rituals). The core challenge is to remember that we live by the images we hold; thus, we are both constrained and enabled by what we view as possible or impossible in our communication behavior.

The cultural analysis process can serve to make us aware of the dominant images held in an organization as well as the images we hold: These images or metaphors influence our communication behavior every day. Cultural analysis can be used to learn how our images of organizations can be obstacles as well as how we can use insights from cultural analysis to become better problem solvers and leaders. For example, if managers became aware of their excessive focus on the structure of an organization (e.g., roles and routines), they might be more likely to explore other metaphors or ways of thinking about their organization. If they were to include reflection on the political frame or power issues (a political metaphor), they might be more likely to reflect on structures in terms of how communication roles need to be clarified as well as communication norms about why and how decisions are being made.

Metaphors matter, and a cultural analysis can help reveal the implicit metaphors influencing the way we communicate and coordinate our behaviors. Part of the power and value of a cultural analysis comes from the fact that organizational members not only create but also maintain and transform organizational meanings and expectations. Thus, the challenge for individual members is how to use insights from an analysis to improve their own use of messages as resources for growth and change for themselves and their organization, rather than focusing on only the constraints embedded in the messages. Such a shift from constraints is made more likely if we understand and reflect on the metaphors operating under the surface. Chapter 4 further explores metaphors as one of the elements of a cultural analysis.

Fourth, this discussion of culture sets the stage for the blended approach taken in this workbook. Are we left with the choice of variable versus root metaphor approaches? Are we to focus on levels of culture or metaphors alone? We do not see these approaches as incompatible. We draw from multiple perspectives, while developing a comprehensive and complex interpretation of culture. *Our focus is on using qualitative research skills to capture cultural elements, themes, and definitions that have practical significance for the organization you study.* We hold four assumptions about culture in advocating a blended view:

- Culture creation, maintenance, and modification are both top-down and bottom-up. Leaders cannot unilaterally create or enforce organizational values and artifacts; however they can be quite influential in shaping the overall climate and values of the organization by what they focus on, what they reward, and how they model organizational life. All organization members must buy in and be genuinely involved for cultural change to occur. Any member of the organization may serve as an impetus for change.

- Cultural knowledge empowers organization members, rather than exposing them to managerial manipulation. Critical theorists have often characterized culture as "unobtrusive control" of employees. Some have questioned whether gaining employee identification with corporate values undermines their own best interests. We believe that promoting more conscious awareness of cultural processes and influences among all organization members equips them more powerfully to achieve organizational change. While cultures can be constraining, as we discussed in the previous chapter in describing structuration theory, they can also be the means of creativity and change.

- Even thick descriptions of organizational culture provide practical implications for organizational growth and change.

- Organizational cultures are both enduring and dynamic. While organizational change at a deep cultural level is not easy or fast, it is possible.

These assumptions are carried in the remaining chapters as we guide you through the process of conducting a cultural analysis. In Chapter 4 we introduce cultural elements that are foundational to the study of a culture. We believe that studying multiple elements encourages a valid and credible analysis as opposed to an exploration of a single feature of the culture. The focus on qualitative research skills (e.g., observation, systematic analysis of organizational texts such as newsletters, and in-depth interviews and open surveys) does not preclude you from using other types of quantitative data (e.g., a standardized survey on job satisfaction). It does suggest that culture is not a concept that can be easily captured through brief or easily constructed surveys. Beginning in Chapter 5 we review various qualitative research skills aimed to sharpen what you do throughout your day—observe, read, talk to others, ask questions.

Our approach has a bottom line of enhancing your performance as well as that of your organization. We will do this by enhancing your awareness of various cultural elements (Chapter 4), sharpening your ability to collect and interpret data about these elements (Chapters 5 through 8), and then guiding your application of insights from the cultural analysis (Chapters 9 through 14). Our experience and that of our students and clients has proven valuable for improving our understanding of organizations and our ability to lead and serve these organizations. Our hope is that the cultural analysis process will assist us in our efforts to be better observers, interpreters, and thus leaders and managers who not only survive but thrive in the organizations that greet us at birth and carry us to the grave.

Connection: Writing a Cultural Analysis Proposal

Depending on your purposes, you may or may not need to create a formal proposal. We have provided an example to guide you in the process. If you gain permission to conduct an analysis, you may still need to use the template below to guide you in responding to common questions. Furthermore, this example provides reminders about the importance of protecting participants via confidentiality. In some cases, you may be in a university context where full Institutional Review Board (IRB) approval is required. We discuss this process further in the introductory section to Step Three. We encourage review of the example below to guide you as you work on Rehearsal 3.3, "Writing a Cultural Analysis Proposal."

To: Chief Executive Officer

From: Your name

Overview

This proposal seeks permission to conduct a cultural analysis of your company. An organization's culture is revealed by the values, history, stories, heroes, practices, and norms that make an organization a unique place to work. Strong cultures have been linked by some research to cohesive work groups, clear understanding and commitment to the values and mission of the organization, and lower turnover.

What is involved in a cultural audit?

We would need permission to interview _____ members of your organization in confidential interviews, preferably during work hours. Each interview would last 45–60 minutes. Interviews would include the following types of questions:

- What is it like to work here?
- What types of individuals get ahead here? Why?
- Does the organization give any employee awards or recognition? For what?
- What types of events does the company sponsor for employees?
- What is different about working here than working at another similar organization?
- What does a new employee need to learn to fit in here?
- What type of individual would not be happy working here?
- What is a story that illustrates what this company is like at its best? Worst?

We would also need permission to "walk around and observe"—to see how offices are configured and decorated, what visitors to the organization encounter, how routine tasks are done, and how employees work and interact with one another. If we could have the opportunity to observe representative meetings or events during the period of the study, that would also be helpful in understanding the culture. We would also do analysis of the website, written publications, memos, and e-mails that are generally available to employees of the organization. The time period of the study would be approximately four weeks.

Deliverable product

Upon conclusion of the study, you will receive a written report summarizing what we learned of your organizational culture and its implication for your company. You will also have an option for an oral presentation of results to whatever groups(s) you may choose within the organization.

What are the benefits to your organization?

A cultural analysis can probe whether values are widely shared among employees, and whether organizational practices support organizational values and priorities. For example, one company we studied was attempting to make a transition to a team-based culture, yet we discovered that all awards and benefits were based on individual accomplishment. Cultural information can also be of value in employee recruitment, selection, and orientation. Knowing the current culture is vital in promoting successful organizational change attempts, as well as in promoting values of ethics and diversity within the organization. Cultural knowledge is also vital to effective leadership.

Considerations:

1. Employees need to be promised confidentiality in order to feel comfortable in offering candid information in the interviews. This means that the source of information will not be revealed at any point in the report or oral presentation.

2. Our study and report of your organization is offered for your benefit and we promise to maintain confidentiality of the information we collect. We would seek your permission if we ever chose to publish any information from the study, and the identity of your company would be protected in any external use if you agreed.

3. It is important that employees receive some feedback from the process. Therefore we encourage clients to release an executive summary of results to employees at the end of the study.

Consultant:

Attach a brief bio, stressing your professional and academic experience. If you are a student, you might emphasize that your work is overseen by your professor, and include a brief bio from your professor as well.

Summary

We can easily get tangled in the web of culture if we do not pause to understand it. A failure to pay attention to how the set is constructed, how the construct culture is defined, can lead to problems. A practitioner, for example, might pick up a cultural survey, measure the culture, and then assume changes suggested by survey results will result in a payoff for the company. Although well intended, such efforts may fail from a lack of understanding of what is being measured. Several major ideas were introduced in this chapter to head off such problems and to lay the foundation for the rest of this workbook:

- The culture-as-a-variable approach focuses on internal (values, rules, etc.) or external (national culture) variables that are thought to predict important organizational outcomes (productivity, employee satisfaction).

- Cultures should be understood as having multiple levels or dimensions. Some levels exert influence on organization members at an unconscious level.

- The culture-as-a-root-metaphor approach focuses on describing the organization. These descriptions differ depending on the way culture is perceived (shared beliefs? shared symbols? shared unconscious processes?).

- Culture can be understood as consisting of three levels: artifacts and creations such as technology, art, and behavior patterns, values held collectively by the group, and basic assumptions held by group members.

- The dominant images or metaphors (prisons, structures, etc.) that are held by members of the organization influence their communication behaviors, for example, the way problems and solutions are identified.

- Culture is often complex and thus not easily captured through brief or easily constructed surveys. Therefore we will rely on a combination of qualitative research methods to improve the validity of the process of cultural analysis.

- Our goal is to guide you in the "how-to" of conducting an analysis as well as the how-to of applying insights for improving such important aspects of organizational life as managing change and ethics.

Rehearsal 3.3 Writing a Cultural Analysis Proposal

Purpose: Develop a formal proposal for conducting a cultural analysis in an organization.

Steps:

1. Identify the person (CEO, HRD manager, etc.) you know to be the one to contact concerning the analysis. It might be useful to have some informal visits first, before sending the formal proposal.

2. Develop a 1- to 2-page proposal in which you:
   - Identify who you are and your relationship to the organization
   - Review the basic goal of a cultural analysis
   - Discuss the advantages or value of the analysis—be specific and when possible connect it with relevant issues within the organization (e.g., if you know turnover has been high, you could discuss the way an analysis often uncovers socialization practices)
   - Gain agreement on confidentiality of individual responses or identifying data collected during the cultural analysis

3. Have a trusted colleague critique or review your proposal before sending it.

4. Schedule an interview to discuss your proposal.

Note: A formal letter of permission is required for your project, even if you are studying your own organization.

4

Step Two—Identifying Cultural Elements

Understanding Roles

Articulate the value of the culture metaphor

★ **Define major cultural elements**

Use multiple data collection methods

Synthesize and interpret cultural data

Identify applications

The burglars came in the back door about midnight. They knew the layout of the restaurant and went right to the office and demanded money from the safe. When I first saw them I was with the store manager by the dishwasher some 30 feet from the office. They wore ski masks and each held something like a pipe. I still recall the command: "Everybody get down and stay where you are." I hit the floor as fast as I could and my manager was right there on the floor with me. We waited and in a few minutes we heard laughter and then a scuffle. I craned my neck and saw the district manager, who happened to be in town to evaluate our restaurant, picking up one of the burglars while trying to pull off his mask. I did not hear what was said next, but in a few minutes both burglars were running for the back door and all that we heard was the district manager's laughter. I do not recall the district manager's name, but I do recall the look on his face when we let him know that it had not been a joke and that he had just thwarted a burglary.

Objectives:

- Gain an awareness of major cultural elements
- Identify a variety of types of cultural data

Stage Terms:

- Elements of culture
- Values
- Symbols
- Stories
- Language
- Metaphors
- Artifacts
- Heroes
- Outlaws

- Rituals

- Rules

- Organizational communication style

- History

- Place

The Making of a Legend?

What stories stand out in your mind from past experiences in organizations? The story above grew from an event in 1978 when Gerald worked as a restaurant manager. The story was repeated often in the coming weeks, and no doubt the legend of the brave manager spread beyond to other restaurants in the chain. This legend illustrates the fact that stories are one of the most common means of transmitting organization culture. They are rich with information about informal and unstated rules and about roles such as heroes and villains.

Most of us seek clarity about our own roles in an organization. Yet it is useful to examine what method acting, a widely accepted approach to actor training, teaches actors about roles (Strasberg, 1987). An effective performance grows from becoming a true ensemble, an acting troupe that has such intimate communication with one another and with the set (props, etc.) that where one scene begins and another ends, where one player's lines end and another's begin are almost indistinguishable. In short, the audience gets the sense that the actors are part of a whole (Vineberg, 1991). What does this analogy say about our roles in an organization? Effective organizational members learn to pay attention to more than their own individual roles. This chapter will introduce you to various cultural elements that help shape and serve as resources for effective individual, team, and organizational culture performances.

The term *elements of culture* may be defined as various facets or windows that reveal the culture(s) of an organization. We understand from structuration theory, however, that symbolic elements create the culture as well as reveal it. Studies of organizational culture may rely on one element, such as stories (Barge, 2004; Brown, 1990; Harter, Scott, Novak, Leeman, & Morris, 2006) or rules (Jabs, 2005; Schall, 1983). Yet to rely on only one element provides a less comprehensive view of an organizational culture. For example, imagine hearing the story at the beginning of this chapter as a new employee. The story may be told to emphasize a safety error in making a joke of the situation, even if the district manager suspected it was a friend playing a prank. Imagine the problems in validity or credibility if you drew conclusions about what was considered acceptable in the culture based on this one story. It may be that the culture really gives limited attention to safety issues, but you would not learn this from a single story. It may be that the whole point of the story was not about safety at all but was told as a "hero narrative" to emphasize to the listener the importance of bravery or protecting the home front.

Indeed, reliance on only one element of culture to draw inferences about effective or appropriate communication behaviors is a source of communication problems for organizations. Furthermore, limiting your analysis can result in overlooking variations in a message found in one element in comparison to different elements. Conquergood (1991), for example, found that various organizational performances (gestures, food, ritual, etc.) express attitudes and issues that are political in nature and often contain multiple meanings and purposes. Thus, simple rituals like a coffee break may reveal information about who is allowed to take breaks and for how long as well as something as basic as what is appropriate talk during a break. The bottom line of this chapter is that an awareness and analysis of multiple elements is central to improving our ability to gain a credible understanding of a culture. We proceed in this chapter by first reviewing eight guides for understanding elements of culture. We then invite you to review and identify examples of specific types of cultural elements. We conclude with a "Connection" on the role of ambiguity in studying cultural elements. You will also find Rehearsals that encourage you to apply concepts to websites as well as activities that provide a close look at stories and metaphors.

> Reliance on only one element of culture to draw interferences about effective or appropriate communication behaviors is a source of communication problems for organizations.

Understanding Elements of Culture

Researchers define and discuss different elements of culture (Bolman & Deal, 2008; Pacanowsky & O'Donnell-Trujillo, 1983). The elements discussed in this chapter are not intended to provide an exhaustive treatment but should give sufficient direction to explore culture. Eight guides should be kept in mind as we discuss these elements. *First, most of the elements we discuss here are surface manifestations of culture that offer insights into deeper layers of assumptions and values.* As we introduced in Chapter 3, Schein (1992) discussed "layers" of organizational culture—artifacts, values, and assumptions. Schein uses the term *artifacts* more broadly than we do in this text to refer to all the objects, rituals, and interactions that characterize the uniqueness of an organization. Artifacts are observable, and values may be inferred from observation of organizational processes. Assumptions exist at a deeper level and form the source for values and artifacts. They often operate at a subconscious level for most of us. We guide you through observational and analytic processes to draw conclusions about deeper layers of the culture from what you can observe.

Second, in the activities we describe in this text, *we are gaining a snapshot of ongoing cultural processes in an organization.* As we described in Chapter 2, in theories of symbolic constructionism and structuration, culture is continually being created and re-created through the interaction of organization members. Depending on the time frame of your project, some of you may have access to a very narrow slice of organization life. Yet we are convinced that even in this rather shallow immersion into cultural observation you will gain skills and paradigms that will be valuable to you in the ongoing analyses of organizational culture you undertake as an organization member or leader.

Third, various elements tend to be embedded in one another. The opening story, as already indicated, contains potential information about organizational heroes, rules, and values. A full description of a ritual, such as a holiday party, will often contain information about organizational language, rules, heroes, and other cultural elements. Or, in the same vein, communication rules may be inferred from an interview designed to gain information about metaphors or stories.

Fourth, the common definitions of these elements will be implied in this text. Specialized definitions of an element may be used in certain texts and articles. For example, a study of stories may focus on various types of stories, such as legends, sagas, myths, or fairy tales. However, for our purpose, the more general terms and definitions will suffice.

Fifth, to stress a point already made, conclusions drawn about a culture should be based on more than one element. Defining a value, for example, based on a single ritual can be misleading. It is best to determine what contradictory or complementary conclusions can be drawn by looking at several elements. For instance, imagine if you worked for a nonprofit focused on educating at-risk children. You join near the end of the year and you find yourself impressed by an organization-wide celebration ritual. You hear stories about successes, including specific recognition of success stories with children. You may be tempted to conclude that the organization is truly effective and concerned about empowering children. However, formally sanctioned events such as this end-of-the-year ritual may not truly capture the extent to which this value set is shared and regarded throughout the year.

Sixth, there is usually a difference between the picture of culture drawn from officially sanctioned organizational sources and the picture drawn from the rank-and-file members of an organization. For example, learning about culture from looking at only the official mission statement, reading an annual report, or listening to the CEO's state-of-the-company address gives only part of the picture. It is often enlightening to ask the employees of an organization what the mission statement is to see if anyone knows it or if their recasting is anything close to the official version. The values of top management are not necessarily the values of the members of the organization. In addition, you will learn more about values from actual interactions of organization members than you will learn from the statement of any organization member, whether leader or employee.

Seventh, the clarity and patterns of the elements you identify may depend on whether the organization you study has a strong or weak culture. Just as there are different definitions of culture, there are different ways to define a "strong" culture. Peters and Waterman (1982), taking a culture-as-variable approach, might describe a strong culture as an appropriate and clear management strategy to align values and symbolism with the competitive environment. The judgment on the culture would come in organizational profitability. Schein (1992) might define a strong culture by the depth and integration of levels of culture. One might ask whether cultural practices were grounded in shared values and assumptions among organizational members.

Louis (1985), in evaluating the strength of subcultures, uses a concept of "penetration" that might be helpful in the assessment of strength of organization culture as well. She offers three types of cultural penetration: psychological penetration, the extent to which individuals hold similar cultural meanings; sociological penetration, the pervasiveness of cultural understandings among employees; and historical penetration, the stability of cultural values and meanings over time.

In strong cultures, values permeate all levels of the organization and all aspects of its functioning. The elements are consistent in their support of overall values and guiding root metaphors. This consistency indicates a strong base of assumptions and values creating the regularities across employees. In weak cultures, however, you may be pressed to identify even common values. Organization members may know little about the organization's history, for example, or have no clear cultural heroes. Symbols are multiple and inconsistent and there are no clear norms to create unity or predictability.

Having a strong culture does not necessarily mean that the culture is positive. Enron had a strong organizational culture, and yet it was one in which ingrained values encouraged employees to take risks and skirt legalities, and the strong culture was eventually part of the downfall that lost many investors millions of dollars as the company collapsed. Table 4.1 distinguishes between strong and weak cultures.

Table 4.1   Comparison of Strong and Weak Organizational Cultures

Strong Culture	Weak Culture
Values permeate entire organization	Values are limited to top management
Elements of culture send consistent messages	Elements send contradictory messages
Most employees can tell stories about history and heroes	Little knowledge about history or heroes exists among average employees
Identification with culture among all employees is strong	Employees identify more with subcultures than with overall organizational culture
Surface cultural elements are tied to employee beliefs and assumptions	Little connection exists between cultural elements and employee beliefs and assumptions
Culture has historical penetration—has existed over a long period	Culture is recent and not well established

With new forms of organizations, the concept of strength of culture is especially relevant. For example, we now see a great many "virtual" organizations with social networking in which members rarely interact face to face and enact their culture in cyberspace. Even in these virtual organizations, it is interesting how culture emerges from interactions as groups develop norms about posting, or as some organization members develop power and status through their interactions. Another recent trend in organization is outsourcing key functions such as security, training, catering, accounting, or other functions. Key organization functions are performed by employees who are not members of the company. How do values get transmitted to such "quasi-employees"? Does such outsourcing weaken organizational culture? Another interesting hybrid organization form much more common is the multinational organization in which organizations display the influence of different national cultures in different divisions of the organization. All such organizational forms present especially interesting targets for cultural study.

Eighth, you may at times find multiple, instead of unitary, organizational cultures. As you collect data on various elements and develop preliminary interpretations, it is important to remember the complexity of culture. Martin (1992) argues that three major perspectives should be considered in viewing the elements or manifestations of culture. An "integration" perspective suggests a cultural unity that is relatively free of uncertainty, one in which values are held consistently from the leader on down. The "differentiation" perspective suggests that the notion of unity is only on the surface. The reality is that subcultures exist that may be in conflict with one another. The "fragmentation" perspective suggests that ambiguity is the norm or "the essence of culture" (Martin, 1992, p. 118). The implications of these perspectives for transitions and change in an organization will be developed in Chapter 8. At this point, however, it is critical to realize that at any point in time, all three perspectives may hold true in an organization. In other words, you may not always discover a "unitary" set of stories, values, or other elements. Keyton (2005) writes about consensus, divided, and fragmented cultures. However, she notes that characterizing cultures in this way may oversimplify the ways that a given culture might contain elements of all three. Martin (2002) concurs with this potential for oversimplification when she writes:

> [S]ome aspects of the culture will be shared by most members, producing consistent, clear interpretations . . . other aspects of the culture will be interpreted differently by different groups, creating subcultures that overlap and nest with each other in relationships of harmony, interdependence and/or conflict . . . some aspects of the culture will be interpreted ambiguously, with irony, paradox, and irreconcilable tension. (p. 120)

Sometimes different geographical or product divisions of a large company may develop their own unique subcultures. Rosenfeld, Richman, and May (2004) studied a large dispersed network culture and found that without strong communication systems, branch offices of a large organization can develop a fragmented culture or one that is differentiated from the overall organization. This differentiation can cause a lack of trust and interdependence and can impact employees' personal growth. At times even departments such as creative services and account services within a large advertising agency may have distinctly different subcultures. In these situations, it is important to probe whether the subcultures share certain uniting elements in their diversity and what might constitute the cultural core that holds together and unites the subculture.

You might also analyze whether the subcultures serve useful purposes for the organization—such as promoting diversity and creativity, matching culture to function of different units, or promoting healthy competition. You may also, however, find that a fragmented organizational culture with competing subcultures is unhealthy and may be a sign of cultural revolution or transition.

Major Elements of Culture

These eight principles for understanding the elements of culture should be kept in mind in the process of identifying and analysis. We provide a list of major elements in Table 4.2, with definitions and examples in the text. We include suggestions for identifying each element; however, we reserve in-depth discussion of element identification for the section on methods. The identification of cultural elements is made easier because we grow up being exposed to them: we hear stories, we participate in rituals, and we learn specialized terms or language. After each element you can jot down your own examples in order to see how familiar you already are with each of the elements. We include a Rehearsal at the end of the section to provide further practice in identifying these elements. Becoming adept at identifying each of these elements will give you a framework for your formal data collection, discussed in the next section.

We have divided 12 elements into five categories for discussion: values (the master cultural element); symbolic elements (symbols, stories, language, and metaphors); role elements (heroes, outlaws); interactive elements (rituals, rules, organizational communication style); and context variables (history, place).

Table 4.2   Categories of Elements of Culture

Values	Master element
Symbolic Elements	Symbols
	Stories
	Language
	Metaphors
Role Elements	Heroes
	Outlaws
Interactive Elements	Rituals
	Informal rules
	Organizational communication style
Context Elements	History
	Place

Values

Definition: the common beliefs and priorities of a group of people. Values are qualities that define a group to its members. They may be the most central cultural construct, on which all other cultural elements rest. In Schein's (1992) model of levels of culture described in Chapter 3, values are the second level of culture, underlying all observable manifestations of culture. Values tell organization members what is most important, what to pay attention to, and how to interpret meanings. Other elements such as heroes or language gain significance because they provide a clue to a key organizational value. When organization members share values, they form a strong force for motivating the performance of employees. Tompkins and Cheney (1985) refer to this motivating force of values as "unobtrusive control." Employees do not need close supervision or an elaborate set of rules to regulate their behavior if they have strongly internalized the values of the organization.

Examples: Enron at its zenith held collective values of boldness, risk taking, and innovation. These values became embedded in its rituals and defined the heroes of the organization (Seeger & Ulmer, 2003; Ulmer, Sellnow, & Seeger, 2011). On the other hand, we have both been in churches that defined themselves as a "healing community" that valued the broken, the discouraged, and scarred individuals. You can imagine that the second value leads to a very different web of culture than Enron's.

Identification: You may find value statements written in conjunction with a mission statement. However, as you collect formal value statements, be sure also to learn about values that are seen, not just heard (practiced vs. merely espoused). You can draw inferences about values from what the organization rewards formally or informally, by the types of individuals who are drawn to the organization, from everyday rituals, and from stories. You may infer values from almost any of the other elements. For instance, values are easily inferred from stories and rituals. Once you determine values, you have the key for interpreting all other cultural elements.

An example of a value shared by members of your organization:

_____

_____

Symbolic Elements

The four cultural elements we categorize as "symbolic elements" have in common their focus on language, nonverbal symbols, and meaning. They are all significant in interpreting organizational culture because they represent an important value or meaning in the culture. The cultural elements include symbols, stories, language, and metaphors.

Symbols

Definition: physical objects or icons that represent the organization. Most organizations develop logos to represent themselves to their public. Often great thought and expense goes into choosing a logo that conveys exactly how the organization wishes to be portrayed. Other symbols can be analyzed as well, such as corporate newsletters, executive speeches, an annual report, building architecture, webpages, and even individuals who come to symbolize an organization.

Examples: One former client of Angi's started out with values of equality and lack of corporate hierarchy. These values led to a corporate headquarters in which it was impossible to distinguish the office of the CEO from the office of a mid-level computer programmer. The indistinguishable offices served as an important icon representing a key value of equality within the company. As the company became increasingly successful and competed for business worldwide with major banks and organizations, the small and unassuming office of the CEO sent a different and less positive message to visitors from potential clients. The CEO and members of the organization were forced to manage the impression of their symbols both internally and externally.

Physical facilities are another example of significant symbols and are especially interesting to analyze. They can include the building(s), layout of rooms, furniture, parking lots, vehicles, and artifacts such as pictures, signs, plaques, visitor reading material in the lobby, and clothing (official and unofficial uniforms). These features of settings can be viewed as significant symbols (Eblen & Eblen, 1987). For instance, Pepper (2008) examined employees' negative reactions to a new building designed to enhance openness and creativity. In use the open building design actually inhibited open communication because of lack of privacy, and in a depressed economy (not anticipated when the building was planned) the expensive building was seen as a lack of concern for employee jobs when layoffs occurred.

Finally, the organizational website is a rich, modern artifact that can yield a wealth of organizational symbolism. It has become the contemporary version of the corporate handbook or newsletter. Not only the content of the website but also the visual layout, the navigation logic, and the security or lack thereof yields information about organizational culture.

Identification: Some researchers have developed elaborate classification systems to study symbols (Axley, 1984; Holmes, 1988). As with other elements of culture, it is important to probe the meaning and importance of a symbol to members of the organization. Often a symbol that might be interpreted in one way by outsiders has a very different meaning internally. It is also important to distinguish between "official" and "unofficial" organizational symbols.

Symbols in your organization:

_____

_____

_____

Stories

Definition: narratives that organization members tell and newcomers hear. They are often a primary form of socialization for new organization members. When you hear the same story or type of story from many different individuals in an organization, it likely has cultural significance. Stories may be told that feature the storyteller or some other organizational member as a main character. Stories are often disseminated organization-wide to encourage members to accept a certain value or rule. Some stories contain explicit "morals" or lessons, while other stories are more subtle and allow the listener to draw conclusions. Stories may take on fantasy or mythic qualities if they begin to deal with larger-than-life characters and do not seem to be situated in time (like fairy tales or legends).

Examples: Stories may be prompted when something goes wrong. As an employee in a retail store, Gerald recalls a cautionary tale told by his manager after a minor accident. The manager used the occasion, with other employees gathered around, to tell about a major accident that cost the company thousands of dollars. Employees, both recent hires and old-timers, were thus exposed to a company value on following procedure. As a consultant in one hospital setting, Angi heard a wide variety of stories about status differences. All the stories had different main characters and different inferences drawn. One story might be about racial differences. Another might be about insensitive doctors being unresponsive to needs of staff. Yet the story type of status differences was strong in the culture.

Identification: Stories may be elicited in a direct fashion: "Tell me about the stories a newcomer is likely to hear around this place." However, as will be discussed in Part III on data collection, the indirect approach is often the most valid way to gain cultural information. Thus, you may simply hear statements during an informal discussion or narratives presented during a formal interview. Stories in these settings may begin with statements like, "Let me tell you what happened when . . ." or "That reminds me of a time . . ." or "The boss often repeats . . ." At times you can elicit stories by asking for an example when interviewees discuss a value or characteristic of the organization. You should be aware that conclusions you draw from a story as an outsider might be quite different from the implications of the story for an insider. Especially interesting are "story types" that you begin to discover in an organization (see Brown, 1990; Smith & Keyton, 2001). Because stories often have multiple elements embedded in them (heroes, values, etc.), Rehearsal 4.2 provides a way to explore your own organizational stories.

Give a story you have heard in your organization that has symbolic significance:

_____

_____

_____

_____

Language/Nonverbal

Definition: the particular vocabulary or terms (argot, jargon, etc.) used by members of the organization as well as the specialized nonverbal gestures, signs, and so on that provide clues to important aspects of the culture (Brenton, 1993). Language distinguishes insiders from outsiders and thus helps define cultural boundaries. The specific terms used by a group, as well as grammar and message construction, are also a means for drawing inferences about a group's metaphors and values.

Examples: A university that stresses its "business plan" or "margin" or talks about its students as "customers" may have adopted a business metaphor. This may be a sign of "mission drift," where economics has taken more centrality than education as the mission of the institution.

Identification: Smith and Eisenberg (1987) analyzed a shift in culture at Disneyland from a "theatrical performance" culture to a "family" culture. They discussed this change by analyzing language patterns in employee interviews and official documents. This shift in metaphor had serious implications for rituals, employee expectations, and values. Not only specific vocabulary but also language patterns can reveal an enlightening view of a culture. Brenton (1993) used critical linguistic analysis to analyze a cultural conflict in a church, looking at language features such as passive or active sentence construction, specificity versus abstraction, pronoun references, and how often certain word types appeared in a text.

Give an example of language that is significant in conveying organizational values or in differentiating an insider from an outsider in your organization:

_____

_____

_____

_____

_____

Metaphors

Definition: figures of speech in which one thing is seen through the lens of another, in which two objects, individuals, or events are implicitly or explicitly compared to one another.

Examples: A small company may describe itself as a family because of close relationships among organization members. The metaphor is consistent with the values of caring, nurturing, and permanent commitments. The values embedded in the metaphor are also found in patterns of rituals, informal rules, heroes, and communication networks that profoundly affect how the company does business. While the metaphor may have great utility, it will pose limits for the company during financial stress. How do you lay off a family member? Why should the bottom line take precedence over the best health care insurance possible when providing for family? It also may be challenged during times of corporate growth and change. While the family metaphor may work well in a small to medium-sized organization, it quickly becomes unwieldy when the company grows larger.

One of our students studied a temporary employment agency that characterized itself as a "pride of lions." All the managers were male, and the agents who processed orders and served employees were female. For some of the employees the metaphor captured role division and gender status differences within the agency, as well as values of interdependence and competitiveness of the environment. In another analysis across organizations, metaphors surfaced as a primary means for describing the experience of workplace bullying (Tracy, Lutgen-Sandvik, & Alberts, 2006). Metaphors, as these examples reflect, promise to provide a rich array of cultural meaning. In fact, Holger, Gross, Hartman, and Cunliffe (2008) argue that metaphor is a key ingredient in language and as such is foundational in holding the culture of an organization together.

Identification: Naturally occurring metaphors, which emerge from language patterns, are generally more valid in cultural analysis than artificially generated ones (Smith & Eisenberg, 1987; Smith & Keyton, 2001). An artificially generated metaphor might be elicited by a question such as, "If this company were an animal, what would it be?" One can infer metaphors from language patterns, heroes, rituals, or other culture elements. For example, if employees use terms such as "battle plan," "chain of command," "search and destroy," and "war games," it would be fair to assume that the culture is influenced by a military metaphor. Metaphors offer insight into rules and values. In the military metaphor example, you would expect to find values and norms of loyalty, obedience to orders, and respect for hierarchical positions within the organization. Rehearsal 4.3 provides direction on using metaphors to initiate the analysis process.

What metaphor symbolizes your organizational culture?

_____

_____

_____

_____

_____

Role Elements

Although some authors, such as Deal and Kennedy (1982, 2000), identify a large number of cultural roles, including high priest, storyteller, and cabal member, we have found two roles especially helpful in understanding cultures. These two roles are hero and outlaw, and they are described below.

Heroes

Definition: individuals or groups who are respected by a large number of individuals within the organization because they embody group values.

Examples: Stories, rituals, and an examination of history reveal the continuing influence of founder-heroes such as Sam Walton and Walt Disney. Stories about Sam Walton still abound among Wal-Mart employees—from his driving a beat-up pickup truck to leading cheers with associates at Wal-Mart stores. A hero may also be someone other than a founder or a CEO though. For example, in one church organization, an 85-year-old church secretary named Helen was widely cited by members as "the heart of the church" and "the custodian of all church stories, history, and procedures." Church leaders had come and gone over the years, while Helen had remained. Her mentoring of new members, her structuring of church services, and her much-sought approval demonstrated her influence over church practices. One member told a story of a minister who did not stay long once he earned Helen's ire. A critical time in any organization is the transition after the death or retirement of a hero. In most cases, the hero's influence remains through prominently displayed pictures and symbols, often-repeated stories, and influence on leadership succession processes. If new heroes fail to emerge over time, however, the organization may drift from its values and history.

Identification: The "hero" may or may not have high formal status within the organization. It is surprising how often you find quick consensus when you begin asking individuals questions such as, "Who is a hero here?" "Who is an organization member you most respect?" "Who embodies this organization at its best?" Within most organizational stories, heroes are easily found. Heroes reveal a great deal about communication rules and cultural values.

Who is a hero in your organization and why?

_____

_____

_____

_____

Outlaws

Definition: individuals who seem to be paradoxes in the organization, who defy organizational practices or values yet remain as valued members of the organization because they exemplify countercultural values that the organization wishes to cultivate.

Examples: Angi belongs to one of the largest Rotary clubs in the United States, with more than 500 members. Most Tuesdays at lunch one can look over a sea of sameness of buttoned-down American business leaders. The shade of tie may vary here or there, and the color of suit may range from charcoal to navy, but the homogeneity is obvious—as are the informal rules of interaction: polite conversation. No rocking the boat with political conversation, raised voices, or divisive topics. That is, until you see Rollie—usually dressed in a Ducks Unlimited sweatshirt and always carrying one of his trademark hand-carved walking sticks. Any time he gets the microphone, which is frequently, he may "Call the Hogs" (an Arkansas football cheer), or call the ducks, or tell everyone about his latest political protégé. Why has he gained almost legendary status when he follows almost none of the rules typical of the culture? Maybe because he embodies the spontaneity, fun, honesty, and bravado that many of the business leaders would like to emulate.

Identification: In interviews you can usually ask a question like, "Who is someone in this organization who is different, who does not follow all the rules but is still valued?" You can also simply observe organizational interaction. Outlaws are usually easy to spot because they are dressed differently and interact with others in noticeably different ways than most organization members. Like heroes, outlaws reveal a great deal about communication rules and cultural values. They may embody subtle subordinate values missed in other elements. Outlaws are particularly interesting to identify and study. If they are expelled from the organization, the reasons for their expulsion tell a great deal about organizational norms and values. If they are allowed to remain in the organization, it may be because they embody important counterculture values (such as creativity in a traditional culture) that the organization wants to support. It is also interesting to discover times of cultural change when a former outlaw becomes a hero, or when an outlaw who was previously tolerated in an organization is expelled or disciplined.

Who seems to break all the rules in your organization, yet is allowed to remain as a valued member? Why?

_____

_____

_____

_____

Interactive Elements

The three cultural elements we have identified as "interactive" exist only in interactions between members of the organization and cannot be observed in a single member. They are a clear example of the theory of structuration explained in Chapter 2. They are created through interaction yet also can constrain improvisation by actors within the culture. These elements are rituals, rules, and organizational communication style and are explained below.

Rituals

Definition: planned and unplanned events that are carried out through social interaction with explicit or implicit purposes and that have multiple social consequences (Trice & Beyer, 1985). Six basic types of rituals (or rites) have been identified: passage, integration, enhancement, degradation, renewal, and conflict reduction (see Trice & Beyer, 1985, 1993). Islam and Zyphur (2009) argue that these various types of rites or rituals are "concerned with (a) transformation, or the shifting of the social positions or statuses of organizational actors, and (b) stability, or the maintenance of a communal set of cultural beliefs and values" (p. 125). They also stress that management is not the only group influencing rituals. Other groups both initiate and maintain them.

Rituals are often the "acting out of values" and form a rich source of data from which to mine inferences about other elements of culture such as values, rules, cultural roles and networks, and heroes. You will most often learn about rituals through observation, thus, we provide a Rehearsal in Chapter 6 (Rehearsal 6.1) with a focus on the six types of rituals listed above. We encourage you to begin an initial reflection on rituals in your organization in the space below.

Examples: informal office gatherings, award ceremonies, organizational practices and procedures, coffee room talk. A specific type of ritual is corporate humor or play. In addition, what members count as humor and play, often in contrast to work, serves critically important functions in the organization. For instance, humor may function to save face, socialize, convey membership, and gain perspective on negative or tragic organizational events (Bolman & Deal, 2008; Meyer, 1997, 2000). In a similar way, play may encourage flexibility and adaptation. In addition, as you attend to the obvious, such as a business meeting, be sure to capture what happens prior to such events. Mirivel and Tracy (2005) identified several forms of premeeting talk. For instance, "small talk" focuses on relationship building, but other less obvious forms, such as "shop talk" involve discussions "about people, events, and issues that link to the workplace" (p. 16). In short, be sure to understand the significance of communication that functions as informal ritualized interactions before the formal ritual.

Identification: One way to identify formal and informal rituals, beyond observing them, is to ask about the events that characterize the organization. For instance, are family picnics or Friday afternoon happy hours common? Or are members rewarded, either formally or informally? Does the organization have rites for recognizing stakeholders outside of the organization (community members, volunteers)? Once you have identified rituals, you can probe for values, rules, roles, networks, and heroes. For example, you might ask questions like: What signs of status are apparent from interactions? How do employees do their work? How do they greet strangers/customers/visitors? How do they interact in meetings?

What is a ritual in your organization? What does it tell you about the culture?

_____

_____

_____

_____

Informal Rules

Definition: "the organization and logic that provide for behavior production" (Sigman, 1980). Informal organizational norms tell what behavior is preferred, permitted, required, or prohibited in organizational life.

Examples: When Angi began as an assistant professor years ago, several colleagues took care to share a story about an assistant professor who, as legend had it, was denied tenure the year after he refused a request by the dean to chair the college United Way effort. She was left to deduce her own conclusions about organizational norms from the story. Was it expected that all employees are active in United Way because of a strong community engagement? Was it prohibited for a junior faculty member to deny a request from the dean? Another example of the significance of informal or unconsciously held rules can be found by looking at decision-making processes. Jabs (2005) explored the value of identifying informal rules in the context of decisions surrounding the *Challenger* space shuttle disaster. One of the four rules she identified was: *subordinates (often engineers) should limit their input according to the interest level and receptivity of the managerial superordinates* (p. 286). These two examples support the importance of identifying informal rules both for aiding individuals adjusting to a new culture as well as to significant decision-making processes.

Identification: Uncovering the complex, often unconscious ways of thinking in an organization that make some actions obligatory, some permissible, some discouraged, and some prohibited is challenging. You may find rules for behavior listed in an employee handbook (no smoking, etc.). However, informal cultural rules, like values, are rarely explicitly stated or written. Because rules operate in the unconscious taken-for-granted realm, some organizational members cannot identify rules when they are asked a direct question about them. In a story about a hero or an outlaw, you may learn what types of behaviors are encouraged or discouraged. You also can uncover rules in field observations of interactions among culture members. When you observe regularities of behavior over time and across actors, the regularity is generally produced by informal cultural rules. Who calls whom by first names or formal titles? Do people arrive early or late for meetings? Who is exempt from the "corporate uniform" and why? What distinguishes those who get promotion and honors from those who do not? What are common threads among those who are fired or voluntarily choose to leave the organization? It is important, once you identify the regularity, to ask organizational members to explain it. Their underlying logic is the key element in identifying the cultural norm or rule. Informal cultural rules are embodiments of organizational values and a direct outgrowth of organizational metaphors (Schall, 1983).

What are informal norms at your organization that may not be written down but still have a strong effect on how actors behave?

_____

_____

_____

_____

Organizational Communication Style

Definition: a collective preference by organization members for certain channels of communication. Usually organizations fall into three "styles": oral/interpersonal, written/formal documentation, and electronic.

Examples: As we have consulted with organizations, we have found that one major aspect of culture involves the collective communication patterns and preferences of the group. Some prefer face-to-face communication in an oral tradition. They value the personal contact and may not "count" that they have received a message until someone has talked to them about it. A typical comment might be, "I saw some memo about that, but no one has actually talked to me about it yet." Cultural socialization and history are conveyed through stories and interactions. A fatal flaw in such a culture would be offering feedback or praise to a group through a memo versus a more personal contact. Change must be achieved by face-to-face appeals and coalition building.

A written culture, on the other hand, places emphasis on standardization of procedure and formal documentary evidence. This communication culture is most prevalent in bureaucratic organizations or in organizations with a high proclivity toward legal actions or grievances. In this culture, oral communication does not "count." A comment in a meeting must be followed by a formal written proposal. A request is not considered effective until it is put into writing. An affirmation would seem incomplete unless it is formalized in writing with copies to all affected parties.

A hybrid of the written culture is the electronic communication culture. In this culture speed and ease of communication are highly valued, perhaps because the pace of change is intensified in highly competitive and fast-moving fields. Organization members are expected to be accessible through e-mail, pager, voice mail, or cell phone at any given time. In this culture, a faux pas might be sending a message by mail instead of by a more rapid channel, insisting on a paper copy instead of an electronic communication, or failing to check messages frequently. Challenges within this culture include information overload, improperly targeted messages, and "flaming," because anger is more easily expressed in impersonal channels. Overload is a problem in an electronic culture because so many messages can be exchanged in a brief time period, and because many individuals are copied on a single message. Communicators often send a message to an entire listserv rather than targeting the message to the person who actually needs it. When additional organization members are copied on an angry or critical message, it can lead to loss of face for the person targeted in the message.

Angi has consulted with a company in the midst of cultural change. Along with changes in organizational structure (eliminating a layer of middle management), growth, changes in corporate ownership that had added more bureaucratic procedures, and changes in personnel, a change in communication culture had gone almost unnoticed, even though it had created major repercussions. The organization before the round of changes had a strong oral/interpersonal communication culture. Employees got things done by knowing the right person at corporate headquarters to call, and cultivating personal relationships across branches took the place of formal communication channels and mechanisms. As part of the corporate change, the company had adopted an electronic communication style. Oral briefings declined. Employees were expected to keep up with policies by e-mail updates and webpage postings. As faces were shuffled in and out, employees no longer knew who was in charge of what and whom to call when emergencies arose. Complaints abounded about the difficulty of navigation, impersonality, and competition among branches. Most of these arose out of grief over losing a comfortable and efficient culture of communication without it being replaced by a clear strategy for how electronic means could serve the same functions as the previous communication culture.

Identification: You can ask organization members in interviews how most people communicate with one another. You can also observe face-to-face interactions, meeting schedules, the inbox (how many paper transactions), and the average number of e-mails per day.

What is the communication style of your organization? How do you know?

_____

_____

_____

_____

Context Elements

The two elements we classify as context elements, history and place, recognize that an organizational culture is substantially shaped by its placement in space and time. An organization located in India will develop different values and norms from one located in France. An organization located in New York City will have a different climate from one formed in Plains, Georgia. Organizations also do not exist in a time vacuum. Their history is vital for understanding how the organization was founded and how it has changed. It is hard to understand present organizational patterns without grounding cultural understanding in the organization's history.

History

Definition: involves knowledge of the purposes of its founding and how it has evolved over the years; it also involves knowing information about the founders of the organization. Learning the history of an organization—the time period at which it was formed, the purposes for which it was formed, the personality of the individual(s) who founded it—can offer great insight into persisting organizational patterns or resistance to change. The insights gleaned from the history are valuable even when organizations have changed dramatically from their initial beginnings.

Examples: One of Angi's clients is a large university hospital with roots as a charity hospital for indigent patients. Even though it has now grown into an internationally recognized medical center, the value of offering universal access to health care remains. Understanding the historic value of access to care explains tensions that result from serving different patient populations.

History reveals the continuing influence of a founder such as Sam Walton or Walt Disney. It is enlightening to determine how much the average organizational member knows or understands about organizational history. In strong cultures, the history is often told and retold. One of our cultural audits was performed in a publishing group that started on a shoestring. Each employee we interviewed and even recent hires could tell about the early days when writers signed on with no salary and just a promise of future profit sharing. Most could tell about the first winter in a warehouse so cold that writers draped a stray cat across their shoulders for warmth as they sat before a typewriter. The history was a vibrant part of the culture because the publishing group did not want to leave behind the value of passionate dedication to creativity. In organizations drifting away from founding values, members often know little about history. In contrast, a founder's values guide the response of an organization facing a crisis (Ulmer, 2001).

Identification: History, like the other elements, is often embedded in stories of heroes or the founding of the organization. Rituals that capture certain common organizational memories are also important places to gain a sense of the history of a place. Artifacts, such as pictures of the founder or pictures of earlier corporate headquarters, also show that an organization consciously tries to build on its history.

What do you know about your organization's history? How does your knowledge affect your present behavior in the organization?

_____

_____

_____

_____

Place

Definition: the complex environment in which an organization resides, whether it is a community, a state, a nation, or a multinational context.

Example: Organizations are products of their environments, as well as entities that shape their environments—the same duality of creativity and constraint discussed earlier in structuration theory. Authors such as Florida (2002) discuss the increasingly important role of place in the new creative economy. Creative employees such as university professors, software developers, medical researchers, information engineers, and others have highly portable careers. They can choose to live and work where they want. Florida points out that the days when employees moved to where the jobs are have passed. Now the creative class chooses to live in environments characterized by technology infrastructure, diversity, and a rich cultural life, and the companies follow. Florida has developed a "creativity index" on which cities such as San Francisco, Austin, Minneapolis, Santa Fe, and Washington, D.C., score high. He posits that companies such as Dell Computers have flourished precisely because they were developed in such rich environments that nourished creativity and innovation.

Identification: This element challenges the researcher to move beyond observation of the internal environment to consider the impact of "place." What are characteristics of the external environment? Big city or small? Homogenous or diverse? Traditional or cutting edge? Prosperous or struggling? How does the environment contribute to the organization's culture? How does the organization contribute to its environment?

How does the physical environment in which your organization is located affect the organizational culture?

_____

_____

_____

_____

Connections: What About Ambiguity?

Elements of culture may be viewed as the primary roles in the organizational culture drama. From your reading of the different elements and reflection on your experiences in organizations, did you notice instances when a rule or story or ritual was complex, multifaceted, layered, or ambiguous in its meaning? For instance, in the burglar story at the beginning of the chapter, the moral of the story might be that even a great manager can make a nearly deadly mistake. Or conversely, it might be that the moral is about bravery in that this manager saved the day by recognizing that these burglars were a joke and not to be taken seriously. The meaning of the tale and the significance to the company depend on who retells it and for what purposes. Is it, for instance, told at an orientation on safety or is it told at a picnic in which the virtues of brave managers are extolled? Part of its value and richness in embodying and shaping the culture results from this very ambiguity.

The notion of ambiguity in meaning is critical to interpreting and applying cultural data. Smith and Eisenberg (1987) and others (Meyer, 2009; Meyerson & Martin, 1987; Morgan, 2007) have drawn attention to the role of strategic ambiguity in organizational communication. Strategic ambiguity involves being deliberately unclear or nonspecific for a strategic purpose. Common assumptions about organizational communication often deal with clarity and certainty about messages and meanings. This is especially true in popular literature about organizational culture. Leaders are encouraged to send clear and specific messages about values and expectations.

However, the importance and existence of ambiguity should not be overlooked. Another way to think about ambiguity is to consider the value of being able to look at something a different way. If all communication were clear and certain, there would be no room for adjustments, change, and alternative perspectives. In fact, the ability to interpret and then translate the meaning of a cultural element in different ways (as allowed by the degree of ambiguity present) is a skill relevant to managing organizational change. In addition, Eisenberg (1984) points out that strategic ambiguity allows for "unified diversity" in which different groups within an organization can feel a common commitment to an abstract value into which each can read its own connotations. Such unity would break down with more specifically drawn goals.

Strategic ambiguity may also be exploited by those wishing to use organizational rituals to initiate change. For instance, Brenton (1993) studied the ritual of "going forward" at the end of a church service as a way to introduce changes in a church organization. Brenton noted how one church member, in conflict with the leadership, utilized this ritual to confess his problems and sins in dealing with a particular issue in the church. His use of the ritual for confession was clearly within the communication rules of this ritual, but his use of the confession to implicate current problems with leadership behavior was part of the ambiguity in the ritual—an ambiguity that allowed him to introduce new ideas and changes. For instance he "defamiliarized" the ritual by making his own statement and praying for himself, while the ritual usually involved allowing a church leader to relay the request for prayer and to pray for the penitent congregant. His changes in the ritual used the ritual that usually reinforced the power of the church leaders to challenge their power instead.

In contrast to the use of ambiguity to bring a change, ambiguity may also be used to resist change, manage risk, or in come cases act unethically. For instance, Meyer (2009) found the use of ambiguous terms such as *unity* allowed for continuity in worship styles in a church setting. His study indicated that leaders worked against those seeking change by claiming the value of "unity." Furthermore, in the context of risk communication, Scott and Trethewey (2008) describe how the everyday talk of firefighters included ambiguous terms that helped them downplay the level of risk in certain aspects of their job. Finally, in the context of crisis management, Ulmer and Sellnow (2000) contend that leaders use ambiguity in ways that privilege their financial stakeholders over others. For instance, in the context of the tobacco industry, Ulmer and Sellnow (1997) argue that biased and incomplete information was used in strategically ambiguous ways that reduced the decision- or choice-making ability of stakeholders.

The concept of ambiguity as related to the elements of culture connects with the notion of culture as a resource. We would want you to see that ambiguity may not be all bad. Yes, there may be times when ambiguity is used unethically and other times it may create a source of confusion or "action paralysis," yet it can be a resource for innovation (Martin, 1992, p. 134) and for organizational renewal (Ulmer, Sellnow, & Seeger, 2009). The competent leader or communicator seeks to tap into culture, its ambiguity, and exploit it to advance ethical performance goals. As in the study by Brenton, the church member recognized the need to work within the culture and did so by utilizing the ambiguity in an existing ritual to effectively introduce a change. We therefore are not merely caught in the web of culture if we are aware of the influence of culture. Consistent with the example above, we can learn to tap into the resource of culture to develop and enact meanings that we view as important to effective and ethical leadership.

Summary

This overview of the major elements of culture suggests just how commonplace most of the elements are in our everyday experience. Although we observe them every day, until now you may not have recognized their value to studying culture. While we may not formally reflect on implied rules or see a coffee break routine as an important ritual, we nevertheless learn, respond to, and enact cultures in a variety of ways. Specifically you should have learned from this chapter:

- Elements often are a "window" on organizational culture.

- Comprehensive organizational analysis should be based on conclusions drawn from multiple cultural elements.

- We should consider both "official" management information and "unofficial" information from rank-and-file organizational actors when we draw conclusions, because culture must pervade the entire organization to be influential.

- Elements are often "nested" within one another. One can learn about values from stories, history, or heroes, for example.

- Part of the richness and challenge of cultural elements is their ambiguity and therefore their ability to convey multiple meanings simultaneously—meanings that may have ethical or unethical motives.

As you have gained an awareness of cultural elements and insight into how to identify them systematically, the next task is to refine your ability to gather in-depth information about each of these elements before interpreting and applying their meaning. Thus, the next section introduces the third step, using multiple methods to collect cultural data.

Rehearsal 4.1 Exploring Websites

Purpose: Identify and evaluate cultural elements that can be assessed from a company website.

Steps:

1. Identify two different company or organization websites. We encourage you to select organizations of interest to you in terms of consulting, career development, or benchmarking. (Example websites can be found at the Student Study Site at www.sagepub.com/driskill2estudy.)

2. Identify as many different elements of culture as possible based on the summary list provided below:

   Values—the common beliefs and priorities of a group of people; they are qualities that define a group to its members

   Rituals—include planned (rites) and unplanned events that are carried out through social interaction with explicit or implicit purposes and have multiple social consequences (see Trice & Beyer, 1984); rituals are often the "acting out of values"

   Stories—narratives that organization members tell and newcomers hear

   Heroes—individuals or a group within the organization that is respected by a large number of individuals within the organization because they embody organizational values

   Outlaw—someone who seems at the fringe, someone who bucks the rules or challenges the system, yet is tolerated and even valued because he or she embodies countercultural values that the group wishes to retain

   Language/Nonverbal—the particular vocabulary or terms (argot, jargon, etc.) used by members of the organization as well as the specialized non-verbal gestures, signs, and so on that provide clues to important aspects of the culture

   Symbols—one of a variety of ways that an organization represents itself to the public: for example, logos, corporate newsletters, representative photographs or graphics, websites, executive speeches, annual reports, building architecture, even individuals who come to symbolize an organization

   Metaphors—figures of speech in which one thing is seen through the lens of another; in which two objects, individuals, or events are implicitly or explicitly compared to one another

History—the time period at which the organization was formed, the purposes for which it was formed, the personality of the individual(s) who founded it

Informal Cultural Rules—the organization and logic that provide for behavior production

References to Place—the environment of which the organization is a part, and the ways in which the external environment influences the organization

Indication of Organizational Communication Style—oral, written, or electronic

Rehearsal 4.2 Getting More From Our Stories

Purpose: Review six major functions of stories before engaging in a practice analysis of stories from your experiences in organizations.

The role of narratives or stories in understanding our organizational communication experiences is common both in and outside academia (Fisher, 1987; Kirkwood, 1983, 1985, 1992). In fact, in consultation with a day care organization, Gerald used stories to improve communication practices (Driskill & Meyer, 1994, 1996a, 1996b), and Angi helped leaders gain insights into their culture by analyzing stories told in employee interviews. Others have identified stories as a significant source for introducing change in which leaders examined the balance of positive and negative stories, and then analyzed story themes to identify values and problems within the culture (Kimoto, 2007).

Reviewing a story is to participate in the ancient rite of storytelling. We are always amazed at the range of events that come to our minds when we review our organizational stories with others engaged in the same review process. The stories range from mundane first job memories, to ethical dilemmas, to examples of the way a change in management practice can reshape an entire work environment. Interactions with mentors or heroes, and the values and informal norms taught by positive and negative experiences, have shaped all our lives in powerful ways. While each of the individual stories has significance in defining aspects of each individual organizational culture, the stories as a whole form a narrative or script of our own organizational drama. Each of the early scenes shapes the action and events of later scenes. A positive experience with an employer will influence how you interpret behavior and evaluate later bosses. For instance, a nurturing boss and mentor might prompt you to take growth-producing risks on another job. Conversely, a negative experience may prompt you to enact your own set of informal rules that limits your willingness to take many risks. An early successful or unsuccessful experience with a group will shape your reactions to teamwork.

(Continued)

(Continued)

Such storytelling demonstrates four important roles of organizational stories. *First, stories function as a type of life review or life construction.* The recalling of past events, this habit of reminiscing, is something we often associate with the elderly. Gerald still hears stories from his Dad of working in Alaska and in China during the 1940s. He has mental and actual pictures of a frozen winter land and of bombed-out buildings. Angi has a prized possession of an audio-tape of her grandfather telling stories of his early days as a circuit-riding preacher in Arkansas and Tennessee and being paid in chickens and produce.

Yet the elderly are not the only ones who engage in this review process. In fact, as soon as we are able to create symbols, we tell stories, we make sense out of the world and do our best to create stories that others will find interesting. The standard question, "So, what did you do at school today?" is an invitation to create a story—to piece together events in a way that will make sense to us and to others. Such a process plays a critical role in our social development and in our sense of well-being. For example, imagine having no stories to tell. Or imagine if all of your stories about organizational life were dark? To be human is to be a storyteller.

Second, stories function as a means of passing on values and norms. Although we may recall past events simply in order to reminisce or to recount an event, these same stories and others often become both an explicit and implicit way to hand on norms, values, and expectations. Rather than simply say, "That is not how we do things around here," a member might socialize a new member by telling about the fate of someone who did things right (or wrong). Gerald can still recall hearing a story 15 years ago about a company's loss of thousands of dollars due to a mistake in a paint-mixing procedure. Of course, he was being taught the correct procedure as the boss told the story.

Third, stories create a virtual shared reality for actors with little common experience. Bormann (1969) writes about narrative functioning to create community among strangers. As we enter into the details of a vivid story, we have a virtual experience of overlapping reality. That is why narrative is such a potent medium for transmitting and creating cultural identity.

Fourth, in these stories, you have illustrated *one route for exploring your own communication practices.* If written in detail, each story would reveal something of the cultural constraints and resources you perceived in each situation (see Eisenberg, Goodall, & Trethewey, 2010). We could determine the implicit theories you held during the interaction, the extent to which you considered options for your response to the situation, and so on. Furthermore, we would learn something of how you frame the story in light of your current values and communication practices. What does the story tell, for example, about your values and ethics? What does it reveal about your reaction to authority? What does it have to say about your relationships with coworkers? What might we learn about your response to change?

Fifth, a specific type of story, a counter-narrative, may empower individuals to enact changes in their group or organization. Counter-narratives function to provide missing, inaccurate, incomplete, and/or damaged social constructions (Papa, Singhal, & Papa, 2006). These narratives suggest positive ways to frame tensions to avoid polarized management practices. For instance, in order to improve decision making, leaders could tell stories of organizations who found a way to transcend the tension between short- versus long-term planning. Such stories would capture the possibility of not focusing solely on short-term profits.

In the health care context, Harter (2009) appeals to "scholars to focus attention on forces that both enable and constrain the transformative and therapeutic potential of counter-narratives" (p. 146).

Sixth, and finally, organizational stories can be used to analyze the culture of an organization. This point will be discussed in greater detail later, but suffice it to say that details from your stories do more than reveal your own practices; they also say something about the context of the stories. That context includes both the broader national culture as well as the immediate organizational culture. For instance, Gerald's research on a multinational firm revealed the employees were aware of the influence of national culture differences but not always clear about how they influenced such things as decision making and perceptions of effective supervisor behavior (Driskill, 1995; Driskill & Downs, 1995).

As a way to review the pervasive influence of organizations in our lives, consider completing the following exercise.

1. **Make a list** of 10 organizations that you have belonged to and/or currently belong to.

2. **Review this list and then, based on your memories of events in the above organizations, write down four organizational experiences** (stories of any type) that come to your mind. Do not take time to analyze or write details. Instead, jot down a phrase in two lines or less that captures the event. If you draw blanks before you reach four experiences, review your list of 10 organizations and ask: "Now, what experiences first come to my mind when I think about my time with organization 'X'?" Put down the first stories that come to mind.

3. **Reflect on the following questions concerning the stories you recalled:**
   - What themes predominated in your organizational stories?
   - Do you have stories of success as well as failure?
   - Do you have stories that you would still rather not talk about?
   - Are there situations that still perplex you?
   - Do you have stories that still excite and motivate you? Did you find examples of counter-narratives?

Rehearsal 4.3 A Game of Metaphors

Purpose: Discern the significance of applying a metaphor to enhance awareness of life in your organization.

Though usually unconsciously, we act out "cultural" scripts of what we view as appropriate and effective communication (Fairhurst & Sarr, 1996). Even in an era of film and videotape, it is hard to see our own performances, our ways of responding to organizational structures. We have neither the eyes nor the objectivity of an outsider for viewing our own actions. A metaphor game can help gain some perspective. Let us illustrate.

(Continued)

(Continued)

If someone were to ask Gerald what it is like to work at the university, one answer would be that it is like being on a "team of circus clowns." The metaphor refers to a department that maintains a sense of humor amid the constant coordination needed to adjust to continuous changes. Faculty sometimes wear faces to diffuse a conflict and are engaged in improvisational acting as they juggle competing demands and schedules.

Angi, in a past role as an administrator at a Christian university, might use the metaphor of a Japanese Kabuki theater—thick masks often concealing personal identities and feelings, with a high degree of drama and traditional ritual.

Now it is your turn. Identify a metaphor or analogy that comes to mind that best captures one of your own organizations. Perhaps you can think of more than one metaphor. These metaphors, as we will see, provide a rich source of insight. For example, Gerald's circus metaphor suggests the expectation of being able to take a joke and other roles of humor associated with workload pressures. The circus clown metaphor also suggests that if you cannot laugh at yourself, your own mistakes and limits, as others laugh with you, then you will not be viewed as an effective member of the organization. Furthermore, you should not spend time complaining about changes, workloads, and so on. Faculty must juggle many duties (advising, writing, teaching, consulting, committee work, etc.). A clown with a sad face is not viewed in a positive light. In action, then, the metaphor does more than provide a simple view of life in the department—it suggests a great deal about our communication behavior and how we define effective or competent communication.

Angi's theater metaphor implies the value of learning tradition so you can perform your role in a way that will be accepted. In a similar vein, Angi's theater metaphor implies that members need to stay in character and not let the mask slip. There is also an implication that improvisation is less valued than scripted organizational rehearsal. Put differently, even if you are not familiar with Kabuki theater, you are likely to recall situations when someone (or perhaps everyone) in your organization values certainty and predictability over spontaneous and less predictable behavior.

Although a single metaphor is far from a complete cultural analysis, the exercise demonstrates one way to begin the process of cultural analysis. If such an exercise were repeated across a representative sample of organizational members, patterns would likely emerge that would capture important elements of the culture, such as heroes and values. Combined with other cultural analysis methods, the identification of metaphors becomes a potent way to portray culture.

After you identify one or more metaphors, reflect on the following questions:

- What does the metaphor reveal about what is permitted in the organization?
- What does the metaphor reveal about what is prohibited in the organization?
- How widely held is the metaphor (i.e., across departments, roles, etc.)?
- What does the metaphor suggest about organizational values?

PART III

Cultural Data Collection and Interpretation

An Introduction to Step Three

Use Multiple Methods for Gathering Cultural Information—Method Acting

The Meeting

You walk into a meeting, and before you sit down you notice that all the seats are taken except the one next to the boss. Everyone stops talking as you quickly, but quietly, sit down. You place your folder in front of you and look at your watch, finding that you were only 2 minutes late. The boss is talking about second-quarter earnings, and as she talks you glance around the room. You see one of your colleagues, hired just months before you, gazing out the window, apparently paying little attention. You shuffle a few papers in front of you to prepare for any questions you might be asked and then notice that several other partners in the firm are engaged in writing notes and are not paying attention. "No one seems to respect the boss" is the first thought that comes to mind.

The boss finishes what appears to be a tirade against poor time management on everyone's part and then asks for comments and questions. You think it strange that she says nothing about the rude behavior of her subordinates. Silence ensues, and while you want to ask a question about discrepancies you observed in the earnings statements, you see almost everyone glancing at their watches and thus you decide to be silent. The boss calls the meeting to an end about 15 minutes after it started.

Articulate the value of the culture metaphor

Define major cultural elements

★ **Use multiple data collection methods**

Synthesize and interpret cultural data

Identify applications

Objectives:

- Explain the importance of using multiple data collection methods
- Discuss the utility of three qualitative methods for identifying the cultural elements
- Implement a plan for protecting human participants in a cultural analysis

Stage Terms:

- Ethnography
- Triangulation
- Institutional Review Board

An
Introduction
to Cultural
Analysis
Methods

If you were the main character in the story at the start of this section, you would be drawing inferences from the meeting you observed. Is it usual for employees to be early for meetings? Why is no one paying attention or asking questions? Why is the meeting so short? While we all observe interactions around us and try to make sense of what we see, we often are not equipped with specific methods for observing interactions and analyzing them in a systematic way. What do we want to accomplish in this introduction to Step Three? We first provide background on the role of ethnography in a cultural analysis, including a brief overview of the major methods discussed in the following three chapters. Next, we provide a table that suggests ways to use specific methods to identify various elements of culture. Third, we provide a "Connections" section to encourage reflection on the significance of using more than one method in a systematic way. We conclude by responding to three FAQ's, including questions about protecting human participants and the institutional review board process.

Ethnographic Methods

Method actors use a variety of tactics to provide a credible interpretation of their roles and the script of the play. They have as their "essential task the reproduction of recognizable reality—on stage (or screen), based on an acute observation of the world" (Vineberg, 1991, p. 6). In a similar vein, anthropologists who immerse themselves in a foreign culture rely on three primary methods of data gathering and analysis: systematic observation, conversational interviews, and systematic analysis of various oral and written texts. Such qualitative techniques are often grouped under the heading of "ethnomethodology" or "ethnography." Goodall (1989) defines ethnography as "representing in words what you have lived through as a person when your stated purpose was to study a culture" (p. xxiii). A professional ethnographer might spend years attempting to integrate herself into the culture to fully understand it. During those years, she would repeat many iterations of observing regularities, asking natives of the culture for their interpretations of the patterns of behavior she observed or their tacit knowledge of the culture, and analyzing field notes, interview transcripts, and cultural artifacts. The results of one layer of analysis would lead to a new round of interviews and conversations.

The cultural analysis process described in this text assumes a shorter time frame for an exploration of organizational culture. Most of you will be doing projects in which you penetrate the culture for only a few months of part-time exploration, applying the same methods an anthropologist uses. Rather than dozens of repeated observations and interviews, you might conduct only a few. Similarly, rather than analyzing every possible text in the organization, you may select strategically among several that are judged most timely. Thus, we have learned that whether we begin with interviews, observations, or textual analysis, the data gained from one method often leads back into the other.

The process of systematic data collection, therefore, may begin with any of the three major methods outlined. Some of you might find it more meaningful to begin with observations, move to interviews, and then analyze texts. Still others will find that textual analysis provides a relatively non-obtrusive way to begin the process. Informal interviews may also provide a useful entry point. Regardless of where you begin, the initial objective is to gain a feel for the organization and its players. This information will form the ground for the next phase of data collection. For instance, if you begin with observations or textual analysis, you may use that information to aid you in developing a qualitative interview guide.

In the following chapters, we first introduce the process of various types of textual analysis. Systematic analysis of organizational texts must be approached with a major caution in mind. You should not automatically assume that mission statements, annual reports, employee manuals, or corporate newsletters are the most significant organizational texts to analyze, because they may reflect more about the ways that upper management wants to portray the culture but may not reflect the daily interactions of employees and their interpretations of culture. Internal memos, employee e-mails, or even coffee room bulletin boards may be truer reflections of organizational culture. We will suggest a variety of systematic methods for analyzing organizational texts. You may also uncover important organizational texts during the process of observation and interviews. Furthermore, textual analysis will be useful when you analyze your field notes from observations and with your interview transcripts or summaries.

Observation will be the second method we introduce. Some of you may be analyzing an organization you participate in on a regular basis, either as a volunteer or an employee. In such cases, you may decide to begin with observation. As noted in the meeting example at the opening of this unit, we all engage in making observations and then inferring from these experiences about how to interact. The process of taking field notes when you observe will challenge you to reflect on a broader array of organizational contexts. Furthermore, you will be asked to distinguish between events and your interpretation of events.

Ethnographic or qualitative interviews and surveys are the third type of method we encourage you to use. Interviews, like conversations with organization members, will help you understand how they interpret the events you have observed. Even if you are an insider to the organization, you will be encouraged to gain a wider array of perspectives on the events you observe as well as the texts you analyze. Any individual in an organization may have a limited perspective on overall cultural patterns. Surveys with open-ended questions that invite narrative responses can also be an effective way to gain interpretive data from a larger sample of organization members. We introduce surveys in combination with interviews because the types of questions covered in each are similar. For instance, in an interview, you might ask someone to describe a metaphor they would use to explain the organization to an outsider. This same question could be placed in a survey to gain responses from a broader sample of organization members.

We are often asked about the use of quantitative surveys in cultural analysis. We have both used quantitative surveys to assess communication in organizations. For instance, we have found the Downs and Adrian (2004) instrument to be of value in assessing member satisfaction levels with certain communication practices, such as horizontal or vertical communication. Other examples of survey instruments focus directly on culture. For example, Glaser, Zamanou, and Hacker (1987) assert that organizational culture can be measured by analyzing how members feel an organization communicates on six factors: (1) teamwork, (2) morale, (3) information flow, (4) involvement, (5) supervision, and (6) communication during meetings. Glaser et al.'s instrument has been used to correlate several of these factors with member identification (Croucher, Long, Meredith, Oommen, & Steele, 2009). You can also locate commercially available quantitative surveys.

Such surveys typically assume the culture-as-a-variable approach. The primary claim made by consultants using these surveys is that the data can aid the company to be more productive or competitive. These surveys have the advantage of gaining a snapshot of participant views on a variety of culture-related topics. For example, one survey assesses such topics as the extent to which participants believe the organization is responsive to change and values an external orientation (Culture Strategy Fit, 2010). Another examines culture along four dimensions: adaptability, consistency, involvement, and mission (Denison, n.d.).

What is our view of these types of surveys? As discussed in Chapter 2, the variable approach is one option for analyzing culture. Furthermore, we believe that the insights from a cultural analysis may hold promise for improving such traditional organizational outcomes as productivity. However, our approach is to view organizations as cultures and to examine culture across a wider array of cultural elements. We believe that this approach promises a richer, deeper, and ultimately more meaningful analysis. Quantitative surveys allow input from a broader range of organization members but reduce data to quantifiable categories. This quantification allows statistical manipulation, averages, and comparisons. The trade-off, however, involves missing the rich symbolic elements that reflect culture—the stories, metaphors, language, rituals, and other elements. Even when asked broad open questions, our experience is that employees do not share as much in-depth information on a written survey as they do in interviews.

Methods and Cultural Elements

As you do your analysis, whether you begin with textual analysis, observation, or interviews, remember that the goal of this collection process is to connect your data back to elements of culture. Thus, for instance, you may conduct an analysis of organizational texts, observation field notes, and interview summaries or transcripts. You may perform a series of analyses of representative texts to tease out a sense of history, language, symbols, metaphors, and other clues that will ultimately lead you to conclusions about organizational values, root metaphors, and other cultural themes. Table III.1 suggests a place to start with each method; it is not a prescription of what information necessarily is paired with each method. Indeed, you can usually find any of the 12 elements of culture revealed in any of the methods we cover in Chapters 5, 6, and 7.

For example, during an observation you might choose to focus on artifacts such as office arrangement, objects hanging on the walls, corporate dress style, and public meeting spaces such as conference rooms or break rooms. In this analysis you might especially look for signs of history—pictures of the founders prominently displayed or historical pictures. You might also look for regularities that would suggest formal rules or informal norms, such as a lack of personal items in offices or conformity in style of dress. You might also find suggestions of heroes—pictures hanging on the wall, prominent office locations, employees who are mentioned frequently and with high regard. You can subtly infer values from the artifacts you observe. How does the organization present itself to insiders and outsiders? In a similar way, interviews or qualitative surveys might serve to follow up on the things you have observed, to ask their meaning from an inside perspective. You would also ask about things it is difficult to observe—things such as stories, representative texts, the influence of place, metaphors, and communication style.

Table III.1   Methods and Cultural Elements Revealed

Method	Focus	Cultural Elements Revealed
Observation	Artifacts	Rules
		Heroes
		History
		Values
		Communication style
	Interactions	Rules
		Heroes, villains, and outlaws
		Rituals
		Communication style
	Language	Metaphors
		Stories
	Symbols	Heroes
		Values
		Metaphors
Interviews/Qualitative Surveys	Place	Values
	Representative texts	Root metaphors
	Heroes and villains	Cultural themes
	Stories	
	Rules	
	History	
	Metaphors	
	Communication style	
Analysis of Texts	Field notes of observations	Values
	Interview summaries or transcripts	Root metaphors
	Representative organizational texts, drawn from organizational communication style (narratives or speeches, documents, electronic communication artifacts)	Cultural themes

Connections: Getting the Best Data

The basic rationale for using multiple methods is that the validity of our cultural interpretations will be improved. The idea of multiple methods is called method "triangulation" and suggests that rather than relying on perceptions from a single method, such as surveys, the effective cultural analyst uses additional methods, such as observations, to enrich the data set (Miles & Huberman, 1984). For example, informal "interviews" in the organization may prompt you to make note of a metaphor used by an employee who says, "Working here is like visiting cyberspace." Observations of work teams or the physical setting may be used to determine the pervasiveness and salience of the metaphor (e.g., is it found in company logos, newsletters, or in language used during meetings?). For instance, if space is devoted each week in the newsletter to applications of the latest and best of technology, then support exists for the metaphor beyond the one-time mention by a single employee. Surveys use triangulation to find a point by identifying two vectors that intersect. Triangulation provides the basis for drawing more credible conclusions about a culture.

Each of us has used the data collection methods outlined in this unit. We may not have consciously walked backstage and taken on the role of anthropologist or method actor. Whether or not we viewed them as "methods" per se, we have been observers of organizational behavior, we have read documents in our organizations to gain knowledge or insight, and in most cases we have participated in informal interviews and possibly in formal surveys. Thus, the process of collecting data about culture, like the notion of cultural elements, is not foreign ground. Put differently, to be a member of an organization is to be a "sense-maker," someone who is trying to make sense of his or her environment (Weick, 1995). This process of sense making is important not only during the first weeks as a new member of an organization, but also during organizational changes and job promotions (Kramer & Noland, 1999). The only way to gain information, to make sense of an organization, is to observe, ask questions, and/or ask someone else to observe or ask questions for us.

These naïve approaches to understanding culture can have great practical significance for the organization member. Angi conducted a cultural analysis in which there was one employee in an insurance company whom no one could stand. The cultural analysis team had probed to understand why this woman was so disliked and rejected by the majority of other employees. All agreed she was competent and hard working. When pressed for details, many of the employees gave the same answer about her failure to fit in. "She brings crackers to the office potluck," several explained, assuming that we would understand immediately the significance of this culinary contribution.

Only in analyzing the culture further did Angi understand the significance. The monthly office potluck embodied several of the organization's defining values and a sense of community and sharing, nurturing, and generosity. All the employees put great effort into bringing creative and tasty dishes. The fact that this employee brought crackers signified to the others that she did not care about the group and that she was cheap. This, of course, signified that she did not share other important group values. The employee probably never grasped the seriousness of her offense or understood why she was disliked by coworkers. She had not picked up on cultural cues about values or the significance of the potluck ritual within the company.

Two "safe" assumptions about our everyday data collection habits prove the value of this approach. *First, we tend to draw conclusions about culture based on sporadic, biased, and incomplete information.* In short, we can improve the thoroughness and validity of our efforts. And *second, incomplete data lead to interpretations that can harm the effectiveness of our communication and thus adversely influence the ethicality and credibility of our leadership efforts.* The hypothetical meeting presented at the start of this chapter is an example of one person's observations. Notice how the story contains a mix of descriptive data ("2 minutes late") and interpretive data ("they must not respect the boss"). The newcomer made a decision not to ask a question based on everyone else's behavior. It is clear, however, that he has much to learn about the function of these meetings and when, if ever, questions can be asked at meetings. In short, the newcomer's observations, his experience of this meeting, form an important aspect of information that will guide his future behavior. The question, then, is how can he improve his abilities as an observer? As a participant in the confusing, often ambiguous world of organizations, how can he move forward from this meeting to contribute to an organizational culture that is more effective and ethical?

Just as consultants and researchers can be critiqued based on their methods used for data collection and interpretation, so can and should we be. If, for example, from the above meeting experience, I fail to ask questions of colleagues even after they present incomplete or inaccurate information at a meeting, then my behavior is no longer simply that of "fitting in"; it can be challenged on ethical grounds.

Rehearsal III.1 Introduction to Method Acting:
The Last Time I Was Wrong

Purpose: Identify the types of informal data you collect and the consequences of relying on these data.

Steps:

1. Recall a time when you drew an inaccurate conclusion about a work relationship, a company policy, or perhaps a change introduced in your organization.

2. What types of cultural data did you use to infer your mistaken conclusion?

3. What other types of data might have helped? What other cultural elements might have helped improve the accuracy of your inference?

Miller and Jablin (1991) point out an inverse relationship between risk and information accuracy when seeking information in organizational entry. The less obtrusive ways of gathering information, such as observing the behaviors of others and drawing inferences, may be perceived as "safer" by the average employee because there is less risk of offending someone or appearing stupid. Yet this less direct way of gathering information can lead the employee to draw the wrong conclusions about the behaviors observed. The more direct information-gaining strategy of asking specific questions produces more reliable data but may be seen as more risky by the employee because of fear of loss of face or being perceived as incapable.

FAQs: Objectivity, Single Method Approaches, and Protecting Human Participants

Will Multiple Methods Result in Objectivity?

A common misconception is that you can somehow create an objective interpretation if you get the right data. We would point out that even triangulated data do not produce an objective view of organizational culture. A researcher always develops subjective conclusions from his or her point of view. Triangulation produces data drawn from multiple points of reference but still contains elements of subjectivity. You will need to accept at the outset that your conclusions about the organizational culture may be different from those another individual might draw.

This does not mean that either is invalid. It does mean that you need to be explicit about supporting your conclusions with data and explaining why you drew the conclusions you did from the data you analyzed. This transparency of logic would allow your readers or listeners to compare the ways in which they might draw different conclusions from the same data set. As we stressed in our introductory analogies, whether "painting by numbers" or "putting together a jigsaw puzzle" the key is to create ethical, credible, and useful interpretations.

What About Examples of Cultural Analysis That Use a Single Method or Single Cultural Element Focus?

Researchers sometimes use multiple methods to obtain information about one or at times two cultural elements. In some cases, however, a more specialized approach (e.g., root metaphor, linguistics, rules) may focus on a particular "element as a method" for interpreting culture. For example, an analysis of stories may be the method used to decipher organizational values (e.g., Meyer, 1995). A focus on a single element, such a metaphors, might be used to gain understanding of a particular phenomenon, such as workplace bullying (Tracy, Lutgen-Sandvik, & Alberts, 2006). The goal of this workbook, however, is to help you perform a more comprehensive cultural analysis in order to produce competent individual and organizational performances. The key is to allow researchers who focus on a particular element to spark your imagination regarding the various methods that can be used to interpret culture. Furthermore, the examples gleaned from these articles are of focused efforts designed to "impress" you with the value or importance of a given element. Our goal is to go beyond the study of one element to gaining a richer description of the culture than can be obtained from a focus on a single method or element. In the following three chapters we explore each method in more depth and offer practical suggestions for how you can use each to gain insight into your organization's culture. We begin with the most basic tool for actors seeking to be more effective at directing and leading the communication practices on the stage—observation.

What Steps Should Be Taken to Protect Participants?

We provide an entire chapter on ethics and hope you have noted the issue of ethics as a theme throughout this book. From a social constructionism perspective, we have a responsibility to be aware of the influence of our cultural analysis on shaping the culture. Science fiction buffs can cite stories of time travelers who have to be very careful in their visit to the past not to take actions that would alter all of subsequent history. There is a parallel in organizational intervention. We need to realize that the questions we ask, how we ask them, and how we use the data all influence the culture of the organization. For instance, if handled improperly, data may negatively influence an employee's job security. You might also ask questions in a way that lead employees to be dissatisfied, or to question the motives of management, affecting organizational trust. We can not stress enough the importance of being diligent about protecting the people in the organization you serve in this analysis process, and being aware of how your activities in the cultural analysis can have an effect on the long-term culture of the organization.

Most universities require researchers using human subjects or participants to seek approval from an institutional review board (IRB). This requirement applies to student projects as well. Your instructor can guide you with the particular requirements and processes at your university. At some universities each student must gain independent approval for each project. At our university, we are able to submit one "blanket" approval form to cover all the student class projects because their methods are all similar. We have provided an example class IRB review form on the Sage companion website, www.sagepub.com/driskill2estudy, in the event your instructor wants to gain approval for each student project under this umbrella approval process.

In general, protection of human subjects is based on three principles contained in the *Belmont Report of Ethical Principles and Guidelines for the Protection of Human Subjects of Research* (Office for Human Research Protections, n.d.), which was issued by the National Commission for the Protection of Human Subjects of Biomedical and Behavioral Research (previously the Office for Protection of Research Risks) in 1979. These three principles include (a) that the study will pose no undue risks to the life, health, or integrity of research subjects; (b) that any risks to subjects are outweighed by the potential significance of the study; and (c) that subjects have the opportunity to give informed consent about their participation in the study.

An informed consent form must contain information about the purpose and procedures of the study, any risk involved, the voluntary nature of participation and ability to withdraw at any stage of the study, and contact information for questions or concerns. It also must inform subjects of the nature of confidentiality and how their privacy will be protected in the study. It will also inform them about what will be done with the information obtained in the study. An example of an informed consent form is included in Rehearsal III.2.

Summary

Before diving into your analysis, you should understand several key ideas in the overview of methods:

- The cultural analysis you will conduct seeks to gather valid and credible data without engaging in the years of data collection that might be involved in an ethnography of an organization.

- We suggest that you use the methods introduced in the coming chapters in an order that is appropriate to your analysis. We introduce systematic analysis of organizational texts followed by observation, then interviews and surveys.

- You have used the data collection methods outlined in this unit, yet your everyday data collection process tends to provide incomplete and biased information that can decrease effective leadership.

- Less direct or obtrusive methods of data collection, such as observations, are safer in terms of influencing participants but may lead to wrong conclusions. Conversely, more direct information-gaining strategies such as formal interviews are less safe but may provide more reliable data because of your ability to gain insider perspectives.

- Triangulation or using multiple methods will result in more credible conclusions about a culture.

- One person's conclusions about the organizational culture may be different from those another individual might draw.

- You should seek to collect information about all of the major cultural elements.

- You should maintain diligence in protecting members of the organization; you may need to gain approval from a university institutional review board before beginning your study.

Rehearsal III.2 Sample Informed Consent Form

Adapt the following informed consent form for use in your cultural analysis. This consent form applies to:

Name: _____

The following information is provided to inform you about the research on _____. Please feel free to ask any questions you may have about this study and the information given below. You will be given an opportunity to ask questions and to have your questions answered. In addition, you will be given a copy of this consent form.

1. **Purpose of the study.** This study is being conducted by [researcher's name and faculty/student status] of the Department/School/College of [subject] at the University of [university name] in order to better understand [research topic]. This research will help [who?] better understand how [process or issue being investigated]. Your responses in the interview are confidential and available only to the [interviewer/researcher/faculty supervisor].

2. **Description of the procedures to be followed and approximate duration of the study.** Participants in the research will participate in [describe data collection process], which will focus on [research topic]. This [data collection process] will last approximately [length of time].

3. **Description of the discomforts, inconveniences, and/or risks that can reasonably be expected as a result of participation in this study.** Discussing [research topic] may be uncomfortable, and [care services] will [or will not] be available to you as a result of your participation.

4. **Description of how confidentiality will be assured and the limits to these assurances, if any.**

5. **Anticipated benefits resulting from this study.**

   a. The potential benefits to you from participating in the study are [describe benefits]. The study may be helpful to increase your understanding of [issue being investigated].

   b. The potential benefits to science and humanity that may result from this study are [describe benefits]. This study will provide information to [intended audience of research results] to help them [intended outcomes of the research results].

6. **Alternative procedures.** [If alternative procedures exist, please describe them here. Otherwise, include a statement that says:] There are no alternative procedures to participation in the interview.

7. **Contact information.** If you have any questions about this study, you can contact the person(s) below:

   Name of Principal Investigator _____
   Department/School _____
   Name of Supervisor (if PI is a student) _____
   Department/School _____

Include name, address, telephone number, and e-mail addresses

If you have any questions about your rights as a research participant, please contact the Chair of the Institutional Review Board at [telephone number].

5 Method Acting

Textual Analysis

> It is easy to create tension by trying a simple experiment. Try lifting something, such as an edge of a piano or a heavy table. At the same time, try to solve a simple mental problem, such as multiplying 75 by 6—an intellectual exercise that would normally involve little difficulty. You will discover it is nearly impossible to do so while lifting the heavy object.
>
> —Strasberg, *A Dream of Passion*, 1987, p. 125

Articulate the value of the culture metaphor

Define major cultural elements

★ **Use multiple data collection methods**

Synthesize and interpret cultural data

Identify applications

Objectives:

- Distinguish among the major types of textual analysis
- Explain major guidelines for analyzing a text

Stage Terms:

- Textual analysis
- Content analysis
- Rhetorical analysis
- Critical linguistic analysis

Step Three: Use a Variety of Methods to Collect Cultural Data

"So, Jane, are you saying you read the company newsletter? Really?"

"Yes, Jamal, and you would do well to pay attention to it. The HRD department takes a lead role in writing it and they often have the inside scoop on what's happening. They have a way of dropping hints in the newsletter that you may not get elsewhere."

Jamal was shocked to learn that in his new organization the newsletter mattered at all. In his prior experience, the newsletter went into the recycle bin without even a glance.

Textual Analysis

Textual analysis is a generic term used for the analysis of any written artifact. Just as an actor in a play must be adept at reading not only the script, but the reviews, biographies of the author, and so on, so also the effective organizational actor must be adept at analyzing texts that give insight into the culture. At an informal level, when you make observations about an organizational trend, pattern, strength, or problem based on reading a document (newsletter, report), you are engaged in textual analysis. The above example makes it clear that organizations differ in the weight given to various written media. However, determining what to read may not be as difficult as determining how to read. In other words, reading just for a quick update is different from reading for cultural information. For those conducting a cultural analysis, reading a newsletter for general updates while also trying to analyze it for cultural meaning may be like lifting the corner of a piano while doing a math problem. Such a process creates tension until you learn to focus. This chapter is about getting you to set aside the math problem to focus on the heavy lifting of textual analysis. You will use textual analysis not only for newsletters and company webpages but also for analyzing your field notes and interview transcripts or summaries.

We briefly review three methods of textual analysis introduced in this chapter before providing more detailed guidance: content analysis, rhetorical analysis, and linguistic analysis. *Content analysis* is a method of creating categories from the text (such as interview transcripts and summaries) and developing a method of counting material related to each of the categories. For example, perhaps you have created four categories of values mentioned frequently during interviews: risk taking, public image, innovation, and profitability. You might then move systematically through your interview transcripts or summaries to see how many interviews mentioned each of the four categories, or how many times the terms came up in interviews. At the end of your categorizing, you might conclude that profitability had been mentioned twice as often as any other value. For instance, one team of researchers explored narratives to determine major content themes related to sustainability practices (Livesey, Hartman, Stafford, & Shearer, 2009).

Rhetorical analysis is typically more qualitative and less quantitative. In rhetorical analysis, the researcher examines the author, background, purpose, strategy, and effect of written or oral texts. Examples of this type of textual analysis are the study of apologies made by sports and corporate figures as well as public officials in the era of public accountability—from Pete Rose and Kobe Bryant to George W. Bush and Barack Obama (see Benoit-Barné, 2007; Bostdorff, 2009; Harter, Stephens, & Japp, 2000; Patel & Reinsch, 2003; Prato, 2000; Scher & Darley, 1997; Sugimoto, 1997; West & Carey, 2006). The rhetorical scholar might investigate the public attitudes or climate in which the apology is offered, the nature of the person offering the apology, the characteristics of the message (Does it take personal responsibility? Does it contain excuses?), and the effect on the intended audience. Although this method of textual analysis is quite involved, it may be appropriate with certain important organizational texts that are cited as the moment of major cultural change or mission redefinition.

A final type of textual analysis is *linguistic analysis*. In this method, the researcher draws inferences from specific language and grammatical structures of messages. The linguistic researcher would pay attention to why a corporate leader chose one term rather than another; why one word was repeated over and over in a text; or the intent or effect of passive verb use, which tends to deny responsibility. For instance, Wasson (2004) examines the use of marketplace or enterprise metaphors. Her analysis gave insight, for instance, to how these metaphors created irony and paradox for employees. One interviewee reflected on how the "enterprise ideology" should have prompted her to feel confident and take control of a project. However, the reality is that the success of the project was not under her direct control. Thus, this employee was ironically "disempowered by being forced to speak as if she were empowered" (Wasson, 2004, p. 190). In another example, Angi in her study of a church conflict (Brenton, 1993) studied two major texts, a statement by a dissident at the church, read ostensibly as an apology to the congregation, and the second a response from church leaders. She found that the statement by the dissident used active voice, stressed agency by specific references to individuals, and used language related to change 14 times in the message. On the other hand, the statement from the church leaders used passive voice, did not include any references to specific people, and used language related to order and stability 24 times. The linguistic features of the messages displayed the different reactions of the two parties in their orientation to change and responsibility.

Perhaps the most powerful argument for using textual analysis is the unobtrusive nature of the method. You can, without influencing reactions from anyone, read and gain useful cultural data. Much can be learned from, for example, such organizational documents and artifacts as memos, written histories, and newsletters or even oral texts such as speeches or videos. Textual analysis also could be used to investigate a culture that no longer exists, or to analyze the past of a current organization through archival material. So, as you might imagine, wise leaders and consultants who want to be effective directors will do their homework at this stage. To make the most of a textual analysis, follow these guidelines:

1. Determine a valid/credible "text" for analysis.

For example, if you examine newsletters, get an organizationally relevant sample. Such a sample may need to include newsletters from both before and after a major change. Or relevance may mean samples from various stages or important periods in the history and annual event calendar of the organization. It is dangerous to draw conclusions from a single artifact or even from a small sample. The danger is much like that to be found in basing your understanding of an organization on one person's views. It is also important to consider official and unofficial samples of written artifacts. In one organization we had done an extensive analysis of a large sample of employee newsletters only to find that most employees considered the newsletter to be corporate propaganda and never read it. We then sought what culture members considered to be more authentic examples of corporate texts. You need to ask yourself who produced a particular text and for what reason when deciding whether it is a credible text for cultural analysis.

You should also consider the organizational communication style when deciding on texts for analysis. Organizational communication style was one of the cultural elements described in Chapter 4. If an organization has a written culture, you should have abundant texts to choose from—from policies and procedures manuals to memos to annual reports. If an organization's style is more oral or interpersonal, you may have to focus on different types of texts. You may be able to find copies of speech texts or be able to find videos of corporate interactions. In an organization whose communication style is electronic, texts to analyze may include e-mail records, Facebook, or other electronic system transactions.

Rehearsal 5.1 Selecting Texts for Analysis

Purpose: Identify relevant texts for analysis.

Steps:

1. Review the list of possible organizational texts to analyze.
2. Put a check mark by those that you have access to in the organization.
3. Put another check mark by those that observation and interviews suggest are particularly credible to organization members.
4. Jot down your sense of the type of cultural data available (values, heroes, etc.).

Example Texts	*Available?*	*Credible?*	*Cultural Data?*
Newsletter			
Annual report			
Website			
Mission statement			
Bulletin boards			
Employee handbook			
E-mail transmissions			
Transcripts of speeches			
Facebook			
Memos			
Affirmative action/ diversity statement			
Employee orientation materials or videos			
Other			

2. Choose your method of analysis.

Content Analysis. The most common method of analyzing texts is content analysis. You will probably use this method for analyzing your field notes and interview transcripts or summaries. You may find it useful for analyzing other written texts as well. The basic technique of content analysis is to let categories emerge from the elements of culture or from your data, and then use those categories to count some feature of the text. You might have a sense after 15 or 20 interviews that you have heard three values most frequently: teamwork, excellence, and accountability. You will go back through the interview notes and summaries with these categories in mind, and perhaps a fourth category of "other." You will count the number of times each of the three values was mentioned, and place a tally mark beside that category for each time it was mentioned in the interviews. When you encounter other values in addition to the three you have chosen as categories, you will place a tally mark by the "other" category. If at the end of the process you find that "other" is larger than any of the three categories you started with, you might need to go back through the notes and decide whether there is another category you need to break out of the "other" category to represent the data accurately. Content analysis is often a trial-and-error process in which you may need to revise the category structure one or two times until you find the categories that fit your data best.

Some researchers use software to aid in content analysis. Thus, if your texts are in electronic format (newsletters, typed field notes, etc.), programs such as *Diction 5.0* (Hart, 2000) enable you to process 30,000 words in 1 minute. This type of software can examine texts for such features as "commonality"—language highlighting the agreed-upon values of a group, or "certainty"—language indicating resoluteness, inflexibility, and completeness.

As you perform content analysis on a text, either by hand or computer, you must decide your measurement unit. What are you counting? In the example above, your unit of analysis was "mentions" in an interview. In analyzing printed texts, different measurements might be more appropriate. You could count the number of pictures featuring management versus employees, or men versus women, or Caucasians versus African Americans. You could count the number of stories on certain subjects, or the number of column inches devoted to various topics. If you were analyzing a smaller document such as a speech, you might focus on counting actual words—how often the word *excellent* appeared in a 10-minute speech, for example. Within a lengthy newsletter, you may want to focus on one area, such as messages from the president or on member spotlights. You can analyze a written artifact at a micro or a macro level. You might, for example, count the number of stories in an overall newsletter on various topics (macroanalysis) or analyze specific words used in a representative paragraph (microanalysis).

You may actually measure square centimeters or inches or do a word count; however, the percentage of an entire newsletter devoted to the issue in comparison to other topics is perhaps more telling. The key here is to use this analysis as *one gauge* of what is important to the organization, based on amount of space allotted in publications.

Rhetorical Analysis. Another technique of textual analysis is rhetorical analysis. Although there are many systems of rhetorical analysis, its simplest form involves an in-depth analysis of a specific speech or text given by an identifiable cultural figure. Because the process is so involved, you would use this on only a very significant organizational text. Suppose you are studying GM's CEO Rick Wagoner's statements and speeches to congress and stockholders in light of the 2008 financial crisis. In rhetorical analysis you would find out more about Wagoner and the events leading up to congress demanding his removal. What factors provide context for these speeches? Then with that appropriate background information you would analyze the message itself. What was the purpose of the speech? What arguments or persuasive appeals were made? How were they supported? What type of evidence was offered? What cultural elements were woven into the speech—History? Values? Metaphors? Symbols? Finally you would analyze the results of the speech. How effective was the speech in providing for smooth transition when he resigned? How did employees respond? What stories are still told about his rise and fall?

Critical Linguistic Analysis. The final method of textual analysis we discuss is critical linguistic analysis. In this method, based on the work of Fowler (1986), you take a small but culturally significant text such as a mission statement, an inaugural address, a press release, or a corporate apology and analyze the language and grammatical patterns to reveal underlying system logic. Although Fowler includes a number of linguistic features in his system, the following are particularly relevant to cultural analysis:

- Pronoun use: As corporate leaders talk and write, do they talk about "we" or "I"? Do they refer to employees as "them"? Do they use pronouns such as "you" that have the effect of finger pointing?

- Active or passive verb use: Do decision makers accept accountability for their actions by using names and active verbs or do they hide behind passive verbs that fail to identify agents of actions? (*The decision was made to eliminate 600 jobs.*)

- Overuse or underuse of certain words or types of words: For example, in a public statement Angi analyzed, leaders in one embattled organization used the terms *rational, orderly,* and *proper* more than 17 times. This was indicative of their resistance to cultural change led by the members of the culture.

- Verb tense: Do public statements talk more about the past with past tense or more about the future with future tense?

3. Link the results of your analysis back to cultural elements and cultural significance.

Like the interview and observation processes, this step is about summarizing your data into a form that is usable. For instance, you might have entries that state the following:

Heroes: Three of the four newsletters gave one eighth of their space to discussing the ex-CEO. This amount of space was about two times as much as for any other person or issue. Interview summaries and articles written by this ex-CEO all suggest that he remains a hero and perhaps a legend of sorts for this organization.

Values: One value was mentioned 43 times in interviews, four times as often as any other value discussed by employees.

Language: Certain terms are used repeatedly in discussing employee pay and benefit concerns. Such terms as *tenure, earned,* and *seen potential* are words used by management to explain a policy change that reduces benefits for employees who have less than 2 years of history with the organization.

4. Ground your interpretation by reviewing the data again.

Take time to reflect on data gathered on the elements. Review data across elements to see what stands out or perhaps does not fit. You should then *make a list of questions about confusing or contradictory issues.* For example, you might find an espoused value in the written documents that is different from the values expressed in employee interviews. The mission statement, for example, might stress the importance of sustainability or community engagement, yet there is not one picture or story in the newsletter that reflects these values. Thus, you should ground interpretations from textual analysis back into the native perspective by asking organizational members about their interpretations.

Summary

Systematic analyses of organizational texts are similar to the intense work an actor does with a script prior to crafting a performance. Textual analysis is an unobtrusive research method and can reveal a great deal about an organization. This chapter stressed the following points:

- Three systematic ways to analyze organizational texts:
  1. Content analysis
  2. Rhetorical analysis
  3. Critical linguistic analysis

- It is vital that you choose a sufficient sample of organizationally credible texts to analyze to learn about the culture. Organizational communication style may influence your choice.

Rehearsal 5.2 Content Analysis

Purpose: To gain experience in noting the types of cultural elements that can be found in various organizational artifacts

Directions:

1. Identify an artifact for analysis (newsletter, etc.).

2. Analyze the artifact using content analysis.
   - Determine the unit of analysis or your focus in the text.
   - Pay attention to the amount of space devoted to certain issues from one document to the next.
   - Identify and give examples of specific cultural elements.
   - Make a list of questions about confusing or contradictory issues.

3. Write a brief summary of insights about at least three of the elements.

4. Write down specific challenges and questions you faced in the process. These issues can be shared with a colleague or instructor who is working with you in this process.

Rehearsal 5.3 Critical Linguistic Analysis

Purpose: To gain experience in using critical linguistic analysis in cultural studies

Directions: Compare the following language features in two organizational texts. These texts can be found online at www.sagepub.com/driskill2estudy. We provide options so that you can contrast mission and company information from two different types of organizations. Tom's Shoes—(http://www .tomsshoes.com/corporate-information) versus Nike Shoes (http://www.nikebiz .com/company_overview) and GM Automotive (http://www.gm.com/corporate) versus Toyota (http://www.toyota.com/about/our_values).

As you examine mission statements and corporate philosophies, pay attention to such language features as:

- Pronoun use

- Passive or active voice

- Words that are overused or underused

- Verb tense—past, present, future

What differences do you note in these texts? Commonalities? What tentative inferences might you draw about how the corporate cultures differ?

6

Method Acting

Observation

Articulate the value of the culture metaphor

Define major cultural elements

★ **Use multiple data collection methods**

Synthesize and interpret cultural data

Identify applications

Step Three: Use Multiple Data Collection Methods to Understand the Elements of Culture

> *To concentrate, one must have an object of concentration; one cannot concentrate abstractly. The simple presence of an object will not induce concentration. If you look at a chair and try to concentrate, nothing will happen. If you start asking yourself simple questions—How wide is the chair? How tall is it? and so on—simple concentration will take place.*

> —Strasberg, *A Dream of Passion*, 1987, p. 131

Objectives:

- Identify four major observation roles
- Describe ways to enhance the validity and reliability of observation data
- Practice recording observations in field notes

Stage Terms:

- Obtrusive and unobtrusive observation
- Complete observer
- Observer participant
- Participant observer
- Complete participant
- Field notes
- Bracketing

Observation

Imagine an actor (or a director) who never took the time to go behind the scenes, research a script or character, or learn the basic methods of acting. We would quickly judge such an actor to be incompetent. However, we all have moments when we realize that our observations can be skewed or biased. For example, based on one interaction or meeting with a colleague, we may form an inaccurate negative or positive

83

impression. However, even with such awareness it is often easier and more comfortable to maintain our casual observation and interaction habits. We may not see a method for or value in reflecting carefully on our daily interactions on the organizational stage.

Awareness of bias in our perception should motivate us to sharpen our observation skills. The goal in this chapter is to improve our understanding of and our ability to enact effective observer roles—the core or foundation of method acting and cultural analysis.

Observation is critical to method actors, as expressed by Lee Strasberg (1987). He calls on training actors to concentrate on the particulars of a process that has become automatic, such as drinking a beverage. Only in concentrating on each element of the habitual behavior can the actor master the subtleties of re-creating a common behavior on stage. The actor must spend many hours in analyzing and practicing a behavior in order for it to appear natural and compelling on stage. Strasberg writes, "The ability to interrupt the automatic functioning of the nerves and muscles in order to create an object's presence for oneself . . . is part of the process of creating reality rather than imitating it" (p. 133).

One value of engaging in a formal cultural analysis is that we become more aware of the way our everyday interactions construct and reconstruct culture. Observer roles can be categorized by examining the degree of "obtrusiveness" or degree of influence the observer has on the members of organizations. "Obtrusive" behavior is that which calls attention to the observer, affecting the flow of behavior being observed. Different behavior may be seen as obtrusive depending on the organization. For example, extensive note taking during a meeting may be the norm in certain organizations, thus taking notes during a meeting would be unlikely to influence the flow of the meeting. Conversely, such note taking during a ritual morning coffee break would be likely to trigger responses from other members of the organization. Reviews of four observation roles followed by observation guidelines are presented as ways to consider the implication of each type of observer role.

Selecting a Method of Observation

There are four major observer roles. Each role involves trade-offs based on such factors as objectivity, insight into interactions, and ethics. As you review these, realize that it is not uncommon to move between different roles. In other words, entering into one type of observation role does not preclude your engaging in another type of role at some other point in time. For example, we have had students begin observation of a given nonprofit as a complete observer and switch to a participant observer as they began to identify with the mission of the nonprofit and get to know the staff and volunteers.

1. Complete Observer

In this role, you observe the culture with or without the organization's knowledge and without direct interaction with members. (Please note, however, that your instructor may require you to gain permission from the organization, even if you are studying your own organization.) To use the drama metaphor, you would be an actor doing research for a role, observing behavior of people similar to the character you are to portray. Assuming this role carries several implications:

- In traditional research terms, the researcher may have increased objectivity due to the lack of involvement with organization members who might bias his or her judgment.

- On the other hand, qualitative researchers would argue that the researcher would possibly also have fewer and less valid insights due to the distance from experience of members.

- The role of complete observer can raise possible ethical problems if you observe individuals without their permission, depending on the purposes of the research. If the organization studied is a professional football team, for instance, and performances are public, then the ethical concerns are less of an issue. In all instances, ethical guidelines must be observed.

- The complete observer role may be best when you do not have full access to the organization, when you have organizational permission to observe the organization, and/or when members' knowledge of your presence would be likely to harm research objectives. For example, individuals considering a career move who are trying to learn more about a particular type of organization may find this method appropriate. If, for instance, they want to learn more about the automotive industry, they may find it useful to show up at a public event or simply to walk through public areas of the organization to learn what they can from the setting and artifacts on display.

2. Observer–Participant

In this role, you would let members know they are being observed, and you would participate partially with them in the organization. This role carries different implications:

- This role somewhat reduces objectivity due to involvement, yet possibly increases validity by interacting with organization members and gaining their insights.

- Some would question validity when members are aware of your involvement.

- You may find adopting the observer–participant role places you on more solid ethical ground due to member knowledge of your involvement.

- This role is best when you have access to the organization and/or when member knowledge of your presence would be unlikely to harm research objectives; for example, observation of meetings to understand norms and interaction patterns for the purpose of enriching the current employee handbook.

3. Participant–Observer

In this role, you let members know they are being studied, and you become involved in the organization. The implications of this role include the following:

- According to a traditional research perspective, it produces reduced objectivity due to high involvement in the organization.

- This role produces increased access to the views and insights of organization members, and the researchers themselves begin to understand the organization from both internal and external perspectives.

- This role places similar constraints on you as an observer–participant in relation to member awareness of your involvement, yet the more organizational members accept you as a participant, the less they are aware of you as an observer.

- Because organization members are aware of your dual role (researcher and participant), you are on fairly solid ethical ground.

- This role is best when you have longer-term access to the organization and/or when member knowledge of your presence would be unlikely to harm research objectives; for example, observation of day-to-day communication to understand positive and negative patterns that would affect training interventions.

4. Complete Participant

In this final role, you become fully involved without letting members know of your observation efforts. The implications include the following:

- You have reduced objectivity due to high involvement and have a high level of insight due to identification with members.

- Possible ethical problems would ensue because of lack of notification of research subjects, depending on the purposes of the observations. For example, if you dropped in on meetings without informing those present that you were also there to evaluate and report their behaviors, then your efforts would be judged unethical because of the potential harm that could result to those present. This approach might also be inconsistent with protection of human subjects if you did not allow informed consent of your observation.

- This role is best when you have access to the organization and/or when members' lack of knowledge of your presence would not influence the ethicality of your research purpose. For example, as a human resources department (HRD) manager you could serve and lead more effectively if you gleaned insights about norms and rules through observation of meetings and rituals.

Standards of protection of human subjects, presented in the overview to this section, are critical in cultural research, as well. If you present a cultural study to the CEO of an organization, and your study inadvertently reveals rule breaking or violation of cultural norms, it could have serious career implications for individuals you study.

One of the observation role options, "complete participant," should stand out as the form of observation we engage in every day. Unless you decide to inform others in the workplace of your analysis efforts, you are a complete participant. As a complete participant you are doing something external analysts and researchers are challenged to justify—"clandestine data collection." The ethical justification for an insider is based on the reality that your observation is doing what all members of organizations do, but simply doing it in a more systematic and planned manner. Nonetheless, realize that, for some, it will be appropriate to seek the permission of a manager or to inform employees of your analysis plans. For example, you may be a trainer in your organization or work in a role that has made you aware of the need for a cultural analysis. After reviewing the value of the study with those you decide to inform, you may want to move ahead with a formal analysis that would involve a participant observer role. Regardless of the role you select, the key is to be aware of the specific issues related to objectivity, validity, and ethics.

Conducting Observations

Once you have decided on the most appropriate role, review the following guides for help in the process of conducting the observation and taking notes. Approach the observation with some theoretical framework or purpose in mind. You cannot observe and record everything. You need to have a rationale for what you notice and record. The elements of culture provide such a framework. Try to notice those things you think might be tied to history, a value, a norm, or a cultural hero. We suggested in the introduction to the section on methods (see Table III.1) that your cultural observation could focus on artifacts, interactions, language, and symbols. We also suggested cultural elements most closely tied to each of these observable organizational representations. Look for things that have cultural significance as you follow these guidelines. Also, at the end of this chapter we summarize these guidelines in a checklist to review as you complete a practice observation in a rehearsal.

1. Make like an alien by making use of various techniques to become a "stranger."

a. Write notes on the mundane, seemingly unimportant events. Improving the quality of our observations, especially if you have been with an organization for much time, involves seeing things with new eyes. We encourage this process in Rehearsal 6.3, "Alien Culture Observation." The first step in this process is taking notes that record information that you have grown to take for granted. For example, if you were an "old-timer" in the case study that began this unit, you would record the setting, the sitting arrangement, and when and how the meeting began and ended. Such detailed notes force you to see situations with new eyes.

b. Mutate metaphors by drawing comparisons or making analogies between things that you normally do not compare (Weick, 1979). Mutating metaphors involves merging or synthesizing two metaphors to capture conflicting values or rules. For example, imagine if you frequently heard two metaphors in your organization: "fast track" and "outer space." As you listened you got the sense that "good" employees were expected to be on the fast track. However, you also heard sarcastic statements about working in outer space with the implication being that there was not a clear sense of what was up or down, because in outer space "up and down" and "north and south" are arbitrary. To capture these two metaphors you might mutate them to create a new metaphor like "working at Organization Z is like being on a corporate ladder without ever knowing which direction is up or down." This mutated metaphor captures what members may be aware of but have not clearly articulated—"We hear about the expectation to move up the ladder but we do not know which way is up!" Such comparisons may clarify or serve to identify a problem in the organization.

Smith and Eisenberg (1987) in their article on Disneyland, for example, indicated that the root problem in employee relations might have begun when employees began seeing their work through the family rather than the drama metaphor. Rules and actions that might have been easily accepted through the drama metaphor became inappropriate when viewed through the lens of family. For example, you might replace a cast member who is incompetent in a role, but you do not fire family. If you were consulting with an organization that had operated primarily through a family metaphor, what implications would a change in that metaphor have for employees? Customers? Helping the organization manage change might involve a metaphor mutation—if employees were able to mutate metaphors they could envision the change in a new way. For example, the mutation might involve both metaphors, "an acting family" that has to determine who is best for what role.

c. Ask "why" and "what function" questions of everything. Though you will have to decide the appropriateness of asking others these types of questions, you should at the minimum reflect on them yourself. For example, you might observe an organization's annual retirement banquet and assume that it indicated a culture in which employee contributions were valued. However, if you asked a member of the organization about it, she might say that there is great pressure for older employees to take early retirement so that less expensive younger employees can be hired. Or she might note that it is a sign that the company values seniority more than excellent performance because the only significant award banquet in the organization is to honor retirees rather than high performers. Once you have made your own possible interpretations, you can make notes to ask organizational insiders how they would interpret the regularities you have observed.

2. If you do not or cannot take notes while observing, reserve time immediately after observation to jot down notes.

Note taking has the potential advantage of improving the quality of the information you collect on the organization. For those who rarely take notes or keep journals, the process will be awkward and feel like a waste of time. Still, the key is to make time for this process of describing what you see. You may think you will remember details later, but chances are you will forget many important details. Doing a thorough cultural analysis requires noting fine details of language, artifacts, and interaction. These are best captured in detailed field notes. Another value of the process of writing involves not just putting words on paper but taking the time to capture events, reflect on them, and in time make sense of them. An enhanced or improved cultural analysis depends on your seeing all the possible "dots" in a connect-the-dots worksheet. Sometimes you draw conclusions—connect dots—without adequate attention to details that could change the shape of the picture. To use the drama analogy, note taking may force you to see a way to interpret the language being used in the play in a different light. For example, a review of notes might reveal a pattern you had not seen concerning the way certain types of conflicts were not discussed. This newly emerged pattern might then shed light on other practices, such as premature closure on decisions to avoid conflict. As shown in this example of conflict, your notes should reflect your observation of things that did *not* happen that one might have expected. For example, why did no one ask questions? Why did no one talk about anything not on the formal agenda? Why do employees have no personal items in their offices?

3. Attempt to include observations of meetings, rituals, and so on as well as observations of less formal interactions, events, and the like.

The tendency, for example, may be to take notes of a ribbon cutting ceremony or a company picnic, but fail to record observations of communication at the coffeepot. Culture, as previously noted, reflects how members experience daily life in the organization. A weekly office meeting or daily coffeepot ritual provides just as much insight into organizational culture as an annual awards banquet. It may be that those coffeepot interactions include significant relationship development rituals that an insider may not see immediately. Such insights may help current employees do more to engage new employees to ensure the latter are not forced to catch on to the importance of the ritual on their own.

4. Use brackets [ ] to help you focus on descriptions instead of interpretations.

"Bracketing" refers to the idea of putting your first impressions, initial definitions of the culture, and inferences or insights inside of brackets. For example, your first weeks spent in observation might surface the way the lounge area has unique rituals with language you did not hear in other places in the building. These observations might prompt you to draw an interpretation or conclusion about the overall culture. Strong personalities in interviews or meetings can also prompt a researcher to draw conclusions early in the process. Indeed, our own ambiguity or uncertainty in a new organization will often prompt us to develop premature ideas. *The key is to bracket these conclusions until you have used other methods and explored all of the elements.*

These premature conclusions, if not set aside, can prompt you to slant your future data collection toward supporting these views. Bracketing them helps you separate description from your tentative interpretations as you process your observation. For example, in participant observation research on an organization that is involved in community building, Gerald is regularly challenged to place his own biases in brackets. The leaders in this organization have differing political and theological positions. It is important for him to bracket reactions to these differences so other information about actual interactions remains in the foreground. The value of such foregrounding is that insight is gained into the way communication functions in the social construction process rather than a myriad of personal reactions. Using the meeting example provided at the opening of the methods section, we provide four different types of bracketed information that might occur while taking notes. Under each type of bracketing you will first see an example of a brief descriptive note and then the bracketed information that provides an example of a type of information you might bracket.

a. *Questions to ask (other) insiders:* There were several new faces today, including two guests. [How would you compare and contrast what happens in a meeting when visitors or newcomers are present versus those times when just the old-timers are there?]

b. *Possible paradoxes, contradictions, root metaphor:* The meeting facilitator briefly introduced the guests, who spoke about a recent statewide political initiative. [In past interviews I recall hearing discussions about being cautious about inviting guests to make presentations. I am not clear on the criteria being used.]

c. *Later comparisons—see how your perceptions change:* The meeting ended with a ritual prayer and then with an additional prayer over a leader who was moving to another state to take on an international role in the unity movement. [The send-off made me think about other meetings that included a special send-off. This particular send-off makes me want to compare the differences in that a value emerged that I had not heard before—a global vision of cooperation among faith leaders. The member seems to be in position to be a hero for this movement.]

d. *Personal reactions/differences:* The guest speakers talked about positive and negative reactions to their political initiative. [I wasn't fully comfortable with the presentation. I am not sure why, perhaps it was that I did not get to hear the full story, the rationale of their opponents. Has this group ever considered inviting those with divergent views to their meetings? This insight makes me consider business organizations that end up with groupthink because they do not have someone or charge someone to voice divergent views.]

5. If a newcomer or an outsider, make use of insiders to check your understanding of jargon and your inferences about cultural elements.

Use informal interviews to check whether your understanding is accurate. We will discuss the role of interviews in greater depth; this guide is a reminder that observation alone is not sufficient.

Often your own interpretation of an artifact or event may be quite different from the way an insider (or a different insider) might interpret the same event. For example, in one study, conclusions were drawn about an organization's culture from its newsletter, only to discover later that no one read the newsletter, thus it had little impact on culture at the grassroots level. Another cultural analysis included a conclusion based on the many positive memos that the CEO sent to employees. They inferred that the culture was positive and supportive. When checking this conclusion with employees, the researcher found that the memos from the CEO had become a joke because they were sent so frequently and so indiscriminately.

6. Review your notes to determine whether they allow you to draw reasonable inferences about most of the cultural elements.

For example, do the notes of a meeting provide enough detail for you to make relatively valid inferences about communication rules? For instance, take a minute to read an edited version of the notes used in one of the previous guidelines:

> There were several new faces at the meeting today, including two guests. The meeting facilitator briefly introduced the guests, who spoke about a recent statewide political initiative. The guest speakers talked about positive and negative reactions to their political initiative. [I wasn't comfortable with the presentation because I didn't get to hear the rationale of their opponents.] The meeting ended with a ritual prayer and with an additional prayer over a leader who was moving to another state to take on an eventual international role in the unity movement.

What inferences could you draw from just this brief section of notes? Notice how even a brief section reveals elements of the culture (e.g., meeting-ending rituals). However, if the above were the entire entry, what questions would you have? What would you have missed? A lack of detail about how the speakers were introduced, as well as participant interactions or reactions to the speakers, is also evident. Also, notice how we excluded brackets that were introduced in the earlier example. The lack of brackets around information means that a later review of these notes would be unlikely to resurface the same questions and observations. If you review notes a week or two later and see a lack of detail, begin to make adjustments. And, again, remember that the goal is to spend a season being a more careful, note-taking observer. This process will pay off in the form of new insights.

7. Categorize notes by elements.

We reviewed elements of culture in Chapter 4. At this point in your data collection, you should take a first step in analysis by entering relevant data from your notes based on these categories (e.g., rules, heroes, history). We provide a Rehearsal activity at the end of this chapter to move you down the road of "performing culture." In particular, as you classify data into elements, you should be aware of two pragmatic goals. First, classifying data into cultural element categories will serve to guide additional data collection by helping you see gaps. For instance, if you have 2 weeks of notes and have been unable to identify a hero or a communication rule, you should let this gap prompt closer and more varied (more times, situations) observations. Second, classifying data into element categories will aid you in the creation of an interview guide or survey. We will cover interviews and surveys in the next chapter. A good set of notes categorized by elements will aid you in gaining the most from these additional data collection practices by helping you identify areas where you need greater clarity or confirmation. For instance, you may have identified what you believe to be a major cultural hero from reading a history of the organization, but the name of this hero never surfaces in informal discussions or formal meetings. Interviews or surveys may help you determine the relevance of the hero's values and vision for the present.

Connections: Getting More From Rites and Rituals

A frequent and rich object of observation is the organizational rite or ritual—either a special event in the organization or a daily routine with cultural significance. As you stand backstage, consider two reasons that something as commonplace and easily observed as a ritual may have more to it than you first realize. First, rituals are an expedient way to gain information on other elements of culture. Islam and Zyphur (2009) argue that a "focus on rituals expedites the research process because, within these forms, it is possible to examine culturally rich phenomena compressed into relatively short periods" (p. 116). For example, an analysis of an annual retreat or a holiday party may reveal communication rules, heroes, and history. In either of these settings, a speaker (guest or manager) may review past events or honor certain events or employees. As you listen, you will be able to glean something about the espoused values of the organization.

Second, rituals function to manage a central organizational tension: stability and change. They aid organizations in transition during a merger or internal change. They also serve to maintain norms and solidarity of values within the organization. Thus, for instance, rituals provide a way to move ahead in the midst of uncertainty about change while maintaining a semblance of order or progress in the midst of flux (Islam & Zyphur, 2009). Six major categories of rituals (Trice & Beyer, 1984) are listed in Rehearsal 6.1. As you reflect on examples in your cultural analysis and/or in your organization, be sure to decipher manifest as well as latent meanings. For instance, the manifest or obvious "surface" meaning of a retreat for organizational development might be the value the organization places on personnel training and planning. In contrast, the latent meaning or the hidden, less obvious meaning might relate to the value placed on renewing and reinforcing friendships in the organization. Notice how in this example, based on Trice and Beyer's (1984) categories, one ritual can serve two functions. For example, the retreat may include a time for play and interaction that serves to bind members together—an integration function. During the same ritual, a renewal function may be served if the key speaker recognizes and reaffirms the current structure of the organization by honoring members who have "climbed the ladder." Yet even the richness of such an analysis should only underscore an earlier point made. If your analysis focuses on a single element, even an element that holds insights for other elements, you are likely to leave the organization with a skewed or inaccurate understanding of the culture.

Rehearsal 6.1 Identifying Six Types of Rites/Rituals

Purpose: Identify various types of rituals in your organization and the elements of culture embedded in each.

Direction: State your example and then possible other elements found in the ritual. For example, a ritual of "passage" in the university might be the "tenure" process. Other cultural elements in this ritual include roles (power structures), language (title changes), and communication rules (how you talk to colleagues and superiors about the process).

1. Passage: facilitates transition into new social roles and status (e.g., Army basic training)

   Example:

   _____

   _____

   Other Elements:

   _____

   _____

2. Degradation: dissolve social identities and power (e.g., firing and replacing)

   Example:

   _____

   _____

   Other Elements:

   _____

   _____

3. Enhancement: enhance social identities and power (e.g., training certification program)

   Example:

   _____

   _____

   Other Elements:

   _____

   _____

4. Renewal: refurbish social structures and improve their functioning (e.g., a retreat for organizational development)

Example:

_____

_____

Other Elements:

_____

_____

5. Conflict reduction: reduce conflict and aggression (e.g., collective bargaining)

Example:

_____

_____

Other Elements:

_____

_____

6. Integration: encourage and revive common feelings that bind members together and build commitment (e.g., office Christmas party)

Example:

_____

_____

Other Elements:

_____

_____

Summary

Observation as a cultural analysis tool is about taking a step beyond what you do every day. The key is to be more observant, more aware of what and how you see. Another difference in systematic observation is the formal recording of detailed field notes. At the end of this chapter we provide additional rehearsals aimed at helping you in the observation process in general and the note-taking process in particular. As you engage in these activities and other observation efforts, you should have a better sense of how to apply the major ideas presented in this chapter.

- There are four observation roles (i.e., complete observer, observer–participant, participant–observer, complete participant); each has advantages and disadvantages.
- Seven guidelines should aid you in the observation process.
  1. Make like an alien by making use of various techniques to become a "stranger."

2. Take notes while observing or reserve time immediately after observation.

3. Include observations of formal meetings, rituals, and the like, as well as less formal interactions.

4. Use brackets to help you distinguish descriptions and interpretations. Bracket items such as questions, possible paradoxes, later comparisons, and personal reactions/differences.

5. Use insiders to check your understanding of jargon and your inferences about cultural elements.

6. Review your notes to draw inferences about the cultural elements.

7. Categorize notes by elements to guide additional data collection to fill gaps; create interview guides or surveys based on your analysis of data in element categories.

- Rites and rituals are particularly rich sites for gathering observational cultural data; however, you should remain aware of the need to explore and gather information about all of the elements of culture.

- As an actor with a renewed commitment to observation, if you enact the various guidelines we have suggested, you should become more adept at competent cultural performance.

Rehearsal 6.2 A Potpourri of Things to
Observe in Cultural Analysis

Purpose: Practice observing a variety of organization settings and events that provide insight to elements of culture.

Directions: Review the following list of questions. Select two or three and attempt answers to these based on the organization you are analyzing.

1. What kind of building houses the organization? What impression does it convey to employees? Visitors?

2. What kind of parking is available? Is there any reserved parking? For whom? Is there any pattern of vehicles in the parking lot?

3. What does the entry look like? What kind of security? A receptionist?

4. Is there a waiting area for visitors? Does it have chairs? What kind of furniture? What kind of reading material? What is on the walls?

5. How is office space configured? Are there "premium" offices like corner spaces or windows with a better view? Who has these offices?

6. Are there offices or cubicles? Are office doors open or shut?

7. Is workspace nondescript or are there personal items? What type of personal items do employees have in their spaces?

8. Do people seem to be working alone or in groups?

9. Are there any items on the walls depicting the history? Photographs of founders? Pictures of early physical locations?

10. Are there pictures of anyone in public office spaces? Of whom? Why?

11. What types of common areas are present? Conference rooms? Break rooms or lounges? Does access to these spaces seem to be restricted?

12. What is in the break room? Do people seem to use it?

13. What is on the bulletin boards?

14. What type of technology do members use? Are there computers on every desk? Recent or vintage? Do employees carry PDAs? Pagers? Cell phones?

15. What do people wear? Do there seem to be status differences indicated by dress? Is dress formal or casual?

16. How do people address one another? First names? Level of formality?

17. Observe a meeting. Where do people sit? Who speaks at the meeting and who does not? Do there seem to be cliques supporting different points of view? Is conflict expressed openly? How long do meetings last?

18. Are awards displayed on the walls? Corporate awards? Individual awards? Team awards?

19. Is there anything in this office to indicate uniqueness based on geographic area, or could this office just as easily be located in Boston as Santa Fe?

20. How much diversity do you observe by race/ethnicity, gender, age, dress?

Rehearsal 6.3 Alien Culture Observation

Purpose: To develop skills in qualitative data collection and analysis through observing an unfamiliar culture and to become experientially familiar with the concept of seeing a culture through "alien" eyes. The process followed here is a short version of each of the steps of a cultural analysis.

Steps:

1. Identify a culture that

   a. you consider "alien" to your own

   b. you have limited or no existing knowledge about

   c. would not be dangerous to observe (!)

   d. you would most likely not observe if not encouraged to by this Rehearsal

(Continued)

(Continued)

2. Arrange a time to visit the culture

   a. Allow a minimum of 1–2 hours

   b. Be sure to gain permission if needed

   c. Take a friend with you if needed for comfort or "fun"

3. Be as unobtrusive as possible

   Remember that unobtrusive behavior depends on the organization. For example, if you visit an open Weight Watcher meeting, unobtrusive might mean keeping things on a first-name basis and not inquiring too much about the background of other participants. In contrast, unobtrusive in an accounting firm might be quietly taking notes during a meeting with the partners.

4. Take field notes during and/or after the observation

   a. Jot down descriptive information related to both verbal and nonverbal communication.

   b. Bracket [ ] information that relates to your own personal reactions, feelings, interpretations.

   c. An example field note entry from an observation of the UK Day Care might look like this:

   The corner of the room is blocked off from the rest of the larger room. The children in the area are in the 2-year-old age group. [I find it strange that they spend most of their day away from older and younger kids.] In the morning, all of the children are greeted with a hug, some children stood limply and did not return the hug while others squeezed back tightly. [Why don't they ask if the child wants to be hugged?] A teacher runs from one side of the area to catch a child about to hit another child with a block. He makes it in time and after removing the block takes the little girl's hand and has her softly touch the little boy she was about to hit. The teacher says, "Remember hands are for touching softly, not for hitting and hurting." [Why didn't he say anything about the boy taking the block from the girl in the first place!]

5. Develop a summary that

   a. provides example data related to at least three of the elements of culture

   For example:

   - **Rules:** Redirect aggression by verbally and nonverbally demonstrating appropriate use of hands. Several teachers were observed telling a child how to touch.

   - **Physical Setting:** The setup of the room provides a way for age-specific teaching and interaction to occur.

   - **Rituals:** Morning hugs are part of the daily activities.

   b. interprets the data (organized by elements) by stating an overall theme

   For example: *Positive use of touch is a mandated and encouraged behavior. Rules and rituals indicate that teachers should initiate touch often during the day as well as encourage children to touch each other in appropriate ways.*

c. infers an overall definition of the culture based on themes and elements

Examples: A paradox, The UK Day Care restricts inter-age touching, but mandates adult–child touching. Or a root metaphor, The UK Day Care is like. . . .

6. Prepare a summary to discuss with a mentor, a colleague, or an instructor.

Rehearsal 6.4 Note-Taking Guidelines

Purpose: Enhance observational abilities by reviewing guidelines.

Action steps: A review of note-taking guidelines is provided in a checklist to assist you. Use this checklist to review the field notes you compiled in the "Alien Culture" assignment to be sure you followed all the guidelines about systematic observation.

_____1. Make like an alien by making use of various techniques to become a "stranger":

a. Write notes on the mundane

b. Mutate metaphors

c. Ask "why" and "what function" questions about everything

_____2. If you do not or cannot take notes while observing, reserve time immediately after observation to jot down notes.

_____3. Attempt to include observations of meetings, rituals, and so on, as well as observations of less formal interactions, events, and more.

_____4. Use brackets [ ] to help you focus on descriptions instead of interpretations.

Use brackets for the following:

a. questions to ask (other) insiders

b. possible paradoxes, contradictions, root metaphors

c. later comparisons—see how your perceptions change

d. personal reactions/differences

_____5. If a newcomer or outsider, make use of insiders to check your understanding of jargon and your inferences about rules and values, and so on.

_____6. Review your notes to determine if you can draw reasonable inferences about most of the cultural elements from your notes.

_____7. Categorize notes by elements to

a. guide additional data collection to fill gaps

b. create interview guides or surveys based on your analysis of data in element categories

7

Method Acting

Interviews and Surveys

Articulate the value of the culture metaphor

Define major cultural elements

★ **Use multiple data collection methods**

Synthesize and interpret cultural data

Identify applications

How employees personally feel, think, and see the company and their work have a significant impact on the character and quality of their work, their relation to management, and their response to innovation and change.

—Deetz, Tracy, and Simpson, *Leading Organizations Through Transition*, 2000, pp. 1–2

Objectives:

- Appreciate the challenges involved in interviewing members
- Apply six general interviewing principles
- Explain the different factors to consider when interviewing as a member of the culture versus as an outsider to the culture
- State the five principles for conducting ethnographic interviews
- Describe basic features of qualitative surveys

Stage Terms:

- Ethnographic interviews
- Levels of communication competence
- Open and closed questions
- Leading questions
- Open Souls Doctrine
- Rapport

Step Three: Use Multiple Data Collection Methods to Understand the Elements of Culture

Method actors, like effective observers of culture, become adept at making observations. They also rely on informal interviews as part of survival on stage. Sandra Bullock spent time observing and interacting with her real-life counterpart for her role in *Blind Side* and even changed her physical appearance to get more into the character. Communication between actors in a scene, including natural reactions and questions of each other, is at the core of the type of interviewing we introduce in this chapter. We introduce you to ways to sharpen your informal, as well as your more formal, interviewing techniques.

Like observations, interviews can range in their degree of formality and obtrusiveness. "Ethnographic interviews" are by definition best when both participants view them as a "friendly conversation" as opposed to an actual interview. In fact, if an informal interview with a coworker became a series of direct questions, fired one after another, your colleague might shut down at some point and say, "Hey, what is this, an interview?" To return to the director metaphor, if the actors on stage sense you are "after them," out to put them on the spot, they will be less likely to help you understand what is going on in their world, in the very play you are seeking to guide and direct.

Interviewing organization members about organization culture is grounded in several assumptions:

• Organizational culture is constructed by organization members and woven deeply throughout organizational sense making. It is not the property of organizational leaders. The values and views of leaders are not culturally defining unless members of the organization share management's values and interpretations.

• Organization members can talk knowledgeably and authoritatively about their own organizational experiences and meanings. Harre and Secord (1973) refer to this as the "Open Souls Doctrine," that one unique attribute of human beings is their ability to reflect and comment on their own behavior. However, organization members vary in their degree of consciousness about cultural values and practices. Harris (1979) and others (Pearce, 2007) have found that individuals range in their mindfulness of and ability to discuss and reflect on their own communication and such influences as culture on their practices. We provide examples of these differing ranges or levels of competence (minimal, satisfactory, and optimal) later in this chapter. Thus, in your interviews, be aware of the need to adapt questions and to rely on other methods.

Before we delve deeply into the particulars of cultural interviews, it would be helpful to discuss general interviewing principles:

Principle 1: Rapport with the interviewee is critical to gaining candid and valid information. The interviewee must understand your purpose, feel some motivation to share information, feel safe, and trust you in order to share sensitive information. It is therefore essential to spend time at the start of the interview building rapport or connection with the interviewee. This initial stage should include a full description of your purpose. If there has been conflict or change in the organization, interviewees may suspect your motives or purpose even when you tell them you are trying to understand the culture. We have both had interviewees tell us they feared the interview because they believed management would use the data to pave the way for further job layoffs or reorganizations, for example.

Motivating the interviewee is also important. This involves sharing the benefits of understanding culture and discussing possible ways that this information can be used to improve working conditions or organizational effectiveness. If interviewees believe that organizational leaders will actually use the information gained for constructive change, they are more motivated to share information. Promising to share results with employees also enhances their motivation. It is important for you to understand, however, that the greatest motivation to participate is intrinsic for the interviewee. Few employees are ever asked about their views or experiences in the organization. Therefore, it is not surprising that being asked to comment as an "expert" on the organization confers a sense of significance and inclusion within the organization. We are continually surprised at how much participants enjoy the process of the cultural interview and how much information they are willing to share.

Rapport is also created through trust and security. Interviewees feel secure when you promise them the interview is confidential and when you create credibility through your communication manner. The promises you make of confidentiality must have a basis in fact. We always negotiate in advance that no raw data from our observation (field notes, surveys, documents) will be available to the organization. We also obtain agreement in advance that we will not reveal the source of interview comments or identity of employees in organizational stories. These assurances are critical to your credibility as a researcher. You must project competence and respect in order to gain this credibility with the interviewee. Box 7.1 captures various stages of rapport building. These stages serve to heighten awareness of normal aspects of the process and factors to keep in mind at each stage. Notice how the higher or more developed the rapport, the more the interview is like a partnership in the cultural analysis process. While such levels of rapport are not necessary for an effective cultural analysis, we see the value of making time to develop such relationships.

Box 7.1 Stages of the Rapport Process

Apprehension is a normal first stage experienced by most interviewees. To put interviewees at ease, focus on low-risk descriptive questions such as describing their job or how they came to work at the company. Adapt to each person. The key rule is to keep them talking.

Exploration is the second stage of rapport in which interviewees may test boundaries to ascertain whether they can trust you. You can help them in trust building by

- repeated explanations of your role, confidentiality, the analysis process, purpose of questions, and the recording process
- restatement of information in their language; speak as you would to someone in their culture

Cooperation is the third stage of rapport building, in which interviewees begin to see a shared purpose for the interview. You can enhance their motivation to cooperate by describing the constructive uses of the interview and by giving attention and significance to the information they are providing.

Participation is the final stage of rapport building. The interviewee becomes an active participant in helping find ways to assist you in learning about the culture. In this stage the control and direction of the interview are shared, and it becomes more of a conversation.

Principle 2: Select the appropriate wording for your questions. Question wording and construction are critical to eliciting the information you want. You have to ask the right question in the right way to unlock the perception of the interviewee. Question construction, clarity, and organizationally appropriate language are all keys to effective cultural interviewing.

Interview questions can range across a continuum from open to closed. *Closed questions* ask for a short, specific answer. They include yes–no answers or questions that ask for a specific piece of information, such as, "What is your title?" "Who is an individual considered a hero in this organization?" "When was this organization founded?" On the other hand, *open questions* such as, "What is it like to work here?" or "Tell me about something that could get you in trouble here" require more expansive answers. Cultural interviewing calls for more open question construction because you are seeking stories, metaphors, explanations, and other rich data to understand organizational logic and values. Some questions, however, are too open to offer sufficient guidance to the interviewee. A question like, "Tell me about this organization" may be open but can also be intimidating to an interviewee who does not know where to begin or what you are looking for. Midrange open questions are usually the most effective.

Not only should questions be open, they also must be clear to the interviewee. Using cultural terms you have learned in this text may seem like jargon to the average organization member. For example, instead of asking about recognition rituals you might ask, "How do employees get recognized here? What kinds of honors or awards are given to employees here?" Or instead of asking about symbols, you might say, "Why is the door greeter important to Wal-Mart?" or "What employee is a perfect example of what Company A stands for?" Sometimes a question is just confusing in its wording or hard to answer. As you start your interview process, it is good to "pilot test" your interview questions with a few sample employees who are typical of the subjects who will be interviewed to make sure questions are clear and understandable.

It is also important to use language appropriate in the culture you are studying. As you observe the organization in your first step of data gathering, you need to pay attention to organizational titles, acronyms, and unique terms. Being able to use these terms appropriately in your questions gives you credibility and taps into culture more easily. For example, if salespeople are called associates, that is culturally significant. You should use the term *associate* in your question and ask what it means to interviewees.

Finally, you may need to adapt your questions as you ascertain through your interaction whether your interviewee has conscious awareness of organizational logic. If the interviewee has minimal competence, he or she may respond to many of your questions with, "I don't know why we do it that way. We just do," or "I don't know exactly what that term signifies. That's just what we call it." With such an individual you might need to shift your questions to asking how things are done, but not asking that interviewee to interpret or explain. With an interviewee with satisfactory competence, you could expect more explanation and interpretation, but such a person could not offer comparative judgments or explain why one pattern was chosen instead of another value or way of interpreting. An organization member at satisfactory competence is immersed in the current system logic and probably cannot understand the system from multiple points of view or adopt a more objective stance of seeing the organization from an outside point of view. Questions for this type of interviewee might ask for interpretation of what this means within the system or why something is inappropriate, but you could not ask why a certain value was privileged over another potential value to guide the organization. A person with optimal competence, perhaps someone who has experience in several different cultures or someone with a more interdisciplinary background, is a gold mine for an interviewer because he or she can understand the culture from multiple viewpoints and often can provide rich cultural interpretations and explanations. (See descriptions of cosmopolitan communication, Pearce, 2000, 2007.)

Principle 3: Use probes or follow-up questions to get the richest and most useful cultural data. For example, stories may emerge after a secondary follow-up question. An interviewee might have said that Mr. Jones is a hero in the organization because he is so compassionate. You ask, "Can you think of an example that illustrates this compassion?" and the response may involve the interviewee sharing a specific story about a time Mr. Jones loaned a car to an employee who had recently lost his car in a wreck. Such stories will tell you more about compassion and how it is defined as a value in this culture. Additional levels of interpretation of the story will tell you other important things about the culture. Follow-up questions require listening carefully for small clues in answers that should be explored further. For example, if you hear an answer like, "Mr. Jones is seen as a hero by some but not everyone," you need to follow up immediately and ask why he is perceived positively by some and not by others. Probes in cultural interviewing are different from strict research protocols in which every question must be asked in the same manner of each respondent. In a cultural interview, you learn most by following up the particulars of each answer, thus the probes may be quite different in one interview than another, even when the initial interview protocol is the same. Box 7.2 gives examples of probe questions.

Box 7.2 Sample Probe Questions

1. Tell me more about that.

2. Can you help me understand why you see it that way?

3. Can you think of an example of that?

4. Do you think most members of the organization would see it the same way?

5. Why is that important in this culture?

6. Are there differences between leaders and culture members in how that is interpreted?

Principle 4: It is important to avoid common interviewing errors. *One common error is asking leading questions.* Interviewers often make this mistake by giving an example when they ask a question, in order to make the question clearer. Unfortunately, the example offered tends to direct interviewees' responses in a direction they might not have gone without the example. If you say, "What are values shared in this organization? Like, is responsibility an important value that is expected of all employees?" the interviewee will either agree with you or think of values similar to responsibility or "virtues" rather than talking about diversity, profitability, or other things that might have occurred to him or her without the example.

A second common error in interviewing is rushing into pauses in the interviewee's answer. In the United States we are uncomfortable with silence. When there is a gap in conversation, we are tempted to rush in with another question or a summary that puts words in the interviewee's mouth. Good interviewing takes patience. Some interviewees need to take time to think through responses. One of the best interviewing techniques is to remain silent while being nonverbally attentive and connected. This use of silence often encourages the interviewee to say more or to go into an answer more fully, revealing rich cultural information.

A third common error is underestimating the significance of interviewer nonverbal communication. How the interviewer communicates nonverbally has a huge impact on the interviewee. Making eye contact, leaning forward, and using encouraging facial expressions and nodding give the impression of interest and attentiveness. Distracting gestures such as checking your wristwatch or drumming your fingers can quickly shut interviewees down or cause them to shorten their answers. You also need to pay careful attention to the interviewee's nonverbal communication, such as when facial expression or physical tension does not match the interviewee's response to a question.

Principle 5: Consider the implications of the way you record the interview. Choosing to audio-record an interview can have implications for interviewee comfort and for data analysis. You also may need to get interviewees to sign consent forms, using forms such as we presented in Chapter 5, when you tape record interviews. Table 7.1 lists advantages and disadvantages of recording interviews. We generally ask the interviewee whether he or she minds if we record the interview. We have also used the technique of setting the recorder beside the interviewee and showing him or her how to turn it off. Control over the taping reduces discomfort, yet we find that few interviewees actually turn off the recorder, and in fact, they often lose consciousness of the recorder once they become engaged in the interview.

Another recording issue is whether you choose to transcribe an interview or summarize it with detailed notes about the answers. Transcribing means you write down word for word what was said in the interview. Summarizing means that you capture the main ideas. A summary might contain a few verbatim quotes of expressions that seemed particularly important, but it contains mostly conceptual summaries. The advantage of transcripts is that you can do more sophisticated analysis with the exact language that an interviewee used. The disadvantage is that transcripts are extremely time consuming to prepare and analyze.

Table 7.1   Recording Interviews

Advantages	Disadvantages
Captures more detail about interviewee answers; allows you to analyze actual language patterns	May inhibit free and open communication and cause mistrust
Frees you from taking notes and allows you to give more attention to the interviewee	Takes more time to listen to interview tapes, to transcribe or summarize
You can focus on the interviewee's nonverbal communication	You may not record impressions gained during the interview; they may be hard to recapture listening to the tape

Principle 6: Consider the advantages of interviewing with a partner. There are advantages to interviewing with a partner. Each of you may notice different things about the interviewee's answers and nonverbal elements. One can take notes while the other asks questions and notices nonverbal elements. The main downside of having a partner is the possible negative impact on interviewee rapport. Interviewees might feel "double-teamed," or it might be more difficult to build as trusting a relationship as with an individual interviewer. It is also easy to compete inadvertently for leadership during the interview in a way that is confusing to the interviewee unless you have carefully planned your roles and interactions prior to the interview.

Principle 7: Consider focus group interviewing. A focus group is a cross between a group discussion and an interview. A focus group usually consists of 5 to 10 members. The interviewer asks broad questions, and members are asked to discuss them. The interviewer plays the role of facilitator, constraining members who are too talkative, drawing out more reticent members, summarizing, and playing devil's advocate. A focus group is a rich source of data because participants are stimulated by one another's answers to think of things they would not have thought of in a one-to-one interview. Disadvantages include the greater complexity of scheduling, the potential for a few members to dominate the discussion, the reticence some have in talking about sensitive cultural issues before others, and the "bandwagon effect" in which members agree with a dominant member instead of thinking of ways their own perceptions might be different. There are various forms of groupware that allow group interaction while avoiding some of the pitfalls of oral group discussion. One product we have used is facilitate.com. This web-based software allows groups to brainstorm, react to one another's ideas, and prioritize. The facilitator can choose whether to make all comments anonymous or allow participants to see the identity of individuals who offer comments.

Special Considerations When Interviewing as an Insider or an Outsider

In Chapter 2 we discussed the considerations in deciding whether to do an analysis of a culture of which you are a member or a culture to which you are an outsider. In Chapter 6 we discussed various observer roles and how each role influences your strategy and the type of data you collect. Your relationship to an organization and its members will also impact your interviewing strategy.

Insider Considerations

If you are a member of the organization, you come to each interview with a relational context. The interviewee already knows you or at least knows you are a member of the organization. Hopefully you have a good relationship with the interviewee so will need to spend less time building rapport at the start. However, there are times when you may bring baggage. You may be part of management, and that could create social distance if you are interviewing a line employee, for instance. You may be a member of quality control, which has a perceived adversarial relationship with production. The biggest hurdle to overcome as an insider is the necessity to ask questions about things you think you already know. You must ask others about their perspectives, and you may find different parts of the organization have different conceptions of the culture than you do. It also is sometimes difficult for the interviewee to answer questions fully and directly for a fellow employee. If you ask them what employees are rewarded for, they will say, "Oh, you know that," and you will not harvest the rich stories and details that might be shared with an outsider. It is necessary for insiders, in the introduction to the interview, to ask interviewees to treat them as if they knew nothing about the organization, and for insiders to prompt and probe during the interview just as if they did not know anything about it.

Another advantage of interviewing as an insider is that you may know more specifics to ask about and be able to start at a deeper level of questioning than an outsider could. You might be able to ask an initial question that would take an outsider two or three probes to reach. You also have more context for interpreting answers. Another negative to being an insider, however, may be confidentiality. Interviewees may be afraid that you would share answers with others in the organization, or that their answers would affect your perception of them and your continuing work relationship. Giving assurances of confidentiality are especially important for an insider.

Outsider Considerations

Outsiders will find it easier to adopt a genuinely naïve position in the interview on organizational culture. They will think of questions that the insider may not think to ask because the insider's cultural knowledge takes certain features of cultural practices for granted. The outsider will have to work harder to develop rapport and trust with the interviewee. Another disadvantage to overcome is substituting your own interpretation for the meaning within the culture. An interviewee might tell you that a stag is the representative symbol for an insurance company, and you might assume you know the reasons why, without finding what the symbol means to culture members. Therefore probes and paraphrasing are especially important when you are an outsider interviewer to be sure that you are checking your interpretations for cultural accuracy.

Connections: Linking Observation With Interviews

In addition to general interview guidelines, it is important to keep in mind the specific considerations for interviewing based both on the unique characteristics of the ethnographic interview and on the data you have already collected. Five specific guides are provided that should be considered as you prepare for interviews.

1. Review the cultural element summaries you drew from your observation in order to develop questions to gain further information about the cultural elements you have observed.

As a general rule, it is best to rely on interviews and surveys to gain information after you have collected other information. This guideline is based on the typical sequence of sense making: We notice something and then we ask about it to gain more detail or check our interpretations.

2. Construct a list of areas from your analysis of other data for possible inclusion. The list might include things like cultural data that

   a. confuse you

   b. lack confirmation from multiple elements

   c. merit further elaboration or clarification to see if your interpretation is shared by other organization members

   d. indicate texts that have cultural significance that you might use for textual analysis (to be described in the next chapter)

   e. can be explored only through direct questions and are not readily apparent through observation, things like metaphors, stories, history, and so on

3. Determine members to interview who represent a variety of perspectives (position, tenure, etc.).

A common bias that enters our interpretation of culture is influence from our information sources. At times, random interviewing can have value in ethnographic interviewing. When you choose respondents for a specific reason, you can overlook important cultural sources. In cultural interviewing, every member of the culture has a perspective that may be valuable. The janitor may be in a position to overhear hallway conversations throughout the building. A part-time employee may have a boundary-spanning role that would be valuable to explore.

It is important to remember in interpretive research that every interviewee "counts." In quantitative survey research, you may treat a statistical deviant as simply an aberration to be dismissed. However, the interviewee who presents information that diverges from the mainstream might be telling you something important about the culture or subcultures within the organization.

One question our students often ask is, "How many interviews are enough?" The answer, of course, varies. It depends on the size and complexity of the organization. In small organizations (25 or fewer members), it makes sense to interview everyone. In larger organizations you must sample. If you were doing an academic study of a very large organization for publication, you might want to sample between 2% and 5% of the organization. In a class project, your sample will be smaller but should be as representative as possible. Ethnographic interviewing focuses more on depth than breadth. It is important to generate "thick" and rich descriptions from fewer people rather than having more, superficial data from a larger sample, as we might do in quantitative surveys. In a practical sense, we often know we have done enough interviews when we conduct three or four interviews without hearing anything new, anything that we have not fully explored in previous interviews.

4. Develop and focus on descriptive questions:

Grand tour questions: Take me on a tour of the company by walking me through the doors at the start of a new day.

Mini tour questions: Take me on a tour of . . . (a specific department or a particular event, such as a meeting).

Orientation questions: What are the kinds of questions that are typically asked (by certain people, positions, times, settings).

Experience questions: Give me an example of experiences you have had (with, at, when).

Native language questions: What does the title Associate mean here? Asked to gain cultural definitions/uses of specialized language.

Hypothetical language questions: If I were to be late to a meeting, how would it be interpreted?

5. Use contrast questions to understand how interviewees construct meaning:

What's the difference between a _____ and a _____?

Example: *What is the difference between a new employee called a "player" and one called a "gunner"?*

These five guides should give you a sense of not only the ethnographic interview process but the content of certain types of questions you might elect to ask. An exploration of Rehearsal 7.1 will help you develop questions.

**Rehearsal 7.1 Sample Interview Questions
for "Reading" a Culture**

Purpose: Develop a cultural interview guide based on suggested questions below.

1. When you were a newcomer to the (name of organization), what was strange, or different, or unexpected about the way things were done here?

2. If you wanted to explain or illustrate to an outsider the essence of (name of organization), both the positive and the negative, what incident(s) would you describe? What do these incidents say about this organization?

3. What should visitors see and to whom should visitors speak if they want to understand this organization? What would they need to understand to "get along" and feel comfortable here?

4. When compared with similar organizations, what is special or distinctive about this organization?

5. What are the principal images or metaphors that people use to describe the organization?

6. What physical impression does the organization and its artifacts create? Does this vary from one place to another in the organization?

7. What kinds of beliefs and values dominate the organization? Officially? Unofficially?

8. What are the main norms operating here? What could people be fired for? What could limit a person's career success here?

9. What are the ceremonies/rituals and what purposes do they serve? What are members recognized for? How is this done? Do other organization members know when someone receives a reward or recognition?

10. What language dominates everyday conversation? What words do you hear in this organization that you wouldn't hear at other organizations? What do they signify about organizational values?

11. What are the dominant stories or legends that people tell? What messages are they trying to convey by telling these stories?

12. What reward systems are in place? What "messages" do they send in terms of what is valued here and what is not?

13. What are the favorite topics of informal conversation?

14. What do you know about the history of this organization? What has changed over the years?

15. Think of three influential people in the organization. In what ways do they symbolize the character and values of the organization?

16. Are there identifiable subcultures or cliques in the organization?

17. Is there a newsletter or similar written document in the organization? Do employees read it? What written source would really tell you something about what the organization is like?

18. How do people prefer to communicate here? If there were a new policy, how would you expect to hear about it? If your boss wanted to thank you for a good job, would you prefer him or her to tell you in a face-to-face meeting or in a note? Do most people communicate by e-mail? Is there anything you would not communicate via e-mail?

19. If you heard a rumor about layoffs or a major change, how would you check it out?

20. How does the surrounding environment (this neighborhood or this city or this country) influence the values and practices of this organization?

21. What is the climate for diversity here? Is there any specific group (African Americans, foreign citizens, Jewish people, women, gays, etc.) that would feel uncomfortable being a part of this organization?

22. Do members of this organization do things together outside of work hours? Who? What do they do?

23. What are special activities or events this organization sponsors for its members? What do they say about the nature of the organization?

Now add a few of your own:

_____

_____

_____

_____

_____

_____

_____

_____

_____

Qualitative Surveys

The process of creating effective qualitative interview questions is identical to that of creating survey questions. For example, imagine not being able to catch a colleague in a "friendly conversation" or even a formal interview and instead sending an e-mail questionnaire. The important point is that just as in an interview, you have to be sure that you gain data that you then check against other information you have gathered about the culture. As discussed in the overview, an array of standardized surveys exists for analyzing culture. However, our conviction is that a grounded analysis is best because it encourages the consultant or leader to gain an in-depth understanding of the culture. A grounded analysis takes an inductive approach, as opposed to a deductive approach that assumes an existing set of categories in advance (Strauss &

Corbin, 1990). Furthermore, a grounded analysis challenges you to devise your own interpretation of the culture rather than one constrained by factors already loaded into a standardized survey. Four reminders for survey development that parallels interviews include the following:

- Establish appropriate rapport for the question (i.e., you may need a brief introduction for your question to make sure interviewees understand your reason for asking)

- Explore question options (i.e., structural, contrast) so as to gain needed cultural information

- Word the question clearly

- Ask the questions of members who represent a variety of perspectives (position, tenure, etc.)

On a final note, remember that writing responses to open questions is time-consuming; thus it is best to narrow your survey to focus on a handful of the most important questions. For instance, you might find that an electronic survey of from two to four questions will glean more cultural information from a wider array of members than seven or eight questions will from a handful of respondents.

Summary

You rely on question asking and responding almost every day. Method actors, like those interested in enhancing the quality of an informal interview process, must become more aware of their questions and how they interpret and respond to those they interview. The interview is an essential technique in gaining cultural knowledge because of its ability to allow you to learn from members about their interpretations and meanings. It is based on the assumption that members can comment reflectively about their own behaviors and interpretations. This chapter covered several key factors, principles, and guidelines relevant to the process.

- Culture members may be at varying levels of consciousness about why members think and act as they do in the organization.

- The quality of your interview data is dependent not just on rapport or technique and preparation but on your ability to evaluate data in light of what you have learned from other players and observations.

- Interviewers must be conscious of six interviewing principles:
  1. Rapport is critical.
  2. Question wording is important for eliciting the information you want.
  3. Probes are critical for getting deeper cultural information.
  4. Interviewers should avoid the common problems of leading questions, rushing into pauses, and discounting nonverbal communication.
  5. The interviewer should carefully consider different methods of recording.
  6. Interviewing with a partner has advantages.

- Be aware of special considerations about interviewing as a culture member or as an outsider.

- Be sure to review the specific guidelines offered about ethnographic interviewing that also apply to surveys (appropriate rapport for the question, explore question options, question clarity, select members who represent a variety of perspectives).

Rehearsal 7.2 Alien Culture Interviews/Surveys

Purpose: To develop skills in qualitative data collection and analysis through interviewing a member of an unfamiliar culture.

Steps:

1. Review your notes from your visit to the alien culture from the previous Rehearsal.

2. Determine areas in which you have confusion or a lack of specific data on a given element (or no data on a certain element).

3. Prepare for your interview by creating a rapport section on an interview guide. Include ways you might build rapport through greetings, description of the purpose of the interview, explaining your role in the organization, assurances of confidentiality, general questions, analysis and note-taking explanation, expressions of cultural interest and ignorance, and incorporating and restating informant's terms.

4. Create the following questions on your interview guide, but remember you will need to adapt to the interviewee by providing more detail in the question, repeating the question, and so on.

   1 grand tour question; 1 native language question

   1 structural question; 1 contrast question

5. Provide a closure/leave-taking section on your guide (appreciation, reminder of purpose and what is ahead, ask for any questions, etc.)

6. Like the observation assignment, develop a summary section that incorporates triangulated and new data and that

   a. provides example data related to at least three of the elements of culture

   b. interprets the data organized by elements by stating an overall theme

   c. infers an overall definition of the culture based on themes and elements

7. Reflect on the strengths and limits of observation and interviewing. What did you understand differently/in more depth after the interview? What did you observe that would have been difficult to understand solely through an interview?

Summary of Step Three: Using Multiple Methods to Collect Cultural Data

The major methods of textual analysis, observation, interviews, and surveys each provide a useful means of gathering cultural data. You should consider the following guidelines a way to provide a credible and valid interpretation. These methods and the call to integrate them into our cultural data collection process are provided as a way to combat a natural tendency we all have. Each of us tends to rely on initial impressions based on a limited number of observations, a few interactions or discussions with a limited number of employees, and perhaps a cursory look at a newsletter. Optimal cultural performance is achieved when we sharpen our ability to collect and analyze data more systematically with each of these methods. If we have a clear grasp of the following guidelines, then we will be more effective in the culture interpretation process covered in the next chapter.

- Triangulate methods to obtain credible and valid data.

- Conduct textual analysis using one or more of the methods outlined: content analysis, rhetorical analysis, and/or textual analysis.

- Select a method of observation and write field notes with bracketed inferences and questions.

- Adopt the curiosity of an outsider, especially when you observe your own culture.

- Apply important principles in the conduct of interviews and surveys, such as selecting interviewees, developing rapport, wording questions in an open and clear fashion, using probes to dig deeper into answers, choosing recording methods, and negotiating the special roles of cultural insider or outsider.

- Draw inferences from each of the methods about cultural elements.

8

Step Four—Synthesizing and Interpreting Cultural Data

Getting Inside the Character

Articulate the value of the culture metaphor

Define major cultural elements

Use multiple data collection methods

★ **Synthesize and interpret cultural data**

Identify applications

Step Four: Develop Your Interpretation of the Culture Through Data Synthesis and Interpretation

I must have at least a dozen pages or more of just notes, and more notes. Of course, I also have draft after draft of cultural elements. The process has been interesting, but it is not realistic. No one can really spend this much time. The pay-off just cannot be worth it!

—Anonymous, Cultural Analysis Student

Objectives:

- Explain the interpretive nature of cultural analysis
- Learn how to combine elements to develop cultural themes
- Create an overall characterization of the culture based on multiple themes

Stage Terms:

- Cultural themes
- Pervasiveness
- Salience
- Central paradox
- Master rule/value

A Time to Interpret

The statement above about data overload reflects a common experience at this stage of the process. It is not uncommon for an initial effort at cultural analysis to become too much. Perhaps the sense of being overwhelmed can be compared to a dress rehearsal of a play when you have doubts about all the pieces coming together, about the ability of your characters to be accepted as "real." The process of "getting inside the character" means that you move to an actual interpretation. Until now the method actor has been devoted to rehearsing the elements, but the time comes to put it together. It is natural to feel overwhelmed at this stage of the process by the sheer volume of data you have collected. Van Maanan (1979) notes that while qualitative data allows richer interpretations and explanations, it is also more time-consuming and complex to analyze. Another source of feeling overwhelmed at this stage is the progression from description to interpretation. In the cultural analysis process, the challenge of the final step of interpreting the culture can seem daunting. However, the reality is that we all hold interpretations of our culture even before conducting formal analyses. The key at this point in the process is to check and change those interpretations by systematically analyzing a wider array of data. The following comments from a few alumni on the value of the process may help give perspective and maintain motivation:

- Evaluating the organization's culture adds another dimension. Although the culture of the organization may not seem to have a direct impact on the immediate, short-term profit or bottom line, it does play a big part in the long-term effectiveness of the organization.

- The basic idea that an organization has a culture was an eye-opener. Since then I've seen the importance of personal fit with the culture. "Problem employees" are often those who won't/can't adapt to the culture and have conflict with those who identify closely with the culture.

- I learned to ask questions in an interview to find out about the culture when I was considering making a job move. I also ask questions of people I'm considering hiring to see if they'll fit with our organizational culture.

- Just simply realizing that an organization has a definable culture has been helpful in dealing with the changes that have and are continuing to occur at the medical facility I work for.

At this point in the process, if you have been collecting data on multiple elements, you likely have more information about your culture than may seem reasonable or "normal." Two factors should help you keep this data overload in perspective. First, this extensive process of analysis is usually appropriate at only certain points in time (e.g., selecting an organization, settling into a new position, during times of organizational crisis or change). Second, as indicated in the alumni comments above, managing the overload of data can have meaningful payoffs. Leaders typically feel like they already operate on information overload, thus the process of collecting cultural data may mean times of feeling overwhelmed by the additional data. Yet recall that at the heart of the process is being a better observer—one who listens intently with ears, eyes, and heart. Becoming more adept at collecting cultural data involves bracketing biases and assumptions about what is the right or the best way to interpret and respond to events in the organization. Therefore, perhaps the most meaningful outcome, one worth wading through the data for, is the potential insight of more effective and ethical behavior for leaders.

Not a Video Recording

Your final analysis may be viewed as a dramatic interpretation of the organization. Consider the drama metaphor as a way to remind you that when opening night finally occurs, when the curtain is being raised, the performance the audience sees will vary depending on the way a director has set the stage, cast the characters, and interpreted the tone and theme of the script. The notion of an interpretation is important in that a cultural analysis does not claim to be an objective and neutral video recording of organizational events. Indeed, the assumption with a cultural analysis is that such an objective and neutral rendering of culture is impossible and undesirable. Instead, the individual "researcher" (or team) works to provide a meaningful, valuable, and valid interpretation. Weick (1995) refers to an interpretive researcher's work as being driven by plausibility rather than accuracy. The researcher must make inferences beyond the directly observable facts and develop an interpretation that fits the facts, even if the fit is not perfect in all respects. At this point in the process you will return to reflecting on the major theoretic frames to guide your interpretation.

The following three-stage interpretive model, also shown in Figure 8.1, attempts to capture a process that is not easily systematized. The process of interpretation is difficult to delineate because interpretation involves insight and intuition. There may be points at which the process is much less linear and systematic than is portrayed in the following model. Nonetheless, it is important that you cover each of the steps in the model with the understanding that you may often move back and forth among the steps.

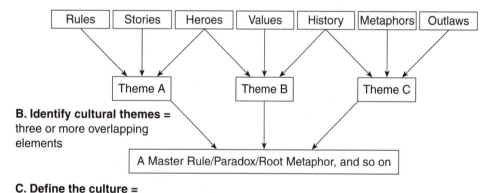

**A. Summarize data by elements:
Multiple methods on most or all elements**

B. Identify cultural themes =
three or more overlapping
elements

C. Define the culture =
three or more overlapping themes

Figure 8.1   A Model for Interpreting and Defining the Culture

A. Creating the Actor's Script: The Elements

Each time you collect cultural information through any one of the qualitative methods, you should sort that data onto summary sheets based on the cultural elements. These summary sheets can be seen as a first step in creating the script—a set of notes that influences the way the actor interprets the character. In order to create these summary sheets, you might take one pass through your interview notes, your observation notes, and your text analyses to consider references to place or to history. You might place each reference to history on a separate note card or in a separate reference citation on your computer. As you look across all those different references to history, you may find patterns, or even contradictions. You would then move to another element, such as heroes, and repeat the process. A few specific guides in this process include the following:

1. Return to the same data set more than once to identify data on elements that may have been overlooked in the first analysis. For example, if you focused on rules in your first analysis of the interview data, return to your data again to explore evidence of values or rituals, and so on. The same piece of data might be categorized under more than one element.

2. Review data in each category to be sure you have collected sufficient information. For example, your initial observations might surface information about all of the elements. A review of your data, however, might reveal limited or unclear information about certain rules, values, and communication styles. These gaps should be a focus of additional data collection efforts. If you do not have clear support or data on an element and you are not able to collect clarifying data, then leave the unclear data out of your final list of elements.

B. Sorting Subplots: Finding Themes

A list of elements does not constitute a final cultural analysis any more than a list of characters and subplots makes a final play. The list of elements is a foundation for getting inside the character, for gaining a valid interpretation of the script, but without the next step all you will have is a list of elements. This second step is to infer cultural themes by surfacing ideas that are supported by three or more elements that also were derived from multiple methods.

Cultural themes can be viewed as similar to values in that they are under the surface, perhaps not ever spoken directly by a member. In other words, a cultural theme has to do with the "pervasiveness and salience" of some important aspect of the culture (Saffold, 1998). *Pervasiveness* has to do with the extent the theme is relevant to various units in the organization. Limited pervasiveness refers to those themes that are relevant to specific departments, while extensive pervasiveness refers to organization-wide themes. For example, in one organization, a theme like "work hard and play hard" may capture just one or two departments, for example, Sales or Marketing. It would have limited pervasiveness in the rest of the organization if the majority of the other units, such as Human Resources or Research and Development, were characterized by a "work hard, but not too hard" theme. In contrast, there may be themes with extensive pervasiveness that cut across units, like, "Get it right the first time."

Salience, on the other hand, has to do with the importance of the theme or its "weightiness" in the culture. The assumption at this point in an analysis is that a theme, because of its repeated presence across elements and methods, is an important one in the organization. A theme might be identified as salient because of the large number of different people who mentioned it, or it might be salient because it was related to almost every element of culture as you analyzed them. It might be, for example, that a theme emerges from an understanding of heroes identified in textual analysis and interviews, rules from observations of meetings, and values from interviews. Across each of these elements you learn something about how the members have come to understand a proper response to conflict or disagreements. You might word the theme as, "silence is the best policy." However, you may find other themes that make the theme related to silence less important or significant. For example, you may learn of other rules and insights from meetings suggesting that conflicts and disagreements are handled in indirect ways, and thus you reword the theme: "Work out your differences without making a big scene." Again, the key here is to make an interpretation that is supported by your data—that stands out above other issues. Just as the actors must decide which aspects of a character to stress, so must the cultural analyst. Your discussion of the theme should give the reader a sense of pervasiveness as well as of salience.

Consider the earlier examples about "how hard to work." Imagine it is a different organization from the one discussed earlier that had mixed views on the subject. As you review data on values, rules, and rituals you might find consistent references to a common attitude about how hard one should work. You decide the attitude can best be captured in the following theme: "Work hard, but not too hard." To support this as a theme, you should be able to summarize data from the elements relevant to this theme (e.g., "Of the 10 people interviewed, all but one made some reference to the 'take it easy' *value*"). In addition, an implicit *rule* surfaced in these interviews that related to promotability. Employees agreed, "If you spend too much time on-task and don't spend time taking it easy and talking to other employees you will not get ahead." And finally, there was a daily *ritual* observed in the organization—a two-and-a-half-hour lunch and naptime was required (yes, this is a hypothetical example, but long lunch breaks are not uncommon in some countries).

Notice how, in the example above, *at least three elements were used that cut across more than one method.* Support from these multiple sources provides a credible reading of pervasive and salient themes in the culture. Support like this is also about finding data that will challenge or check your biases about an organization. Of course, as you develop support by reviewing field notes, realize that other examples and relevant observations may occur to you that you failed to record in your notes. If this happens, be sure to document these important observations. As you develop themes, remember that your analysis does not end there. These themes are used to help you provide a general characterization of the culture or the "defining plot."

Rehearsal 8.1 Finding a Theme

Purpose: Take 5 minutes to practice developing themes

Steps:

1. Briefly state examples of three elements (heroes, rules, stories, etc.) from your observations, interviews, and/or textual analysis that appear relevant to one another.

   Element A:

   _____

   _____

   _____

   _____

(Continued)

(Continued)

   Element B:

   _____

   _____

   _____

   _____

   Element C:

   _____

   _____

   _____

   _____

2. Identify connections across these elements by developing a theme that captures the core idea that links these elements.

   _____

   _____

   _____

   _____

3. Determine the relative pervasiveness of this theme. How widely spread is this theme in the organization? You may determine this by checking the sources you used for the various elements (e.g., organization-wide meetings vs. interviews in one department?).

   _____

   _____

   _____

   _____

4. Determine the relative salience of this theme. How important is this theme to organizational outcomes such as productivity or employee satisfaction? How often was it mentioned? How many elements supported it?

   _____

   _____

   _____

   _____

C. The Defining Plot: "What Is the Culture?"

You walk out of a play, an art gallery, a music performance hall and think about what you just experienced. The effort of translating the symbolic forms of music or art into words is difficult: something is always lost. For example, a book/opera like *Les Misérables* might leave you with a mix of feelings and ideas, such as "power in love," "the mystery of mercy," and "the self-destruction of evil." These word pictures attempt to capture themes in the play. Yet another step can be taken if you then distill these various themes and attempt to answer the question, "So what was that *Les Misérables* story about, anyway?" The process of distilling themes into a clear statement about culture is the third step in this interpretive model.

An overall characterization or representation of an organization may appear to fly in the face of the convention that organizations cannot or should not be reduced to specific labels or monocultural characterization (Martin, 1992). However, a general and overall characterization does not mean that you must oversimplify the organization you have studied. Indeed, the answer to the question, "What is the culture?" may take a number of forms, each of which provides room for characterizations that are complex and creative. We provide four major options to aid you in this process. Each of these methods for characterizing a culture should be seen as a tool for thinking out of the box. We added a fifth method for defining the culture to encourage you to create your own interpretive approach.

1. Is there a central paradox underlying the themes?

A paradox is a contradictory statement that is nevertheless true. By a central paradox we mean a contradictory true statement that captures the core of the culture. Thinking about paradoxes in the organization can help you and members make sense of values and themes that may be the source of confusion or high levels of uncertainty. For example, "Chaotic Order" might capture a number of themes relevant to an organization characterized by standard policies and procedures that guide creative endeavors that are known for causing chaos in the organization. Often the crux of the culture is best depicted in tensions and contradictions—for example, the contradiction between espoused values and organizational practices.

2. Is there a master rule/value underlying the themes?

The notion of a master rule or value implies that a number of themes merge to suggest an overarching guiding principle that permeates the organization. For instance, using the example above, if paradox is not the sense you get from your reading of the culture, you might note that the culture can best be captured by drawing attention to the way employees are expected to follow an implicit communication rule in all that they do: "Speak first of new ideas and ways of doing things before critiquing old ways." Or you might find that one value, such as, "The Customer Comes First," permeates descriptions of rituals, heroes, history, and stories.

3. Is there a root metaphor underlying the themes?

The idea of a root metaphor, like a master rule or value, suggests that one thing serves as the source or explanatory idea behind multiple themes. Root metaphors can capture multiple elements and provide a valuable way to examine an organization (Morgan, 2007). One church we studied was captured with the metaphor of "a healing community." This metaphor guided the theology of the church, the role of its leaders (often anointing sick members with oil and praying for their healing), the large percentage of disabled persons who regularly attended the church, the design and use of its building, and common rituals within the church.

4. What are the deeper assumptions underlying these themes?

In the earlier chapters of this text, we used Schein's (1992) categories to talk about layers of culture. At the surface level, culture is created and displayed through the kinds of elements you have been collecting and interpreting over the course of your analysis. At a deeper level are values that underlie all the elements. The relationship between the surface manifestations of culture and the values may or may not be understood by organizational actors. Still more likely to be operating at unconscious levels is the bedrock foundation of culture, which are assumptions. What unstated assumptions underlie the cultural elements you observed? Assumptions about status differences? Assumptions about goals or accountability? Assumptions about effectiveness?

5. Are there [fill in the blank and be creative!] underlying the themes?

The process of interpretation is a creative one. Interpreting a central paradox, a master rule, a root metaphor, or underlying assumptions may not be the most useful or meaningful approach with the set of elements and resultant themes you have identified. In fact, before you ever complete the process of identifying elements or themes you may have had a hunch or a word picture in your own mind that defined the organization. Recall that the intent of being more thorough or systematic in the process of answering the question, "What is the culture?" is to be able to provide credible support for your position. Yet we recognize that this process may sometimes be intuitive and that the formula or steps we encourage may work in the reverse. For example, you may have created your own characterization before attempting a thorough data collection. If this is the case, the process of analysis is one of determining just how accurate or well supported your characterization is once you dig deeper. Even if you did not begin this process with a sense of how you might define the culture, you may find it useful to go beyond the first three suggestions to create something of your own. Again, just be sure the overall characterization is clearly supported by multiple themes and elements.

One last factor to consider in your interpretation is to ask yourself, "What is not here that I would expect to see?" Martin (1992) refers to this type of analysis as probing silences and empty spaces. Angi once served as a consultant to a children's home trying to survive a leadership transition. As she questioned the board members about the strengths and weaknesses of the organization, she was struck by the absence of any language about the care of children. Board members talked about the strength of leadership, the business plan, the endowment, and the new facilities, but no one talked about the children. The silence made it clear that the nonprofit organization had drifted from the clarity of its original mission and values.

When you write your analysis, you might experiment with creative forms of writing in presenting your results. Often the products of ethnomethodological research read more like short stories than formal research papers. They may include extensive quotes or narratives from interviews with culture members. They may include narratives of key episodes you observed. Rehearsal 8.4 provides an example template, but you will find a variety of example papers on the book's Student Study Site, www.sagepub.com/driskill2estudy.

Summary

At this stage of the analysis, your immersion in the data and your own creativity as an interpreter become all important. You should have a sense of seeing the organization you are studying in a new light or with a clearer understanding. Like an actor who has hung out behind the scenes to interact with other actors, who has studied the script and gotten inside the character, you should know more than the other actors about the set, the stage, the relationships among the players, and what makes this particular troupe and performance unique. The themes you have already discussed as well as other relevant data should support your general characterization of the culture. Before moving to the application section, be sure you have a clear grasp of the following aspects of the interpretation process:

- Cultural analysis is an interpretive process; characterizations of the culture will likely vary from person to person.

- Cultural themes grow from combining multiple elements and methods.

- A general characterization should be based on multiple themes and may take the form of paradoxes, master rules/values, root metaphors, and/or other ways to capture the organizational culture.

Rehearsal 8.2 A Practice Stage

Purpose: Develop skills in observation and content analysis of data so you can make interpretations of an organizational culture

Major Steps:

1. Complete 2 weeks of observation notes.
   a. A minimum of 3–4 hours a week in observation
   b. A variety of observation settings (e.g., meetings, informal interactions, formal rituals)
   c. Notes that include bracketed information (about inferences and questions)

2. Use interviews or qualitative surveys to explore cultural interpretations of organizational actors.
   a. Choose a representative sample of interviewees.
   b. Develop rapport.
   c. Use relatively open questions to elicit accounts, stories, and explanations.
   d. Follow up answers with probes.

3. Content analyze a representative text or texts.
   a. Choose representative and credible texts that match the communication style of the organization.
   b. Use content analysis, rhetorical analysis, or linguistic analysis.

(Continued)

(Continued)

4. Create a document summarizing data by elements of culture.

   a. Be sure to make clear reference to observation notes (date, etc.) and/or content analysis text (date of newsletter, section, etc.); the key here is to have summary data that can easily be traced back to notes.

   b. Be sure you have several examples of most, if not all, of the elements.

5. Analyze your summary of elements to determine major themes.

   a. A theme equals a description of the culture drawn from common ideas that surface in three or more of the elements.

   b. State the theme and the supporting elements. Be specific.

   For example: In a day care organization a theme was: "Supportive touch is a mandated and encouraged behavior." Rules and rituals indicate that teachers should initiate touch often during the day as well as encourage children to touch each other in appropriate ways. Furthermore, during a weekly staff meeting a story was told of a teacher's aide who was fired because he did not take time to hug and encourage children through positive and appropriate touch.

   c. Aim for a minimum of three themes.

6. Create an overall characterization of the culture based on themes and elements.

   a. An overall characterization is a general statement that attempts to capture the core of the culture.

   b. An overall characterization does not mean that subcultures do not differ or that the culture is unified across all levels and divisions of the organization.

   c. Themes and relevant elements provide support for the characterization you have developed.

   d. Review Chapter 8 for options in developing an overall characterization of the culture.

7. Checklist for reviewing major steps of the Rehearsal:

   _____ Interpretation section with themes and an overall characterization

   _____ Appendix with a paper trail (for validity and reliability/consistency checks)

   _____ A copy of your field notes

   _____ A description or copy of the text you used for content analysis

   _____ A copy of notes from any other method used (survey, interviews)

   _____ A copy of your summary data for each element

   _____ A completed reliability check by a trusted colleague, a mentor, a classmate, or a member of the organization to make sure your account is consistent with how organizational members interpret the culture

Note: Though the idea of a reliability check seems at first "too academic," it should be part of our interpretive processes—we check our perceptions with others. The guide sheet in Rehearsal 8.3 can be used for a trusted colleague, mentor, or classmate to review your work.

Rehearsal 8.3 Reliability/Validity Check

1. Observation process:

   _____ Clear rationale for the observer role that was selected

   _____ Clear understanding of ethics involved in the choice

2. Check field notes: Check for improvement (from weeks 1–3) in the following:

   _____ Detailed descriptions

   _____ Use of brackets

3. Check text analysis:

   _____ Clear rationale for choosing this set of documents

   _____ Representative sample

   _____ Credible

   _____ Method of analysis documented and explained

4. Review summary of each element:

   _____ Are there gaps that indicate the need for more data?

   _____ Can you trace examples back to field notes, text, interviews?

   _____ Focus on descriptions? Free of judgment?

   _____ Examples clearly fit each element according to characterization of element?

   _____ Missing details? (information sufficient, makes sense?)

   _____ Method triangulation on most elements: examples from text analysis and observation and/or interviews/surveys?

5. Check themes for

   _____ Method triangulation: examples from content analysis and observation and/or interviews/surveys?

   _____ Data triangulation: examples from three or more elements?

6. Check an overall characterization for

   _____ Theme triangulation: support based on two or more themes (may include other well-developed elements)

   _____ Method triangulation: support from text analysis and observation and/or interviews/surveys?

Rehearsal 8.4 Cultural Analysis
Write-Up Guides

Directions: This final checklist should guide rather than dictate your writing process. These suggestions are intended as guides to developing a highly credible report for other members of the organization. (You will also find a variety of example papers on the Student Study Site at www.sagepub.com/driskill2estudy.) Of course, who your audience is (members of one department vs. executive leadership team) will dictate format. Remember, the goal is to "tell the story" of your analysis in a convincing manner. In this suggested outline, you are focused on elements, themes, and your characterization of the culture. After we cover application topics, we will discuss ways to develop implications of your findings.

Introduction:

_____ Draw interest to your analysis

_____ Discuss the importance of your analysis

_____ Develop credibility—references

_____ Preview main sections

Body:

I. Overview of analysis

_____ Background of organization (mission, structure, brief history)

_____ Methods (discuss data collection, rationale, time spent)

_____ Refer to Appendix with notes on each element

II. Major Themes

_____ Minimum of three; each supported by data from three or more elements

_____ Clear, convincing support from Appendix/Text/Book

_____ Clear tables/data summaries

(e.g., examples, frequency counts, quotes, paraphrases)

_____ Written to capture the richness of cultural data

III. Overall description of culture

_____ Supported by themes and elements

_____ Clear articulation of the rationale for the characterization

Conclusion

_____ Restate major goals and major conclusions and benefits

_____ Review the process (strengths of analysis, lessons learned)

References (complete; consistent format)

Appendix

_____ Synopsis of inferences on all elements (e.g., list all the rules)

_____ Copy of interview/survey guide if used

_____ Copy of Executive Summary (when applicable)

_____ Field notes

_____ Texts used for analysis

PART IV

Cultural Analysis Application

An Introduction to Step Five

Identifying Applications for Cultural Analysis

Articulate the value of the culture metaphor

Define major cultural elements

Use multiple data collection methods

Synthesize and interpret cultural data

★ **Identify applications**

Good managers contemplating mergers today routinely consider cultural match as an important criterion in deciding whether to proceed or draw back. Major organizational changes succeed or fail depending on how well leadership grasps the symbolic details that are so easy to overlook and works to integrate them into the change strategy. All modern managers are expected to understand these concepts and practice them in their daily managerial life. Who would have thought it so twenty years ago?

—Deal and Kennedy, "Introduction,"
Corporate Cultures, 2000, p. iv

Objectives:

- Explain implications of culture for important organizational activities and processes

- Apply cultural data to assess an organization's commitment to diversity, approaches to change, leadership styles, and integration of ethical principles and overall organizational effectiveness

Stage Terms:

- Diversity
- Organizational change
- Symbolic leadership
- Ethics
- Organizational effectiveness

An Approach to Answering "So What?"

Certainly actors undertaking the rigorous training of method acting must ask themselves at some point, "Will this really make me a better actor?" As they try to focus concentration on drinking a cup of orange juice, undertake animal studies, learn to channel emotions from previous experiences, and increase their concentration on stage, they have to wonder about their ability to transfer these activities into the creation of better stage and screen performances.

In the same way, students and organizational leaders often wonder whether the rigorous study necessary to understand their organizational cultures has a payoff. What is the practical significance of understanding organizational culture? How does it lead to more effective individual and organizational performance? In Step Five of our five-part method, we address these questions.

Five Examples

In Chapters 9 through 13 we develop five examples of applications of cultural knowledge: diversity, organizational change, symbolic leadership, ethics, and organizational effectiveness. It is valid to ask, "Why these five?" If we understand culture as a root metaphor for the whole organization, as we explained in Chapter 3, then culture is inherently tied to everything that goes on in an organization. We believe this is true. We chose these five as examples of cultural application because they are significant organizational processes or outcomes, and because they have a compelling and clear linkage to organizational culture. We hope that as you see the connection between culture and these five topics, you will move beyond this textbook to consider other applications of your cultural insights. For example, we hope you will begin to explore how culture relates to employee socialization, to technology innovation, to creativity, and to an unlimited number of other topics.

It is also fair to ask whether a cultural perspective brings anything new to the understanding of leadership, diversity, ethics, change, or other organizational processes. We believe that the cultural lens does have much to contribute to understanding organizational life. Take diversity as an example. Most organizations desire to harness the power of diverse perspectives among employees. Yet many organizations approach diversity only through superficial training programs and organizational practices that never become rooted in the deeper levels of organizational culture, values, and assumptions. Until diversity becomes deeply woven into the organizational culture, it fails to change the organization in fundamental ways.

Organizational ethics is a similar case. If an organization tries to become more ethical through training or adopting new accounting processes without changing the fundamental ideology coded into organizational stories and metaphors, the result will be superficial. We make arguments about the value of a cultural perspective on each of the topics covered in the next five chapters of the text.

In Chapter 9, "Casting Against Type: Diversity," we explore the linkage between organizational culture and embracing diversity. We approach this in two ways: how organizations can become more multicultural, and how marginalized actors in an organizational culture can understand dominant cultures for the purposes of professional development, gaining a voice, and initiating change. Too many organizations have launched diversity programs in a compartmentalized way—with an office that reports to the human resource director, several levels removed from the CEO. We point out that the culture, as a whole, must support a commitment to diversity if the value is to permeate an organization.

In Chapter 10, "Improvisation: Managing Change," we address the reasons why strong cultures often resist major change. We offer examples of organizational leaders who have initiated change without sufficient knowledge of the culture or sufficient collaboration with organization members, leading to unsuccessful change efforts. We explain how change can be introduced more effectively by using key elements of the culture rather than changing in opposition to the culture.

In Chapter 11, "An Honest Portrayal: Ethics," we explain our perspective that ethical principles must be deeply ingrained in an organizational culture in order for them to exert an unconscious influence on employee decision making and behavior. We explain how recent ethical lapses such as the Wall Street risk-taking that caused a global economic crisis can be understood as a reflection of organizational culture.

In Chapter 12, "The Director's Chair: Symbolic Leadership," we consider that culture creates a frame for viewing effective leadership performance. Effective leaders must understand how they are constrained by culture, as well as the role they play in creating, maintaining, and transforming culture. We argue that one of the most important characteristics of effective leaders is more than their technical expertise, it is also their ability to use symbols to create identity and shared vision. We offer opportunities for you to evaluate your own symbolic leadership abilities and to assess leaders in your organization.

Chapter 13, "Reading Reviews: Organizational Effectiveness," summarizes the application of a cultural analysis to the organization by discussing effectiveness and how all the previous application topics contribute to organizational performance. We discuss different ways to evaluate the relationship of culture and organizational performance, and offer tools to assess the effectiveness of your organization in light of cultural data.

We hope that the chapters exploring Step Five will assist you in recognizing that cultural analysis is not only fascinating but also practical for organizations and their members.

9

Casting Against Type

Diversity

Articulate the value of the culture metaphor

Define major cultural elements

Use multiple data collection methods

Synthesize and interpret cultural data

★ **Identify applications**

Step Five: Identify Applications for Organizational Diversity, Change, Ethics, Leadership, and Effectiveness

Thus creativity has come to be the most highly prized commodity in our economy. . . . Hiring for diversity, once a matter of legal compliance, has become a matter of economic survival because creativity comes in all colors, genders, and personal preferences.

—Florida, *The Rise of the Creative Class*, 2002, p. 5

Objectives:

- Explore the paradox of culture and diversity
- Promote skills for understanding organizational subcultures
- Explain the importance of diversity in today's creative economy
- Describe the progression organizations take in becoming multicultural
- Explain the essential nature of cultural understanding for minority subcultures within the organization

Stage Terms:

- Diversity
- Multiculturalism
- Marginalized groups
- Hegemony
- Dialogue
- Cosmopolitan communication
- Mentoring
- Creative economy

Here's a trick: Create a strong and vibrant culture in which values are shared, employees are socialized into a common way of creating meanings, and at the same time maintain a diverse workforce with enough tension to promote creativity and innovation. This is the essential paradox of culture. Strong cultures tend to reproduce themselves. New employees are hired because they are a "good fit" with existing employees. Cultural values and norms are so strong that employees are socialized to accept the "company way" or they leave. Diversity is a clear example of Eisenberg, Goodall, and Trethewey's (2010) concept of creativity and constraint. The very cohesiveness enabled by a strong culture can be a constraining force on difference and change.

The flip side also can be true. If a company strives for diversity in hiring and consciously chooses individuals quite different from the existing employee base, culture can become eroded over time. History is forgotten, rituals lose their meaning, and values fade. Subcultures compete for organizational dominance. These changes in culture may be positive in the long run but are disruptive and difficult at the start. Zak (1994) offered an ethnographic study of a blue-collar organizational culture newly diversified by race, gender, ethnicity, and class due to legal mandates. Veteran employees sought to maintain cultural identity and hierarchical position through linguistic strategies such as inside humor, exclusive language, and horseplay. Because of the frequent conflicts between newcomers and veterans, management stepped in to increase control and enforce punishments, leading to cultural fragmentation and resentment. In the context of religious organizations, efforts to move away from the norm of segregation on Sundays are occurring. However, the challenges are complex. In a case analysis of several multiethnic congregations, Emerson (2006) describes inevitable tensions concerning the identity of the church based on the ethnicity of the leader or leadership team. Inevitably, if a church is founded and led by one person, members and other leaders may sense power inequities. Thus, as might be anticipated, DeYmaz (2007) includes the need for diverse leadership teams in his model for healthy multiethnic churches.

Defining Diversity

Cox (1993) defines cultural diversity as "the representation, in one social system, of people with distinctly different group affiliations of cultural significance" (p. 6). This definition is useful because it recognizes the role of perceptual identification and cultural significance in defining diversity. For example, an African American female who identifies more with her social class and gender than with her race might not add to the diversity of an organization in which her race is underrepresented. A Caucasian male who identifies more as a disabled person than as a majority male might add to diversity. Cox's definition also stresses cultural significance of the group affiliation. For example, in a traditional church structure that is composed predominantly of intact nuclear families, introducing a church leader who identifies himself as a single or divorced male would have great cultural significance and add to diversity, while a divorced individual in another organization would have little cultural significance. Conversely, a multinational firm with a dominant Asian Indian culture would enhance diversity more with the inclusion of employees from a country with vastly different assumptions about hierarchy and power distance (Hofstede, n.d.), such as Germany, than from a country with similar assumptions, such as Pakistan.

Thomas (1996) takes a more inclusive view in defining diversity. Arguing that diversity has become understood by many as a new word for affirmative action and focusing attention primarily on African American employees, Thomas defines diversity as "any mixture of items characterized by differences and similarities" (p. 5).

He notes that this broader definition encourages organization members to focus not only on differences but on similarities as well and to explore the contours of difference and sameness. He also says that his definition refers to the collective (all-inclusive) mixture of differences and similarities, using the metaphor of a jelly-bean jar. In looking at the diversity, you consider not only the last color added to the jar but the overall mix of colors and what each adds to the jar. Finally, he states that a broader view of diversity can stretch beyond artificially constructed demographic differences to consider functional or methodological diversity as well, for example. Diversity thus becomes a holistic way of thinking about organizational complexity.

Hays-Thomas (2004) adds additional rationales for a broader definition of diversity such as Thomas's. She says that when diversity is understood as accommodating only a few legally protected classes of employees, it may engender resistance or resentment from other employees. The broader definition also draws on rich social science research from fields like group dynamics and decision making, noting the superiority of heterogeneous workgroups. In addition, the broader definition helps organizations understand that meeting legal requirements is only one rationale for diversity but that more important rationales lie in potential for innovation and organizational effectiveness. Hays-Thomas writes:

> By conceptualizing diversity in terms of environmental complexity and change, Thomas takes a powerful conceptual leap. He shows us that the challenges posed by diversity management are just one aspect of life in an increasingly complex organizational world. Complexity of thought and flexibility of behavior are required for success in contemporary organizations. An important consequence of this perspective is that diversity management is seen as a form of organizational development and change as well as a set of processes for increasing effectiveness and harmony in a workforce that varies along important dimensions. (pp. 11–12)

We concur with the value of these far reaching rationales. However, beyond these pragmatic values, we would underscore the historic and consistently stressed rationale of ethics. In short, creating equal access and opportunity is also the right action to take.

We take two different approaches to diversity in this chapter. The first approach helps you to assess the commitment to diversity within your organization and to understand the importance of culture in shaping a truly diverse organization. The focus of this first approach is on organizational development and change. The second approach is an individual strategy that recognizes that not all organizations fully embrace a culture of diversity. If you are part of an organization that does not embrace diversity, we suggest ways to enhance your organizational performance and even serve as an agent of organizational change if you are a member of a marginalized organizational group.

Creating Multicultural Organizations

The process of enhancing diversity practices is not a simple one. Take a minute to consider your experiences in work, nonprofit, and/or religious organizations. Few of us can claim that each of our organizations has fully embraced diversity. Yet, in our consulting, research, and leadership roles, we have seen cause for hope. We conclude this section with practical ways to improve diversity practices. To set the stage, we review four imperatives for creating organizational cultures that value diversity. While such information is not new to many, it might be useful if you need to remind a client, coworker, and/or supervisor of reasons to engage in improved diversity initiatives.

Next, we provide cautions and pitfalls to avoid in drawing conclusions about diversity from your data. We then suggest several principles to guide diversity initiatives.

Imperatives for Valuing Diversity

First, globalization processes and demographic shifts in the workforce make the need for improved diversity practices evident. Earlier, we stressed that nearly two thirds of U.S. organizations conduct business internationally. If you live on the Euro-Asian, African, or Australian continents, odds are that you will either work for a multinational or do business in a diverse setting. In the United States, projected demographic shifts for the next 40 years makes the need for improved diversity practices evident as well. As Table 9.1 indicates, the Caucasian population of the United States is projected to become a "majority minority" by 2050. According to the 2000 U.S. Census (U.S. Census Bureau, n.d.), those who identified themselves only as "white" constituted 71.6% of the population in 2000 but will be only 52.5% by 2050. The Hispanic population is projected to increase most dramatically, from 11.3% of the current population to 22.5% in 2050. The African American population will increase more slowly, from 12.8% to 15.7%. The Asian American population will also increase, from 3.5% to 7.2%. Population gains will come from higher birthrates among some minority populations as well as immigration patterns. Foreign-born citizens and legal immigrants will also constitute a growing portion of the U.S. workforce.

The trends and projections captured in Table 9.1 are commonly mentioned in the news and in classes on management and organizational development. The common assumption is that these U.S. demographic shifts will result in organizations that enjoy the benefits of increased diversity—multiple perspectives from differing cultural value sets and/or synergy from increased contact and collaboration between different cultural and ethnic groups (Moran, Harris, & Moran, 2007).

Second, for those employed by the U.S. workforce, age diversity will increase. While a higher percentage of older workers will work longer due to economic downturns that have played havoc with retirement accounts, a new wave of younger workers (sometimes called the "Net Generation") will enter the workforce in huge numbers. The Net Generation is the largest generation since the Baby Boomers. Tapscott (2009) documents that the Net Generation (born between 1977 and 1997) now constitutes 27% of the U.S. population, compared to 23% for the Baby

Table 9.1   Projections of U.S. Population by Race/Ethnicity

Race/Ethnicity	2000 Percentage of Population	2050 Projection
African American	12.8	15.7
Hispanic	11.3	22.5
White	71.6	52.5
Asian American	4.4	10.3
American Indian/Native, Eskimo, & Aleut	0.9	1.1

SOURCE: The full table of these trend data can be found online at www.sagepub.com/driskill2estudy.

Boomers (born between 1946 and 1964), 15% for Generation X (born between 1965 and 1976), and 13.4% for Generation Next, born after 1998. Net Generation members have well-developed technological skills but very different orientations toward work from their parents and grandparents. They are dismayed when they join an organization and find technical systems less advanced than those they used in high school, policies forbidding social media at work, seniority policies that diminish their roles in the organization, and inflexible work hours that value "desk time" over work productivity. They are also impatient with cultural assumptions that encourage newer employees to "pay their dues" by silently observing current practices before speaking or promoting change. Younger employees expect to have voice and exercise influence from the start.

Third, organizational cultures, even with changes in demographics, still face entrenched stereotypes and assumptions. Cleveland, Stockdale, and Murphy (2000) express the feminist viewpoint that despite their differences, most organizational cultures have been built upon male stereotypes and assumptions. They write,

> American organizations tend to expect and reward high levels of dedication and commitment, long hours, and placing the demands of work ahead of the demands of nonwork responsibilities. . . . Most U.S. organizations were built by and for men (usually White men), and it should come as no surprise that men fit better than women in many instances. Perhaps the biggest challenge in building organizations that fit women as well as men is to examine critically the values and assumptions that define work and work organizations. (pp. 381–382)

They advocate pluralistic rather than monolithic organizational culture. Rather than expecting each culture member to adapt to a single set of values and expectations, a pluralistic culture will create systemic organizational change to adapt to the dynamism of a diverse workforce. The assumptions favoring males are an example of the deep and unconscious assumptions that form Schein's (1996) third level of culture.

Finally, solving the dilemma of culture and diversity takes on additional urgency in the present "creative economy." Richard Florida (2002) has written an intriguing book, *The Rise of the Creative Class: And How It's Transforming Work, Leisure, Community, and Everyday Life.* In it he argues that the U.S. economy (and to a large extent the world economy) has become based not only on information but also on creativity, an economy in which hardware and software innovation, biomedical research, e-commerce innovation, and entertainment are driving our total economic growth.

Florida points out that an essential ethos of the new creative class involves diversity. Members of the creative class feel that innovation can flourish only in an environment of stimulation and creative tension. As companies compete for the top creative talent, diversity is a key edge. Florida has conducted extensive statistical research showing that the fastest growing economic areas show excellent statistical fit with areas rich in diversity. Florida (2002) writes,

> One indicator of this preference for diversity is reflected in the fact that Creative Class people tell me that at job interviews they like to ask if the company offers same sex partner benefits, even when they are not themselves gay. What they're seeking is an environment open to differences. . . . When they are sizing up a new company and community, acceptance of diversity and of gays in particular is a sign that reads, "nonstandard people welcome here." (p. 79)

"When they are sizing up a new company and community, acceptance of diversity and gays in particular is a sign that reads, 'Nonstandard people welcome here.'"

Cautions: Avoiding Two Extremes

While these imperatives should motivate reflection on diversity practices within organizations, two cautions should be noted when studying multinational or culturally diverse organizations. First, diversity in an organization does not necessarily result in diverse values and/or perspectives. Cultural generalizations about value differences may or may not hold true from person to person. Thus, while an organization may appear diverse in terms of color or nationality, the value sets of those individuals may or may not be dissimilar. A Thai immigrant who has spent his whole life in Bangkok working for Citibank, for example, may have more organizational values in common with a native from New York City than with his own countryman who has spent his life in a rural area of Thailand. This point echoes Cox's (1993) definition, earlier in this chapter, of cultural identification in defining diversity. Organizations also sometimes create barriers that prevent the full advantages of a diverse workforce.

Dodd (1998) suggests that caution in generalizing about differences must be balanced by another equally important second caution—acting as if differences do not exist or do not matter. In his research, Gerald has heard comments from more than one manager revealing the assumption that "we are really the same," or "yes, I see some differences, but it is really just a personality thing, not a cultural issue." At one level it is important that supervisors recognize a difference even if they attribute it to a personality difference. At another level, however, being blind to the pervasive influence of cultural differences can handicap an organization.

In one multinational company Gerald found that the minority Asian Indian population, as well as the majority U.S. population, tended to overlook differences with two results—mismanaged conflict and missed opportunities for creatively tapping into value differences. In one situation, differences in supervisory style were creating tensions with employees. Asian Indians in management roles assumed that close, immediate supervision was effective. U.S. employees tended to prefer less "over the shoulder" approaches. Neither side had an understanding or acceptance of this national cultural difference. Furthermore, neither side realized that if managed well, not only could these tensions be lessened, but both supervisors and employees would have the opportunity to tap into their value differences to solve problems more effectively. Rather than remain in a stalemate over the difference, dialogue might have resulted in more creative approaches to supervision and teamwork (Driskill, 1995; Driskill & Downs, 1995).

This organizational culture lacked a vision for managing differences in a way that could result in creative responses to difference. Thus, casting a diverse set of players on the organizational stage with the hopes of creative outcomes involves more than just having diverse cultures or personalities present. Creative outcomes also involve more than being aware of differences or effective cross-cultural conflict management. Leadership must develop core and defining values about valuing and tapping into the creativity gains promised by diversity. Such values must be grounded in practices that address pragmatics such as language and perceptions of difference. For instance, Lauring (2007), based on a study of 14 Danish multinationals, argues that a lack of shared language and perceptions of differences tends to fragment work teams, thus actually decreasing opportunities to tap into the richness of the diversity. For instance, one interviewee commented:

> It is most often easier with only Danes. The meetings become more formal when conducted in English rather than Danish. There is less ping-pong across the table—less informal talking. That is a bit negative. It can be good to have the informal talk because it strengthens the group socially. (p. 5)

This comment reflects something of the challenge of tapping into diversity in constructive ways. Despite the challenges, a number of processes are available to increase diversity and creativity.

Fostering Diversity and Creativity

Given these cautions, we seek to identify processes that will allow us to create cultures that value diversity. Cultural data will often reflect information about diversity initiatives. For instance, one student conducting an analysis was overwhelmed by the conflicting and competing views of diversity within one unit of a large organization. Some interviewees boasted about various diversity practices. Others quietly spoke of the surface nature of these practices. In this section, we first review a model for reflecting on stages of multicultural development. We find these stages a useful device for stressing the journey or process rather than an either/or dichotomy. Next, we integrate several principles for improving diversity practices.

A Diversity Development Model

In the chapter "Becoming a Multi-Cultural Organization," Taylor Cox Jr. (1993) reflects on his years of experience as a diversity consultant for some of America's larger corporations, in stressing the importance of deep cultural change in supporting diversity goals:

> The root cause of many failures to manage and leverage diversity is a misdiagnosis of the problem. The problem posed by diversity is not simply that there are not enough people of certain social-cultural identity groups in the organization. Nor is it primarily one of making insensitive people more aware that identity matters, although this is certainly part of what needs to happen . . . the more significant problem is that most employers have an organizational culture that is somewhat between toxic and deadly when it comes to handling diversity. (p. 12)

So how can an organization create a strong culture that fosters diversity and creativity? Holvino, Ferdman, and Merrill-Sands (2004) present their model of multicultural organizational development (MCOD), developed by Holvino (1998) in a previous monograph (see Table 9.2), proposing that organizations go through six phases as they move from monocultural to multicultural organizations. In the first or exclusionary stage, organizations explicitly and actively base themselves on the values of one cultural group and explicitly privilege that group in organizational practices and norms. In the second phase, which Holvino terms the "passive club" stage, organizations are less openly exclusionary but still admit only new organization members who are similar in values and perspectives as the dominant group. Stage three is a transitional stage of compliance. In this stage the organization may not actively exclude organization members who are different from the current dominant group but also does not make affirmative changes in management or cultural practices that would seek out diverse new members. Stage four is the transitional stage of positive action in which the organization becomes committed to including others, especially those in legally protected categories. The organization begins to tolerate differences created by new members. The fifth stage is the beginning of multiculturalism that Holvino calls "redefining." In this stage the organization tries to expand its definition of inclusion and diversity. Leaders and organization members attempt to identify and change barriers to diversity. In the last stage, that of true multiculturalism, the organization actively includes a diversity of groups, styles, and perspectives and becomes a continuous learning organization with changes in basic assumptions and values that capture the benefits of diversity.

Table 9.2   The Multicultural Organizational Development Model

Monocultural		*Transitional*		*Multicultural*	
Exclusionary	*Passive Club*	*Compliance*	*Positive Action*	*Redefining*	*Multicultural*
Actively excludes in its mission and practices those who are not members of the dominant group.	Actively or passively excludes those who are not members of the dominant group. Includes other members only if they "fit."	Passively committed to including others without making major changes. Includes only a few members of other groups.	Committed to making a special effort to include others, especially those in designated target groups. Tolerates the differences that those others bring.	Actively works to expand its definition of inclusion and diversity. Tries to examine and change practices that may act as barriers to members of non-dominant groups.	Actively includes a diversity of groups, styles, and perspectives. Continuously learns and acts to make the systemic changes required to value and include all kinds of people.
Values the dominant perspective of one group, culture, or style.		Seeks to integrate others into systems created under dominant norms.		Values and integrates the perspectives of diverse identities, cultures, styles, and groups into the organization's work and systems.	

SOURCE: Holvino (1998). Used with permission.

Diversity Action Steps and Principles

As you reflected on the above stages, we hope you took time to identify where you would locate your organization. It might help to think of the stages as a continuum rather than discrete stages. Put differently, it might be that your organization shares characteristics across stages and/or has moved back and forth between strategies. You also may find that some forms of diversity (such as gender) might be valued and promoted while other forms (such as ideology or sexual orientation) are not. To aid the process of encouraging reflection on cultural data in light of diversity, we provide four additional suggestions.

First, reflect on your data in light of options that organizations have in response to diversity. Thomas (1996) created a Diversity Paradigm in which he theorizes that organizations can create eight action options regarding diversity:

- Include/exclude by deciding how much diversity to admit to the organization
- Deny by claiming that differences do not matter and all are treated the same
- Assimilate by expecting "minority" components to conform to norms of the dominant culture
- Suppress by burying/removing differences from your active consciousness
- Isolate by creating "niches" for diversity within the organization
- Tolerate by accepting but not valuing differences
- Build relationships by treating diversity as an interpersonal issue
- Foster mutual adaptation by valuing differences; all members of the organization work to value and learn from one another

Thomas notes that only the last option leads to a multicultural organization, while the others form a progression of increasing comfort with the idea of diversity.

Second, consider how communication practices may contribute to cultural patterns that promote or inhibit organizational diversity. For example, Kirby and Krone (2002) document ways that employee communication influenced employee use of family leave policies. In their study, employees without young children felt that family leave policies were unfair and placed additional workload on them. They especially discouraged males from taking paternity leave. The negative talk about work–family policies resulted in low usage rates of policies designed to accommodate diversity among employees.

W. Barnett Pearce (1989) stresses the importance of communication practices in shaping the multicultural organization. He notes four forms of communication, which correspond to other stages of multiculturalism in this chapter: monocultural (in which organization members cannot see past the dominant cultural pattern); ethnocentric (in which members see other cultures but act in ways that indicate their own culture is superior); modernistic (in which members are completely relativistic and communicate as if all cultures are equal and none can be preferred over others); and cosmopolitan (a form of communication in which we can value our own cultural practices while appreciating and seeking to understand the perspectives of others). Grimes and Richard (2003) posit that cosmopolitan communicators

> can make important contributions to diverse organizations because they do not ignore differences but instead fully recognize, appreciate, and collaborate across them. . . . [They] consider functional conflict as a learning opportunity rather than a threat. Such characteristics will improve the quality of thought, performance, and decision making. (p. 18)

Third, consider specific changes needed to move toward "true multiculturalism." Holvino, Ferdman, and Merrill-Sands (2004) share their vision of what a multicultural organization looks like:

> In essence, we define a multicultural, inclusive organization as one in which the diversity of knowledge and perspectives that members of different groups bring to the organization has shaped its strategy, its work, its management and operating systems, and its core values and norms for success. Furthermore, in multicultural, inclusive organizations, members of all groups are treated fairly, feel included and actually are included, have equal opportunities, and are represented at all organizational levels and functions. The ultimate goal in working with diversity is to weave it into the fabric of the organization. Working with diversity connects directly to the work of the organization and the people within it. It implies that diversity is the work and responsibility of everyone, not just managers and leaders. It suggests that diversity is an asset to be used and developed, rather than a problem to be managed. Finally it projects a sense of dynamism and continuity. (pp. 249–250)

They claim that to achieve such a multicultural organization three changes are necessary: (1) structural changes such as recruitment practices, policies, equal pay and benefits, policies on work/family balance, holidays, and so on; (2) cultural changes in values, beliefs, and ideologies that are reflected in language, rituals, metaphors, and work styles; and (3) behavioral changes, eliminating behavior that conveys stereotyping and negative intergroup relations. Florida (2002) concurs with

---

**Rehearsal 9.1 Assess the Multiculturalism
of Your Organization**

Purpose: To apply the material from Holvino, Ferdman, and Merrill-Sands to your organization

1. Where would you place your organization on the continuum of moving from monoculturalism to multiculturalism? Why?

   _____

   _____

   _____

   _____

2. What structural changes in recruitment practices, policies, pay and benefits, holidays, work–family balance, and the like would support multiculturalism?

_____

_____

_____

_____

3. How do employees' communication patterns contribute to or inhibit multiculturalism? Are certain voices muted in the organizational dialogue? Does employee communication about diversity policies limit policies' impact?

_____

_____

_____

_____

4. What behavioral changes are necessary to promote more effective intergroup relations?

_____

_____

_____

_____

the need for these types of changes. He writes that this evolution of culture in some of America's largest corporations has indeed occurred to attract and retain creative employees. The cultural transformation is marked by casual dress codes, flexible work schedules, open loft-style office spaces, communal hangout spaces, abundant art, and new perks such as concierge services.

Fourth, support and encourage organizational subcultures within the overall culture. Steve Jobs did this at Apple Computer when he developed the subversive, renegade team that created the Macintosh computer. This group was supported and encouraged in flouting organizational norms to foster creativity and a sense of being "outlaws." Most creative teams in advertising agencies are granted similar latitude in breaking organizational norms of dress, scheduling, and work habits to foster an environment that nourishes creativity.

The danger with the second approach is evident. If more and more distinct subcultures flourish, employees may come to identify more closely with the subculture than the overall parent culture, and the subculture's values and norms may eclipse and/or change the dominant culture over time. These subcultures can also be one way that an organization isolates diverse elements rather than creating a multicultural approach to changing the overall organization. Different subcultures can also compete with one another, as the Mac division did with the Lisa division at Apple Computer. While competition is not always negative and some cultural change and evolution may be positive, if competition is not effectively managed it can fragment and weaken cultures.

Enhancing the Ability of Marginalized Groups to Read Dominant Cultures

In an ideal world, all organizations would be in the process of becoming multicultural. However, in the real world some organizations are blind to the value of diversity or uncertain as to how to move toward multiculturalism. Because organizations vary so widely in regard to inclusion, it is also crucial for members of marginalized groups to understand the dominant organizational culture. Being able to read the dominant culture can provide critical information to guide employment choices, as well as promoting individual career development. We offer this section as a way to improve awareness of the experiences of marginalized groups as well as to provide practical guidance. Both organizations and individuals have responsibilities in enhancing cultural awareness. Organizations can develop mentoring, dialogue, and training, as we suggest later. Individuals can learn to ask the right questions, participate in informal organizational activities, seek out mentors, and form their own communication networks to enhance cultural knowledge. As you analyze your cultural data, you may find themes that emerge related to the experiences cited in this section. If this is the case, we encourage you to reflect on the suggestions for improving the experience of these groups.

Developing Awareness: Minority Experiences and Muted Voices

Marginalized groups are those whose interests and styles are not privileged within the organization. Such groups face a number of challenging obstacles. Rosabeth Moss Kanter (1977), in her classic book *Men and Women of the Corporation*, offered a numerical minority hypothesis: that tokens (one of only a few representatives of their category in a larger dominant group) face similar pressures whether a woman in a male-dominated profession, an African American executive in a European American–dominated team, or an American manager in a Japanese subsidiary of a multinational corporation. One obstacle facing each of these tokens is the lack of access to informal channels of information that would yield tacit understanding of organizational norms. Allen (1995), based on her review of the literature, concluded, "Persons of color tend to have limited access to social networks, blocked mobility and often do not have mentors or sponsors" (p. 150). For instance, Amason, Allen, and Holmes (1999) document the stressors experienced by Hispanics in the acculturation process. Again, the limited access to supportive networks contributed to the challenges they faced in adjusting.

Rehearsal 9.2 Are You a Privileged Member of Your Organizational Culture?

Purpose: To develop awareness of your relative position of advantage over members of marginalized groups.

1. Have you ever left an employment interview wondering if your race or sexual orientation was a factor in not getting a job?

2. How likely is it that your direct supervisor will be of your race and gender?

3. Do you have to use two languages or idioms, one for social and the other for professional?

4. How many times in a year do you walk into a meeting in which you are the only member of your representative group?

5. How likely is it that someone of your group would be available as a mentor within your organization?

6. Are holidays associated with your religion standard organizational holidays, or do you have to ask special permission to observe them or take personal vacation days?

7. What would be the reaction of your colleagues if you took the person you live with to an office party?

8. How many times have you been asked to speak for all members of your race or gender in a business conversation?

9. Would questions be raised if you chose to select or promote a member of your race or gender?

10. Are you ever invited to a club or restaurant for an organizational function where you feel uncomfortable as a member of your group?

11. Do you have to rely on laws to ensure equal treatment of your group?

12. Do you ever have to seek assistance or alternatives to be able to enter an office or to use a restroom because the facilities were not designed for you?

13. Do you often feel you are chosen for committees or assignments not because of your qualifications or interests but to represent your minority group?

In a similar vein, O'Brien (1980) noted that women in male-dominated workplaces faced the double jeopardy of being less likely to understand informal norms in the workplace and being judged more harshly than their male counterparts when they violated informal norms. In Angi's dissertation research (Laird, 1982) she found that female supervisors working in an oil-well cable manufacturing plant could articulate organizational norms and values as well as their male counterparts in oral interviews, yet when asked to enact the rule in an applied episode they did not show the same situational intelligence as almost all their male counterparts. In a consulting study a few years ago, she asked all the tellers in a large bank chain what it took to become an officer of the bank. All the white males knew it took hard work, good results, face time, and service in certain "approved" community organizations. Every woman and racial/ethnic minority she interviewed declared with confidence that they would become an officer with hard work and diligence. Not one mentioned the expectation of face time or community service. How did all the males know? It likely is because this "tacit" information is learned through informal communication networks—on the golf course, at the Friday happy hour, at the company hunting lodge—all venues from which the tokens are too often excluded. It is this very "social networking" that Richard Florida's Creative Class rebels against as they seek a meritocracy built on talent and performance rather than social connections.

The experience of minorities goes beyond problems faced in "learning the ropes." Meares, Oetzel, Torres, Derkacs, and Ginossar (2004) examined responses to mistreatment in the workplace. They document various forms of mistreatment that occur both at the interpersonal and the institutional level. Their analysis includes documentation of various ways minorities construct "muted narratives" in response to mistreatment. For instance, minority responses to mistreatment tended to fall into narrative categories such as "muted, but engaged," "angrily disengaged," and "resigned." The authors stress that ambiguous policies about mistreatment were a major source. While management had acknowledged problems for several years, no action had been taken to create clear definitions or ways to address mistreatment. In fact, minorities faced a dilemma regarding options for responding effectively. The researchers state:

> If they work to resist mistreatment, they are placing themselves in a position where they are likely to face more mistreatment. If they react to the mistreatment by becoming disengaged, they are indirectly recreating the power structures and giving up the chance of being heard. (p. 21)

As this study on mistreatment suggests, the challenges faced by marginalized groups are varied and complex. Thus we consider several communication practices that are most likely to create a culture that embraces diversity.

Strategies for Marginalized Groups: Mentoring, Dialogue, and Multicultural Training

We recognize an ethical dilemma as we propose strategies for marginalized groups to understand the dominant organizational culture. Numerous critical theorists (see Clair, 1993, 1998; Mumby, 1997) have pointed out that when marginalized groups adapt to the dominant culture, they reinforce the legitimacy of unjust cultures that privilege the interests of some groups over others. They call this process hegemony, the participation of marginalized groups in their own domination. Our response is that marginalized groups must understand the dominant culture in order to change it. Often the means of domination through unconscious cultural patterns can be the means of liberation when marginalized groups understand and use cultural patterns to support their own interests.

Either organizations or individuals can take primary responsibility for ensuring that members of culturally significant minorities have resources to learn about cultural expectations. In this section, we will explore three such options, recognizing that one strategy alone is unlikely to align an organizational culture with a value for embracing diversity.

Mentoring Programs

One strategy is to install formal mentoring programs, in which a senior member of the organization is paired with a new employee to "show him [or her] the ropes." These formal mentoring relationships rarely produce the same results as naturally occurring mentoring relationships based on perceived mutual benefit and professional attraction. The assigned mentor spends less time with the mentee and does not interact in the informal ways that would produce a cultural understanding of the informal relationship.

Chao, Waltz, and Gardner (1992) and Cotton (1995) compared results and levels of satisfaction between individuals who had been involved in informal and formal mentoring programs. While they found that both groups expressed greater socialization and career progress than employees who had not been mentored at all, satisfaction was much higher in informal mentorships, and those relationships also resulted in higher salaries for mentees.

Kreps (1983) writes of another interesting way that organizations have sought to help all new employees with enculturation. RCA developed extensive video orientation programs, telling the new employee not only of policies and corporate data but also cultural information about history, rituals, heroes, and norms.

Another mentoring strategy has been developed by minorities themselves in organizations such as minority fraternities and sororities, all-female professional networking groups, and communities of immigrant populations. These alternative information networking groups may give the edge that formal programs lack.

African American fraternities and sororities are an especially interesting social networking phenomenon. More than 1.5 million people, predominantly African Americans, participate in nine fraternities and sororities associated with the National Pan-Hellenic Council, according to its website (www.nphchq.org). The fraternities include Omega Psi Phi, Kappa Alpha Psi, Alpha Phi Alpha, Phi Beta Sigma, and Iota Phi Theta. The sororities include Alpha Kappa Alpha, Delta Sigma Theta, Zeta Phi Beta, and Sigma Gamma Rho. Unlike many Caucasian college sororities and fraternities, the organizations of the National Pan-Hellenic Council (NPHC) are formed as lifetime networking groups to give members an alternative to exclusive corporate and social networks. The council's website states,

> Each of the nine NPHC organizations evolved during a period when African Americans were being denied essential rights and privileges afforded others. Racial isolation on predominantly white campuses and social barriers of class on all campuses created the need for African Americans to align themselves with other individuals sharing common goals and ideals. With the realization of such a need the African American Greek-lettered organization movement took on the personae of a haven and outlet which could foster brotherhood and sisterhood in the pursuit to bring about social change through the development of social programs that would create positive change for Blacks and the country. Today the need remains the same. . . . A lifetime commitment to the goals and ideals of each respective organization is stressed. The individual member is also expected to align himself with a graduate/alumni chapter following graduation from college, with the expectation that he/she will attend regular chapter meetings, regional conferences and national conventions, and take part in matters concerning and affecting the community in which he or she lives. (National Pan-Hellenic Council, 2004)

Members of the National Pan-Hellenic Council have become an economic, political, and social force. The organizations also create a strong and effective alternative networking structure. Recently we interviewed an African American applicant for a tenure-track teaching position at the university. Angi was fascinated when her associate dean greeted the young man and proceeded to tell him every member of his fraternity on campus and leading members of the community who were also "brothers." Listservs for the fraternity offer opportunities to seek career guidance, reestablish connections after moves, or offer social support.

Such constructive efforts provide alternative networking/mentoring structures to counteract the exclusion of many women, racial/ethnic minorities, international employees, and other marginalized groups from informal communication networks in many organizations. They may offer the best long-term opportunity for learning cultural information in alternate ways.

Dialogue Groups

Mentoring programs provide a key strategy for empowering marginalized groups. However, the need also exists to do more to engage employees in discussing their experiences through regular feedback systems. Imagine, for instance, entering an organization and learning from a mentor and from orientation that discussions are held each quarter to learn of minority concerns and issues. Then, over time, you discover that information from these sessions is integrated into management training.

In fact, the very organization that was reported earlier, in the study by Meares et al. (2004), was involved in such a process. The researcher had been called into a large, 1,000 member research and development organization because of a history of reports on mistreatment. In the process, they found that the organization was beginning to turn the corner on the problem by allowing forums and dialogue groups to form to openly address the concerns. In the process, such issues as the ambiguous policies were addressed.

Engaging members in dialogue groups should not, however, be undertaken in a casual way. We would encourage tapping into an array of resources provided on the Student Study Site at www.sagepub.com/driskill2estudy. We concur with W. Barnett Pearce and Kim Pearce (2000; see also Pearce & Pearce, 2004) with the following list of six core assumptions that should influence dialogue initiatives:

1. Dialogue is a form of communication with specific "rules" that distinguish it from other forms.

2. Among the effects of these rules are communication patterns that enable people to speak so that others can and will listen, and to listen so others can and will speak.

3. Participating in this form of communication requires a set of abilities, the most important of which is remaining in the tension between holding your own perspective, being profoundly open to others who are unlike you, and enabling others to act similarly.

4. These abilities are learnable, teachable, and contagious.

5. There are at least three levels of these abilities, including the abilities to respond to another's invitation to engage in dialogue, to extend an invitation to another to engage in a dialogue, and to construct contexts that are conducive to dialogue.

6. Skilled facilitators can construct contexts sufficiently conducive to dialogue so that participants are enabled to engage in dialogue in ways they would not without the work of the facilitator. (see p. 162)

The promise of dialogue groups, if implemented based on the above guiding assumptions, is that they create communication practices that begin to shape the culture. Stories, for instance, begin to be told of employees finding voice and of leaders willing to address problems before they get out of hand.

Multicultural Training

Dialogue groups, however, suggest the need for developing intercultural or multicultural communication competency. Earlier in this chapter, we discussed the growing reality of diversity in the United States. Beyond growing diversity in this country, we have stressed throughout this book the rapidly expanding number of multinationals. Friedman (2005), in his best-selling book, *The World Is Flat*, recounts his experiences in connecting with business leaders in India. As he reflected on those experiences, he concluded that, contrary to popular belief, the world is flat. Indeed, a typical day for us mirrors the experience of an increasing diversity. For instance, Gerald interacts daily with three faculty in his department, each from different national cultures, and students from such far-ranging places as Senegal and Pakistan to Taiwan and the Bahamas. Furthermore, a neighborhood friend recently shared about his initial concerns and ultimately successful efforts to adapt culturally to a group of Asian business leaders. He was to receive and host these leaders in his role as operations manager of a Dutch-owned company located in Arkansas.

The reality of the "flat world" indicates the need to go beyond mentoring and dialogue groups. We encourage organizations to take initiative in developing intercultural communication training. Such training should be adapted to the experience and needs of participants. Training activities and assessment practices should fit existing models for developing intercultural competence (Driskill, Arjanakova, & Schneider, 2010). One central practice is to engage participants in an increased awareness of cultural identity. Jameson (2007) provides one valuable resource in this area. She stresses:

> Those whose professional lives depend on being able to communicate effectively in intercultural contexts need greater self-insight about the hidden force of culture. To help achieve this goal, the field of intercultural business communication should more strongly emphasize how to understand one's own individual cultural identity: the sense of self derived from formal or informal membership in groups that impart knowledge, beliefs, values, attitudes, traditions, and ways of life. (p. 200)

Beyond integrating aspects of improved insight to identity and communication, effective training should go beyond sending employees to an hour or even a day of training. In one stellar example, Heifer International, a global nonprofit working to address hunger and poverty in more than 50 countries, took major strides to demonstrate to its employees the benefits of working in a diverse environment. As part of a larger diversity initiative undertaken by Heifer leadership, Gerald was invited to develop and present a full-day's training on intercultural communication. Heifer took additional steps, including empowering employees by providing opportunities for future trainings and by continuing to provide opportunities for employees to share information related to cultural competency development.

When done well, such training initiatives can be part of a set of practices that reflect a commitment to empowering employees from diverse backgrounds. Such training, therefore, should be focused on the types of diversity present in the organization. Generational diversity training programs, as well as gender, and national or ethnic trainings, indicate another level of commitment to create a culture where the diverse backgrounds of individuals truly enrich the culture of the organization. Resource links for intercultural training can be found on the Student Study Site, www.sagepub.com/driskill2estudy.

Summary

In this chapter we have summarized a variety of approaches for integrating the value of diversity into organizational culture. Those various approaches, along with their advantages and disadvantages, are summarized in Table 9.3. The challenges and opportunities presented by diversity are real. The choices you make in response to cultural data may result in improving the quality of life and creative outcomes for your organization. We have provided a survey (Rehearsal 9.3) as a way to assess

Table 9.3   Creating Diverse Cultures

Method	Advantages	Disadvantages
Creating diversity as a central organizational value	Ends duality of culture and diversity Sends clear message through multiple channels	Difficult to change culture Top leadership must support and lead by example
Encouraging diverse subcultures	Creates pluralistic cultural values and norms	Can erode community and identification Can set up battles for organization identity
Formal mentoring programs	Give equal access to informal cultural information	Not same effect as natural mentoring relationships
Organizational orientation including cultural information	Recognizes the importance of culture Gives all access to cultural information	Much cultural information is tacit
Minority networks for personal and professional development	Empowering	May not have cultural insight to share

your perceptions of the value your organization places on diversity. In all, we trust that you have found practical tools for using cultural data in the context of diversity. Seven major ideas were stressed in this application section.

1. Strong cultures can prevent organizations from embracing diversity because of hiring biases and expectations for new employees to embrace cultural norms and expectations.

2. Organizations can fall along a continuum of development between monoculturalism and multiculturalism.

3. Structural, cultural, and behavioral changes are necessary for organizations to become more multicultural. Employee communication also plays a key role in the social construction of multiculturalism. Pearce (1989) calls this type of communication cosmopolitan communication.

4. Women, racial/ethnic minorities, international employees, and other marginalized groups are often disadvantaged because they are not part of informal communication networks that transmit cultural norms and values.

5. Working toward pluralistic cultures in which diversity is a central organizational value seems the best long-term solution. In the meantime, mentoring or conscious culture socialization processes can help to level the playing field.

6. Naturally occurring mentorships have advantages over formal mentoring programs. Networks specifically formed to advance the interests of women and minorities also show promise in creating cultural change.

7. Enhancing the experience of minorities should also involve well-designed dialogue or feedback groups as well as intercultural training that equips employees for a diverse workplace and thereby creates a culture that embraces diversity.

Rehearsal 9.3 Diversity Survey
(Created by Angela Brenton for a hospital client)

Purpose: Assess your perception of diversity values with your organization.

Directions: Please respond to each of the following questions on a 5-point scale in which 5 indicates Strongly Agree; 4, Agree; 3, Neither Agree nor Disagree; 2, Disagree; and 1, Strongly Disagree.

1. My job is important to this organization.   1 2 3 4 5

2. I enjoy my job.   1 2 3 4 5

3. I have received adequate training
   to do my job.   1 2 3 4 5

4. My opportunity for advancement in this
   organization is good.   1 2 3 4 5

5. Hiring and promotion decisions
   are made fairly here.   1 2 3 4 5

6. Top management supports respect for diversity   1 2 3 4 5

7. This organization has a clear policy on sexual harassment.   1 2 3 4 5

8. I know how to file a harassment complaint.   1 2 3 4 5

9. I know how to file a discrimination complaint.   1 2 3 4 5

10. Individuals guilty of harassment in this organization
    are disciplined appropriately.   1 2 3 4 5

11. Individuals guilty of discrimination in this organization
    are disciplined appropriately.   1 2 3 4 5

12. Employees of different racial and ethnic groups are
    treated equally in organizational policies and practices.   1 2 3 4 5

13. This organization treats men and women equally
    in organizational policies and practices.   1 2 3 4 5

14. Discrimination on the basis of race, gender, religion,
    age, disability, or sexual orientation is not tolerated here.   1 2 3 4 5

15. I have experienced discrimination in this organization.   1 2 3 4 5

16. Someone I know has experienced discrimination in
    this organization.   1 2 3 4 5

17. I have heard offensive comments of a sexual nature here.   1 2 3 4 5

18. I have heard offensive racial or ethnic language
    used by employees in this organization.   1 2 3 4 5

19. Employees of different racial/ethnic groups and genders
    communicate well with one another.   1 2 3 4 5

(Continued)

(Continued)

20. My supervisor shows appreciation for individual
    differences (i.e., ethnic, gender, age, disabilities,
    sexual orientation, etc.).   1 2 3 4 5

21. My supervisor accommodates the needs of employees
    who are responsible for the care of children or older adults. 1 2 3 4 5

22. I have the opportunity for flextime on my schedule.   1 2 3 4 5

23. I have the option of job sharing.   1 2 3 4 5

24. I find it difficult to balance work and family responsibilities. 1 2 3 4 5

25. This organization would benefit if more women
    were promoted to managerial or leadership positions.   1 2 3 4 5

26. This organization would benefit if more racial/ethnic
    minorities were promoted to managerial and leadership
    positions.   1 2 3 4 5

27. I would feel comfortable working with someone
    who is openly gay/lesbian.   1 2 3 4 5

28. My supervisor shows respect for me.   1 2 3 4 5

29. This organization makes accommodation for
    employees with disabilities.   1 2 3 4 5

30. My supervisor shows favoritism to some employees.   1 2 3 4 5

31. I have input into decisions that affect my job.   1 2 3 4 5

32. This organization is a good place to work.   1 2 3 4 5

33. This organization cares about the health
    and welfare of employees.   1 2 3 4 5

34. What is your employment status?
    A. Part-time
    B. Full-time

35. What is your gender?
    A. Male
    B. Female

36. What is your racial/ethnic classification?
    A. Caucasian
    B. African American
    C. Hispanic/Latino
    D. Asian/Pacific Islander
    E. Middle Eastern
    F. Native American
    G. Other

37. How long have you worked at this organization?

    A. Less than 1 year

    B. 1–5 years

    C. 6–10 years

    D. 11–20 years

    E. More than 20 years

Note on Survey Analysis: We computed cross-tabs of each question by employment status, gender, race/ethnicity, and tenure to determine if there were differences in job satisfaction, relationship with supervisor, training opportunities, or reactions to diversity by demographic characteristics.

10 Improvisation

Managing Change

Articulate the value of the culture metaphor

Define major cultural elements

Use multiple data collection methods

Synthesize and interpret cultural data

★ **Identify applications**

- This merger was tougher than others in that we were expected to do a full banking computer conversion in 12 hours.

- Things change so often around here that we do not even call it change.

- If it were not for a supervisor making extra effort to listen to our gripes, I am not sure I would be handling these changes so well.

- [The] way we handle our differences, more than the positions we take or even who wins the arguments, will shape the evolution of our social worlds. (Pearce, 2007, p. 216)

Step Five: Identify Applications for Organizational Diversity, Change, Ethics, Leadership, and Effectiveness

Objectives:

- Identify examples of major forces that drive change
- Articulate five assumptions about the relationships between change and organizational culture
- Explain four perspectives on the way organizations view change
- Develop a change plan for an organization based on insights on managing change

Stage Terms:

- Substitution
- Evolution
- Loss
- Integration
- Differentiation
- Fragmentation

A standard part of the training for method actors involves improvisation—creating scenes and characters without the security or structure of a script. In improvisation, characters must draw on their creativity and inner experiences to create a reality with one another when neither knows what is coming next. Although improvisation is seen as creative and fun for many method actors, it is often stressful for organizational actors. It is our position in this chapter that understanding organizational culture is essential to achieving substantial and lasting changes in organizations. The cultural perspective is a unique viewpoint on organizational change for several reasons: (a) It focuses on how organizational practices are interwoven with deeper (but unseen) layers of organizational beliefs and assumptions, (b) it helps organizational leaders understand resistance to change (or at least what they may interpret as resistance) and helps them develop successful change strategies, and (c) it suggests collaborative and symbolic strategies necessary for successful organizational change. This chapter first reviews some of the forces that prompt change before discussing major assumptions regarding culture and change. These assumptions then inform five principles intended to guide your application of cultural data. We conclude with a Connection focused on managing the dialectic tensions involved in change.

Forces Driving Change

A list of factors that cause organizational changes in policies, practices, and core values is not difficult to generate. If you generated your own list of change-inducing forces, what would you include?

Rehearsal 10.1 Forces Driving Change

Purpose: Reflect on forces or factors that have resulted in changes in your organization.

1. _____

2. _____

3. _____

4. _____

Your list probably includes such things as competition, changes in the environment and technologies, government regulations, economic conditions, generational changes, globalization, mergers, and/or rapid growth. You may also have included factors that cause an individual in an organization to undergo adjustments and changes that are beyond typical organization-wide changes, for example: promotion, firing, transfer, or retirement.

Assumptions About Culture and Change

We offer six observations about the relationships between culture and change that underlie some of the theories and practical suggestions about change in the last part of the chapter:

First, not all organizational change is cultural change. Changes in technology, leadership, business strategy, or even the competitive landscape often are surface changes that do not alter the basic underlying assumptions and values of an organization. At times we even talk about how an organizational change is going to "re-shape" our whole organizational culture, when in fact it does not. Several examples will illustrate. While we were writing the second edition of our book, the health care debate was raging in Congress. As far-reaching as some of the implications may be, powerful cultural forces have lobbied successfully to ensure that the basic structure of health care financing and delivery would not be altered. Private insurance companies would still serve as the intermediary for financing. The government would still assume gap financing for those who cannot afford private coverage. A second example is a large health care organization Angi has served over the years as a consultant. The organization began more than a hundred years ago as a charity hospital. Even though it has grown to a large and successful academic medical center with nationally recognized centers of excellence in research and clinical treatment, vestiges of the charity hospital culture remain and shape practices today.

While many organizational changes are not cultural changes, employees tend to view changes through the lens of cultural values. A bureaucratic culture trying to become more service oriented may still view customer service as following correct procedures. Traditional faculty members may feel threatened by online instruction and express conviction that it cannot produce the educational quality of face-to-face instruction. We are convinced that the reason why many organizational change efforts, such as diversity or ethics, are not ultimately successful is because they are implemented at a surface level of training and rules without ever penetrating the deeper values or assumptions of the culture.

Second, change, like culture, is symbolically constructed. When leaders initiate an organizational change, they may have a rationale in mind for the change. However, they cannot necessarily control the ways in which organization members will interpret or react to the change. Jian (2007) refers to employee sense-making as one major factor creating unintended consequences of planned organizational changes. McKinley and Scherer (2000) write that change often produces a reassuring sense of order and control for corporate executives but cognitive disorder, stress, and lack of control for rank-and-file employees. Ford and Ford (1995) discuss resistance strategies that employees may use to reconstitute the meaning or practice of organizational change, such as attributing different motives to the change, or complying with the change superficially instead of embracing its intent. Deetz, Tracy, and Simpson (2000) offer an insight on the different reactions of management and employees to major change:

> Business leaders rarely anticipate the extent of the resistance to planned changes. One reason for this is that the leaders have had more time to think about the change and more fully understand the reasons for it. But equally important, leaders often have less to lose from it. Employees, on the other hand, are surprised, do not understand the reasoning, did not participate in the choice, and see themselves as having much to lose. (p. 39)

Bridges (1991) likens the change process to a marathon with thousands of runners. Runners start in tiers. The competitive runners start first. The "Sunday runners" are so far in the back of the pack they cannot even hear the starting gun. By the time the Sunday runners have eased into a trot, the competitive runners have neared the finish line. Too many managers are typical of the frontrunners; they are impatient with employees who cannot seem to catch a vision of the finish line.

We have encountered this phenomenon of different constructions of change personally in the past few months. Angi, as dean of the college, called together two departments to suggest that they explore the idea of merger to create a professional school. While she stressed that she was proposing the idea only as a proactive investigation that might enhance the position of both departments and that the decision rested totally with the faculty and staff of the two departments, the faculty and staff developed their own rationales for the impetus for the action—desire to reduce budgets, political motives about the leadership of the two departments, or other rationales. Only through consistent and open discussion did some of these attributions subside.

Third, not all cultural change is purposeful. As we discussed in Chapter 3, cultures are both enduring and dynamic. They are always being created and re-created in the interactions of their members. Kuhn and Corman (2003) claim that cultures evolve in a subtle process as new organization members or new conditions introduce values, assumptions, and practices that are slowly integrated with existing culture. Sometimes these changes are adopted by consensus and sometimes they develop through political wrangling and conflict. Alvesson (2002) calls this an organic social movement that is generally not controlled from the top of the organization. At times cultures can follow the same laws of entropy as other social systems with values that were once functional for an organization becoming dysfunctional over time.

Fourth, the stronger the culture, the more likely the members will be resistant to change. Of course this is not always true because some cultures are built on a strong assumption that continuous change is essential. However, for most cultures, the more ingrained and entrenched the cultural assumptions and values, the harder they are to change. We have found in our work with churches, universities, and government bureaucracies that they can have particularly entrenched ideologies, which are difficult for members to change even when those ideologies are dysfunctional. Lyon's (2007) analysis of communication at Merck concurs about the problems of a strong culture. Entrenched patterns at Merck contributed to unethical communication practices resulting in the death of thousands of patients taking Vioxx. Put differently, a strong culture is not necessarily a good one or an effective one. As we will discuss in the chapter on effectiveness, the notion of a strong culture as an effective one is not accurate.

Fifth, initiation and active support by leaders are necessary but not sufficient for cultural change. Executive management, according to Keyton (2005), initiates most planned organizational changes. This may be due to their belief that new practices or strategies are necessary for corporate success or survival. Yet because culture is cooperatively created, leaders cannot always be successful in forcing cultural change on employees without a cooperative process. Eisenberg and Riley (2001) claim that some cultural change efforts fail because leaders are pushing an ideology that conflicts with strongly held cultural assumptions and values. Jian (2007) advocates the critical role of dialogue in managing a process of change. He offers a process model of organizational change that "emphasizes that both senior management and employees are change agents positioned in two different roles: initiation and implementation, respectively" (p. 24). He writes:

To facilitate system integration and manage tensions, senior managers should be able to create opportunities of employee participation in change initiation, attend to critical communication events by emphasizing dialogue and negotiation, and participate themselves in change implementation among local employee groups. Such two-way participation will foster shared interpretive schemes and transform tensions into constructive energy. (p. 25)

We discussed in Chapter 3 that culture is paradoxically both a top-down and bottom-up process. It is difficult to sustain a change effort in any part of the organization if there is not leadership support and commitment, but at the same time leaders cannot force change in culture without the active participation and commitment of employees or organization members. We have all been part of an organization in which the mission statement is not embraced beyond the executive suite. The customers of organizations interact most frequently with organization members at the bottom of the organizational chart. If the value or ideology does not pervade the whole organization, then it does not exist to the average stakeholder.

Principles for Managing Change

These five assumptions about culture and change have implications for how we introduce and communicate change. We have derived the five principles from the change and culture literature to guide you in the process of analyzing your data in light of change processes.

1. Adapt communication to the varied meaning structures held in response to change.

Change is a pervasive aspect of organizational life. As indicated in the opening section of this chapter, varied responses and reactions to change are part of all our experiences. Marris (1974) argues that disruptions in "meaning structures" are what people most resist in change processes, not the change itself. Put differently, individuals hold different levels of "psychological safety" in response to change depending on how they view or interpret the form of the change. Forms of change, according to Marris, can be categorized as follows:

- Substitution: a change in which one item of meaning is exchanged for another (e.g., a new boss)
- Evolution: gradual shifts in values, meanings (e.g., a gradual move from a family business to a larger business employing nonfamily members)
- Loss: significant change in the avenue a person had used to achieve attachment, success, and competence (e.g., job loss due to a plant closing or a transfer resulting in new duties and new colleagues)

Alvesson (2002) writes that Marris's categories of change can be complementary for the individual organization member. For instance, a new employee or a new role created in an organization may also prompt experiences of gradual, evolutionary change or a sense of loss.

In *substitution,* the organization member gives up one cultural meaning for another. Alvesson (2002) uses the phrase "every-day reframing," which is an informal process in which opinion leaders promote new patterns of interpretations of practices or policies. This process of substitution or reframing does not always occur easily. Smith and Eisenberg (1987) give the example of Disneyland, which shifted from a theater metaphor to a family metaphor with some harmful consequences for the organization. A family metaphor became inconsistent with hard business decisions management had to make. You do not lay off family members. The authors suggest that Disneyland could recover its original culture by substituting the original theater language and rituals for the family elements that had replaced them. At times, when change is perceived as substitution rather than loss, it may be easier for organization members to accept because they are not left with a void. When there is strong ego attachment to the culture, however, even substitution may be difficult to accept.

In *evolution,* change seems gradual rather than abrupt. In the taken-for-granted reality, employees may not even be aware of gradual changes. Alvesson (2002) views this type of change as an organic process in which values and assumptions slowly shift and change over time. Those most likely to react negatively are employees with longer tenure who are most likely to remember "the way things used to be." At times there is a moment of cultural comparison that may make organization members more aware of the change. Such awareness may prompt reflection on whether changes are perceived as positive and/or negative. In our university culture, we have both seen this process of evolution occur. For instance, in the area of valuing international or intercultural competency, there has been a gradual shift. Twenty years ago there were pockets of administration, students, and faculty who valued the development of this competency in the learning process. Today, when we pause to reflect, we both see substantial growth in the number of units as well as practices on campus that reflect this value. This change has resulted in the centralization of some functions, such as study abroad. This centralization is not received well by all but has meant a growth in opportunities for students. As in all evolution, this is likely the way many of us experience change in our organizations.

In *loss,* change is sudden and shocking, producing resistance and grief. Alvesson (2002) uses the term *revolution,* in which important cultural tenets are abandoned suddenly. Recognizing change can be experienced as loss can be useful in anticipating normal and expected reactions. Depression, grief, denial, anger, sadness, and holding on to the past are all responses to loss. Thus, in managing changes viewed in terms of loss, communication skills of reflection and paraphrasing may be more appropriate than arguing with someone to "get over" a normal process. In particular, Bridges (1991), in an excellent and practical book on change, offers several suggestions to help employees let go of the past as they respond to a sense of loss.

- Identify who is losing what.
- Accept the reality and importance of the subjective losses.
- Do not be surprised by "overreaction."
- Acknowledge the losses openly and sympathetically.
- Expect and accept the signs of grieving.
- Compensate for the losses.

In all, the value of paying attention to change management as a meaning-management process places a greater emphasis on understanding the organization's culture(s), because symbolic ("sense-making") processes are at the core of understanding change.

2. Recognize different assumptions concerning change held by individuals, subcultures, and organizations in general.

The first principle focuses on the need for an awareness of the differing ways individuals experience change. In a related way, organizations hold different assumptions about change in general. As we discussed in Chapter 4, Martin (1992) reviews three variables that influence how members interpret culture: (1) "the relationship among cultural elements or manifestations" such as values and rules, (2) the degree of consensus among organization members about the culture, and (3) the "orientation to ambiguity" or uncertainty (p. 190). Based on these three variables, Martin characterizes organizational cultures as integrated, differentiated, or fragmented. These perspectives can also help in understanding why one organization experiences change so much differently from another organization. After reviewing each perspective, we will present implications for this framework in the change management process.

The *integration* perspective focuses on consistency in cultural elements, organization-wide consensus on issues or policies, and has a negative orientation toward ambiguity. Those holding this perspective believe shared values come from inspirational leaders who unite organization members, often in response to the external environment. The strength of the culture is often seen in its stability and in the continuity of organizational values and practices. It is clear from this perspective how change is seen as destabilizing and threatening to group identity. Keyton (2005) notes that change often happens more slowly in consensual culture organizations because there is value in reaching wide agreement on proposed changes. Developing this level of consensus on change can take time.

The *differentiation* perspective focuses on the differences in values and assumptions among members of the organization and on the tensions among subcultures competing to define organizational values and practices. For example, you may have noticed differences in your analysis between a marketing department and a research department about the values or norms of the organization. One of your themes might have been paradoxes or tensions among organizational values. Change, from this perspective, is viewed differently by various subcultures in the organization. Some subgroups may applaud a change consistent with their values while others may feel loss and disconfirmation. Keyton (2005) indicates that change may happen more rapidly in a differentiated culture, yet change may be restricted to a subculture rather than permeating the entire organization.

Finally, a third perspective, *fragmentation,* assumes an inherent complexity in cultural elements, accepts a multiplicity of views on organizational issues rather than organization-wide or even subculture consensus, and accepts ambiguity and change as normal. A researcher operating from a fragmentation perspective assumes that values and meanings are only partially shared among organization members and that cultural consensus is more surface than real. For example, while all organization members say they value diversity, the term may have completely different meanings and implications among employees. Members of a divergent culture welcome diverse views and do not see problems with varying values or interpretations of events. For example, a computer research laboratory may thrive because it accepts the norm of uncertainty and embraces such uncertainty as a resource and motivation for creativity. Change, from this perspective, would not even be noticed because change is par for the course. Yet because of the ambiguity, not all members might agree about the application of the value to specific practices or events.

Martin's (1992) model provides a way to *contextualize change* by directing attention to the meaning organizations attach to uncertainty or ambiguity in the environment. Table 10.1 highlights examples of each of these perspectives by providing a metaphor, the degree of consensus within the organization about how change is viewed, how ambiguity is viewed, assumptions about the source of change, and finally implications for each perspective.

Table 10.1   Three Perspectives on Organizational Culture and Change

	Integration	*Perspective Differentiation*	*Fragmentation*
Metaphor	Clearing in a jungle	Islands of clarity in a sea of ambiguity	Jungle
Consensus	Organization-wide	Within subcultures	Issue specific
Ambiguity	Denial	Channeling	Acceptance
Change	Revolutionary	Incremental	Continual
Source of change	Leader-centered	External/ internal catalysts	Individual catalysts
Implications	If superficial, controllable; if deeper, difficult to control	Predictable and unpredictable sources and consequences of change	Uncontrollable due to continual change

SOURCE: Adapted from Meyerson and Martin (1987).

The jungle metaphor for each of the three perspectives captures the importance of understanding how an organization views change. Each metaphor holds implications for how the organization views effectiveness and what, if anything, needs to be done to manage change. The difference, for example, between an organization seeking and accustomed to organization-wide consensus on issues (integration) versus an organization accustomed to continual change (fragmentation) is clear. For one, change typically must be monitored and initiated by top leaders; for another, change is something everyone is involved in adapting to each day. Thus, new leaders not tuned in to a fragmentation culture with the norm of accepting change may run aground. Their failure may be inevitable if they attempt to manage change based on an integration perspective with the focus on top management taking charge and managing the process.

> We should not confuse our analytic frameworks with reality.

Understanding these perspectives provides an awareness of our own as well as an organizational comfort level with ambiguity. Martin (1992) provides a critique of these three perspectives and in doing so reminds us that reality is not contained in just one of the three boxes. With her, we realize that any framework may cause you to fail to ask other important questions of your cultural data.

While Martin does not provide a clear "fourth box," she does suggest questions that you might ask that get beyond her boxes. For example, she suggests examining cultures in light of the focus or intent of changes that are introduced by management: Does management introduce change solely for its own interests? Do they seek change that would be less oppressive to lower ranked organization members (Stablien & Nord, 1985)? These questions underscore a key component of effective change management: We should not confuse our analytic frameworks with reality; they, like culture, are constructs intended to help us manage meaning. Rehearsal 10.2 provides an opportunity to make application of these ideas to your organization.

Rehearsal 10.2 Adapting Change
Messages to the Culture

Purpose: Develop communication strategies based on the way an organization views change.

Steps:

1. Review your analysis data to determine organizational perceptions of change. Examine each of the three options: integration, differentiation, and fragmentation.

2. Develop a communication strategy appropriate for the organization, remembering the concept of multiperspective thinking. In other words, go beyond the boxes to synthesize an approach sensitive to the way change is viewed in the organization. For example, the organization may place a high value on consistency and clarity, which suggests certain top management efforts to establish direction. However, there may be subcultures or minority cultures that have a greater acceptance of uncertainty. Thus, change management strategies should go beyond a simple approach that addresses a unitary or integrated view of the culture.

Metaphor A: It Is a Jungle Out There

Culture: A stable force with high consistency among manifestations of culture

Change: Results in a loss of psychological safety if clarity is not maintained

Subculture Variation: _____

Strategy: Leadership creates messages to indicate control over change process, reduces ambiguity by clarifying roles and norms and processes in place to maintain stability and meaning.

(Continued)

(Continued)

Metaphor B: The Jungle Is Not All Out There

Culture: Stable within units, but diverse and unpredictable across units

Change: Accepted unless viewed as an effort to disturb subculture clarity or autonomy

Subculture Variation: _____

Strategy: Leadership stresses and defines sources of change that can be controlled by the organization and those factors that are beyond their control. Organizational responses are developed as a longer-range incremental approach that will be reviewed and adjusted as new information is gained. Messages focus on maintaining clarity and meaning in areas most significant to the organization.

Metaphor C: We Are Part of the Jungle

Culture: Cultural manifestations are accepted as unclear and inconsistent

Change: Not noticed as a problem unless underlying value system disturbs perspective of acceptance

Subculture Variation: _____

Strategy: Leaders encourage continued acceptance of the reality of the change process. Policies are reviewed that encourage empowerment of subcultures and individuals to respond to change and to serve as catalysts for future change.

Metaphor D: Conflict in the Jungle

Culture: Cultural manifestations perceived by workers as manipulated for management interests or gain

Change: Viewed as a tension between management and employee interests

Subculture Variation: _____

Strategy: Leadership encourages dialogue and negotiation on issues of importance to the employees and management. Symbols and rituals are used to unify and find common ground to encourage sense of value in the process of making sure the change brings benefit to the entire organization.

"The choice that individuals and societies ultimately have before them is thus really a choice about the kind of contradiction that is to shape the pattern of daily life." (Morgan, 1986, p. 267)

---

3. Understand how cultural elements can be used to implement and manage change.

One assumption we discussed earlier in this chapter focused on how a strong culture can inhibit change efforts. What is key, then, in any culture, is respecting the elements that symbolically carry and create the culture. In his book *The Heart of*

Change, Kotter (2002) stresses the emotional and symbolic dimensions of change. He notes that too often leaders approach change through an analytic procedure, assuming that if they produce enough data that organization members will be able to analyze the data and understand the need for change. On the contrary, Kotter posits that we do not think our way to change as much as we are motivated to change through our feelings. He offers examples of leaders using creative symbolic stories and demonstrations to *show* employees the need for change, with the assumption that seeing produces feelings, which will enable change. In other words, once leaders understand the importance of culture and have a good understanding of the current organizational culture, they can use cultural elements to support change efforts. A few examples of the power of these cultural elements should prompt us to reflect on cultural data in a more competent manner.

Values, as a deeper level of culture, can be used as a bridge to new rituals or practices. Angi was a management consultant for a bank for several years. It was known for its exceptional customer service. As banking was deregulated to offer more financial services, the bank rolled out a plan to encourage employees to "sell" more products and services to bank customers. They offered significant financial incentives and were surprised when few employees achieved their selling goals. After interviewing several employees, she concluded that the resistance to selling was based on employees' perceptions that selling compromised their service to employees. She encouraged the bank to drop the financial incentives and to focus instead on explaining to bank employees how the new products could serve existing customers, to tell stories about the elderly lady getting 1.7% on a large balance in a regular savings account who could earn 6% with the same money in a mutual fund. Sales soared once employees "reframed" the new sales practices within the strong cultural value of service.

Cultural elements such as rituals can also assist in grieving losses or symbolically welcoming new practices. For instance, Bridges (1991) suggests these additional practices to enhance the success rate of change efforts: "Mark the endings"; "Treat the past with respect"; and "Let people take a piece of the old way with them." One can easily imagine introducing a ritual that would accomplish all three of these suggestions. You may plan, for instance, a prelaunch event that marks the end of a particular practice or structure. During this event, individuals could be prepared to honor what they will miss, rather than just assume all that is old or passing is not valued. Furthermore, reminders of the "old way" could be kept in the form of mementos or artifacts. Anniversary celebrations could include reminders of the history that demonstrate respect for the contributions of the past. In one organization Gerald participated with, an anniversary event resulted in reconciliations between members who had left the organization 10 years earlier with hard feelings. Such rituals have a way of both affirming the past and at the same time recognizing the value of the change. Cultural heroes, in such events, can also be positioned as leaders of change.

4. Realize that process is everything during periods of cultural change.

It is not so much where you end up as how you get there that will impact employees' reactions to change. Even a good change that is badly handled will be damaging. Two keys to good process are communication and participation. Change processes are destabilizing and increase uncertainty. Providing as much information as possible, as often as possible, helps reduce this uncertainty. As Bridges (1991) stresses, "Give people information, and do it again and again." Yet, process is not simply about sending out the facts. One major medical institution implemented a new value statement constructed by upper management. The CEO then e-mailed the list of values to the employees. Three years later, a member in the Organizational Development department talked with Gerald about formal processes that they were now implementing to help employees buy into these values.

Employees, as you might expect, tend to support what they help create. Involving employees in every stage of the change effort will reduce their feelings of being passive victims and will encourage their ownership of the change effort. In another medical organization, Gerald was contacted to provide assistance in the midst of a merger process. The lack of focus on the process had resulted in one physician becoming the scapegoat for much of the grieving and sense of loss in the organization. To complicate matters, this physician was from another country. Thus, Human Resource Development (HRD) managers and senior managers tried to determine whether part of the problem was to be found in employees' having to adjust to a national culture difference. A closer examination of the two organizations that had merged showed that the issue was not as simple as the collision of two national cultures. The core issue was that the controversial physician represented an organizational culture that valued research productivity while the other organization valued patient care. In short, the merger got on track only when HRD focused on process and gave more time to training rituals that allowed discussion of value differences.

The focus on process can be supported by tapping into Bridges's (1991) idea of the neutral zone—the time during which employees have left behind the familiar but have not fully entered the new. He writes,

> Given the ambiguities of the neutral zone, it is natural for people to become polarized between those who want to rush forward and those who want to go back to old ways. And given that polarization, it is natural for consensus to break down and the level of discord to rise. Teamwork may be severely undermined, as may loyalty to the organization itself. Managed properly, this is only a temporary situation. Left unmanaged, it can lead to terminal chaos. (p. 79)

Bridges notes that the neutral zone is important because old ideas and practices have to have time to die before employees are ready to embrace the new. It should be a place where you take time to define *what's over and what isn't*. It can also be a time of innovation and creativity when old norms and restraints are loosened and new rules have yet to develop. Communication strategies such as reframing metaphors, sharing information, reducing uncertainty, and building connections assist employees in realizing the positive potential of the neutral zone.

5. Co-construct a clearly communicated vision with a practical transition plan to inspire and offer guidance.

Most employees are reluctant to set out for foreign territory unless the leader can share some inspiring vision of what lies ahead. Deetz and colleagues (2000) stress the importance of communicating a vision that is linked to shared values within the organizational culture:

> A vision without the voice of a prophet can neither inspire nor guide. Undercommunication usually occurs when the vision remains a property of upper managers. They may be clear about where they are going, but the various instructions and directives they send out do not carry the vision. These often make little sense and fail to inspire. (p. 45)

Bridges (1991) notes that even an inspiring vision can be frustrating without a specific transition plan. Such a plan should serve as a roadmap for realizing the vision. The vision and the plan must work together. Either without the other is incomplete. Kotter (1995) outlines eight steps for major organizational transformations. As you read his guidelines, keep in mind ideas we introduced earlier—change management is most effective when leaders pay attention to elements of culture and when communication and participation are high throughout the process:

1. Establish a sense of urgency.

2. Form a powerful guiding coalition.

3. Create a guiding vision.

4. Communicate the vision.

5. Empower others to act.

6. Create small wins along the way.

7. Consolidate improvements and create more change.

8. Institutionalize the new culture. (pp. 59–67)

His steps, of course, would need to be filtered through the information you gather about how the organization views change. If change is par for the course, the organization likely already has a strong framework and norm of empowering others to act to manage change.

Connections: Managing the Dialectics of Change

If you were to review your cultural analysis, including elements, themes, and an overall characterization, you would likely find embedded in it insights on change management. You might learn, for instance, of changes that have gone well, of mergers that have left residual ill will. A cultural analysis may help explain or even predict possible problems during a change process. The guides we have provided in this chapter seek to provide insight on how to manage these potential challenges. Pepper and Larson (2006), based on a case analysis of a merger, argue for identifying and then responding to identity tensions that are embedded in the change process. An identity tension grows from members who have developed a certain level of identification or attachment in relation to organizational values (Scott, Corman, & Cheney, 1998). For example, one medical specialty organization experienced major difficulties when it expanded to work with a state-run agency. In initial interviews, comments were made about who was to benefit from this new association. It was clear that most of the energy was being used to negotiate the new political territory. Even as they continued to spend energy there, leadership had become aware of a higher turnover rate and much lower employee satisfaction. They noticed that employees called on to spend more time in the state agency did not feel valued and that they were experiencing a loss of meaning in that some of them had worked with the smaller, "family" culture of the home organization for more than 10 years. Efforts to manage this expansion were soon augmented with greater employee support through more regular ritualized meetings that allowed them to grieve for their loss. These same meetings became an opportunity to reaffirm the employees' value to the organization. In this process, leaders were sensitive to the issue of managing challenges to identity in the changes associated with expanded work roles.

This example illustrates several of the change management practices we have stressed thus far, such as meeting to grieve losses. We see value in a specific questioning process designed to identify tensions. Table 10.2 captures questions useful to identify specific identity tensions. This process requires leaders and change agents to be more involved with those most influenced by changes: employees. Because tensions are "constructed in the daily discourse of organization life," you should reflect on cultural data in ways that will help surface or unveil these tensions (Pepper & Larson, 2006, p. 65).

Table 10.2   Sample Questions to Access Cultural Identity Tensions

Sample Questions to Access Cultural Identity Tensions

Assimilation–autonomy:

What should [the other company] do to be more like you?

What about you would we not want to change? What do you value most about who you are as [acquired company] members?

What are you willing to give up and/or change in the merger-acquisition (M/A)?

Consensus–command:

How do you make decisions here?

How much do you value your decision-making norms?

How much tolerance is there for other types of decision-making practices?

Each of the above questions provides a resource in the tension identification and management process. Attention to member responses and then an effort to negotiate changes during transitions, such as mergers and acquisitions, is key. To conclude this chapter, we provide a Rehearsal to encourage thought about ways to manage change. Your goal should be to devise an approach that does not limit your interpretation or change management strategy to a single tactic or strategy.

Summary

Guiding and promoting change through collaborative processes will no doubt remain one of the most critical leadership skills.

We stressed five assumptions about culture and change:

1. Not all organizational change is cultural change.

2. Change, like culture, is symbolically constructed.

3. Not all cultural change is purposeful.

4. The stronger the culture, the more likely the members will be resistant to change.

5. Initiation and active support by leaders is necessary but not sufficient for cultural change.

Regardless of the source of the change (merger, resizing, etc.), five principles should be considered for change managers whether they are executives or informal organizational leaders:

1. Adapt communication to the varied meaning structures hold in response to change.

2. Recognize different assumptions concerning change held by individuals, sub-cultures, and organizations in general.

3. Understand how cultural elements can be used to implement and manage change.

4. Realize that process is everything during periods of cultural change.

5. Co-construct a clearly communicated vision with a practical transition plan to inspire and offer guidance.

Rehearsal 10.3 A Change Plan

Purpose: Apply change principles by developing a plan.

Overview: Choose a project that would be a significant cultural change within either your own organization, your cultural analysis organization, or another organization with which you are very familiar. Outline a plan for how you would approach leading the change, using principles from your reading. Make sure that your project narrative addresses the following issues:

1. What change is envisioned? Why is this change a cultural change?

2. Discuss how you would prepare individuals in the organization for change.

3. Describe the change process. How long would it take? Who would be involved? What would be the steps toward change?

4. Describe how your plan would accomplish the following:
   a. Encourage employees to confront and deal with losses
   b. Use a neutral zone creatively
   c. Make a new beginning involving purpose, picture, plan, and part in the plan for each member of the organization
   d. Ensure continuity of cultural values
   e. Use cultural rituals to support and enable change
   f. Ensure as much security as possible during transition
   g. Keep the lines of communication open

Rehearsal 10.4 A Change Case

Purpose: Application of change principles to a situation.

Dean John Smith was hired by a research-intensive university to become Dean of the College of Science and Mathematics. He had served as a program director for a major national science foundation for 10 years before assuming this role.

(Continued)

(Continued)

He had previously held a tenured faculty position at a university, but had no university administrative experience. He inherited a college in which 40% of the faculty were older than 55, the college was dead last in the university in grant activity, the number of majors was declining, and the quality of facilities for instruction and research were substandard. The college had been led for 4 years by a series of interim deans during unsuccessful searches for a permanent dean.

During his first year as dean he led the faculty (in the face of some resistance) in a major and ambitious strategic planning process. The plan produced by the process set ambitious goals that would require about $3 million in new investment. He also instituted the following actions:

- He required all faculty members to integrate Internet instructional tools into their classes, with the goal of developing online instruction that would attract new students.
- He overruled a faculty decision to award promotion to a popular faculty member he considered did not have sufficient research productivity.
- He made public comments disparaging the quality of the current faculty and put pressure on senior faculty members to consider early retirement.
- He requested that the university offer his faculty no summer teaching contracts to force more faculty members to seek outside grant support to provide summer income.
- He developed assertive (some perceived them as aggressive and competitive) appeals in the Dean's Council for why his college should receive additional funding for salaries, graduate assistantships, and facilities.

Results of his efforts were mixed. The number of majors and student semester credit hours increased in the college. The number of grant submissions increased, although his faculty did not have a high ratio of awards to submissions. A number of senior faculty members chose early retirement, and the dean hired bright new faculty members to take their places. His evaluations by faculty members in his college were the lowest for any dean in the university. Many of his colleagues on the Dean's Council viewed him as brash and noncollegial.

Questions:

1. How would you evaluate these change efforts?
2. Were such reactions by members inherent in making major change and to be expected?
3. What type of cultural orientation to change existed prior to the change efforts (integrated, differentiated, fragmented)? How did this affect reactions to change?
4. What might have been done differently to gain more acceptance of change? Reflect on Kotter's guidelines from the chapter. Also consider Pepper and Larson's identity questions.

11 An Honest Portrayal

Ethics

Articulate the value of the culture metaphor

Define major cultural elements

Use multiple data collection methods

Synthesize and interpret cultural data

★ **Identify applications**

Step Five: Identify Applications for Organizational Diversity, Change, Ethics, Leadership, and Effectiveness

> *To preserve our deeper desires amid the pressures of the modern corporation is to reserve our souls for the greater life we had in mind when we first took the job.*
>
> —David Whyte, *The Heart Aroused: Poetry and the Preservation of the Soul in Modern America*, 1998, p. 298

Objectives:

- Learn the major value tensions that influence communication and ethics
- Develop critical questions to ask concerning culture and ethical value tensions

Stage Terms:

- Value tensions
- Economizing values
- Power aggrandizement values
- Ecologizing values
- Teleopathy
- Organizational conscience

Too Much Bad News

When the curtain is raised or when the screen lights up, as audience members we hope for nothing more and nothing less than an honest portrayal. Method actors are trained to develop a devotion to the "power of truth in acting" (Vineberg, 1991, p. 7). In short, effective acting is not about pretense but honest portrayals that bring truth to the heart and mind.

When the curtain is raised on cultural performances, we hope for the same. In fact, what we deem not only as right and wrong but what should or ought to happen is at the heart of many complaints about life in organizations. Labor unions continue to battle management for power and resources. Disenchanted citizens hear again and again of CEOs with incomes that rival the budgets of third world countries. In fact, a 2008 report shows that S&P 500 executives pocket 344 times the daily pay of average workers, about $1.5 million a year. Compensation levels for the top 50 equity and hedge fund managers are at $588 million a year (Anderson, Cavanagh, Collins, Pizzigati, & Laptham, 2008). Daily news reports bring bad news about another CEO indicted or sentenced. The names of the organizations and their respective CEOs are now too numerous to track. However, sentencing news of Enron, ImClone, and Tenet Health Care executives was eclipsed by the financial crisis in 2008 that was rife with unethical leadership practices. To add to these moral failures, more than two thirds of Fortune 500 firms have been convicted of serious crimes, ranging from fraud to illegal dumping of hazardous wastes (Eisenberg, Goodall, & Trethewey, 2010).

Beyond headline news events that have rocked our global economy, other stories receive less attention. The unethical communication practices associated with workplace bullying (Tracy, Lutgen-Sandvik, & Alberts, 2006) and sexual harassment (Keyton & Menzie, 2007; Richardson & Taylor, 2008) impact millions. Furthermore, the unethical communication practices of pharmaceuticals such as Merck have caused death and suffering (Lyon, 2007; Lyon & Ulmer, 2010).

Given this litany of bad news, it is not a surprise that organizations continue to call for assistance in dealing with the problems associated with unethical behavior and value conflicts. In the search for guidance in the ethical arena, we are drawn to an occasional moral or ethical hero, such as the case of Malden Mills' president Aaron Feuerstein. After a fire destroyed his textile plant, he kept employees on the payroll despite the cries of shareholders to do the opposite (Ulmer, 2001; Seeger & Ulmer, 2001). The "1996 Botwinick Prizes in Business Ethics and in Ethical Practice in the Professions" was presented to Feuerstein for his ethical leadership (Columbia Business School, n.d.). More recently, despite speculation that bankruptcy could have been avoided had he not been so generous with his employees, he maintained his position of no regrets. The guiding ethical principle for Feuerstein, growing from his religious faith, was that of acting for the larger goal, not for the moment, for doing the right thing (Shafron, 2002).

Ethical heroes such as Feuerstein are rarely in the news. Yet, fortunately, he is not alone. For instance, Bunnatine Greenhouse, at the cost of her job, stood against an improper no-bid contract to Halliburton in the reconstruction of Iraq. Basseem Youssef fought against post-9/11 discrimination that targeted Arab Americans within the FBI. In corporate America, Cynthia Cooper and Sherron Watkins were recognized by *Time* magazine as "Persons of the Year" in 2002. They were instrumental in exposing Enron and WorldComm scandals (National Whistleblowers Center, n.d.). Ethical heroes stand out as they enact behaviors that display such virtues as honesty and integrity.

Rehearsal 11.1 Ethical Heroes

Purpose: Reflect on experiences of being influenced by individuals who have modeled ethical behavior.

Most of us can tell a story based on what we have heard or experienced related to gross financial inequities, harassment, bullying, and/or lying. It may be harder to identify an organizational hero who stands out as a person of integrity and/or moral courage. Write about a story you have heard and/or a person you know who has displayed such virtues. As an option, review the list of over 30 whistleblowers at www.whistleblowers.org.

1. What was the situation they faced?

   _____

   _____

   _____

2. What did they do that makes them stand out?

   _____

   _____

   _____

3. What communication behaviors did they enact that created an honest portrayal?

   _____

   _____

   _____

Identifying guiding principles or virtues of ethical heroes can serve as one approach to ethics. In the context of deciphering cultural data, such principles may provide a benchmark or a place to reflect on themes or cultural values that merit revision. Yet, it is our view that ethical values and assumptions must be deeply grounded in organizational culture to have a guiding influence on employee decisions and behavior. If ethics become compartmentalized, or if they reside only in organizational practices at the surface level of culture, such as formal mission statements, they will fail to become a guiding force or anchor for the organization.

In this chapter we argue that ethical lapses, for the most part, are not simply moral failings of individuals but reflections of cultural values and practices deeply ingrained in organizational cultures. Goodpaster (2007) describes the organizational tendency to approach organizational decision-making without consideration of ethical values as *teleopathy*. He defines teleopathy as "the unbalanced pursuit of purpose in either individuals or organizations" (p. 28). He writes that principal symptoms of teleopathy are fixation on personal goals, rationalization, and detachment of moral values from decision making.

Goodpaster draws on Piaget's (1932) model of moral development of children in arguing that the antidote to teleopathy is in balancing rationality and respect in decision making. He defines rationality as focused on criteria by which a person or group measures success for self. Respect, on the other hand, takes others' needs, goals, and interests into account in decisions, not just instrumentally as they contribute to your own goals but as deserving consideration in their own right. Piaget's model of moral development explains that children proceed through stages of egocentrism, compliance with norms, and interdependence. In egocentrism, children are focused only on what they want and have little awareness of others around them. As children grow and develop, they learn external norms and rules about interacting with others. It is only with maturity that children reach the stage of autonomy or understanding of interdependence, in which they understand the ways in which they are interdependent with others and develop a genuine desire to orient their own needs with needs of others, not out of compulsion but because of an understanding that their own best interests depend on the well-being of others.

In a similar way, Goodpaster says that organizations develop a corporate conscience when they move through a similar set of stages of moral reasoning. An organization locked in teleopathy may not be aware of its impact on external stakeholders or larger social systems, or may regard such considerations as irrelevant in organizational decision making. Our response in national policy making may be to impose sanctions or oversight mechanisms on ethical lapses, yet these responses take organizations only to Piaget's second stage of moral reasoning: responding to external norms or constraints. It is only when organizations move to a genuine understanding of interdependence that places self-interest and public interests as intertwined rather than competing that Goodpaster says we can claim that organizations are ethical and operating with conscience or morality.

We concur with Goodpaster's claims about ethics in organizations. The approach we take in teaching and consultation is to examine cultural data in light of value tensions in the organization. We focus on a model that assumes that key value tensions are an inherent part of organizational communication. This model, when applied to a rich array of cultural data, provides a way for leaders to enrich their understanding of and ability to proactively address ethical concerns. In particular, this chapter is designed to encourage the development of four manifestations of corporate ethical awareness that Goodpaster (2007) stresses: (1) reflectiveness (taking time to think about goals and how decisions are made), (2) humility (actively seeking feedback from employees and stakeholders to test organizational assumptions), (3) anticipation (proactively revisiting ethical standards to avoid value drifts and ethical entropy), and (4) community involvement in which organization members are personally involved with communities the organization serves. Before discussing three specific value tensions, we provide a context for this approach.

Value Tensions and Ethics

We have stressed throughout this workbook that organizational cultures do not exist in a vacuum. Effective organizations must find ways to exist and thrive in the national and international cultures that they seek to serve. The challenges organizations face in adapting and responding to the external culture are especially salient in the case of ethical issues. As an organization develops its own value system for evaluating ethical behavior, it must at the same time be responsive to the larger societal value system (Nicotera & Cushman, 1992; Weaver, 2001). In fact, Hofstede (n.d.) and colleagues, based on a study of 16 country cultures, point to certain U.S. values that contributed to the financial crisis in 2008. They identified the negative impact of the primary focus in the United States on values such as individualism and short-term orientation. U.S. business leaders, for instance, scored higher than those in any of the other countries on seeking personal wealth and this year's profits.

Examining the norms of a given culture via customers and business partners, however, is not sufficient. The lament of sales, marketing, and development specialists in multinationals is often that bribes and corruption appear to be the norm in certain societies. The U.S. government has passed laws and interpretive guides. Intercultural specialists also provide additional insight on how to respond to bribery and corruption (Knoten, 1999). In addition, we have provided several links on the Student Study Site, www.sagepub.com/driskill2estudy. Nonetheless, the challenge of knowing when to "do as the Romans do" and when to take a stand for a certain principle is not easily resolved. For example, if you learn that it is the norm to pay an extra fee to build an additional storage building for your company, do you take on a local bureaucrat about the ethicality of the fee knowing it may mean months of delay, or do you pay it realizing that you may be hit with other hidden fees later? Furthermore, what do you do if you learn that your own organization has developed a culture that allows for practices such as paying bribes that you know the society "back home" would not consider ethical? A cultural relativist position would encourage you to view the fee as a tip, while a cultural universalistic position would challenge that view by noting the differences in power relationships and motives between a tip and a bribe.

As of this writing, an example of a value conflict facing a U.S. company in an international context is the operation of Google in China. In order to operate in the world's most populous country, Google at one time agreed on limits on operation imposed by the Chinese government, including censorship and privacy limits. As time went on, such limits brought Google under criticism at home as their actions seem to betray U.S. values. Google was faced with a difficult choice. Would they stay in China with the government limits on their operation, giving de facto support to such limits by compliance, or would they withdraw from the country with the result of denying billions of Chinese access to Internet information? Add to this dilemma recent charges by Google, denied by the Chinese, that multiple efforts were made to hack into and gain access to accounts that would identify communication by and from civil rights activists (China Rights, 2010). Google eventually decided to leave the China mainland and base operations offshore to escape the value dilemma. Furthermore, Google leadership faces an additional dilemma. In their race to provide public access to documents and books, multiple lawsuits are pending as authors and publishers claim copyright infringement (Kirschbaum, 2009; Saltmarsh, 2009). Both of these situations illustrate the types of ethical and communication tensions that are part of our world.

Given the challenges faced in a diverse and multicultural society, organizational cultural leaders need to be equipped to meet ethical challenges. One approach to communication and ethics is to gain an awareness of values tensions that are an inescapable part of organizational life. Frederick (1995) discusses three general value clusters in light of human culture. He argues that these value clusters are tied to each other and inform our efforts to encourage good decision making about ethics and value conflicts. His primary claim is embedded in the context of an understanding of the challenges we face.

> Business practitioners . . . confront many daunting problems. Some of the more important issues are lagging productivity, burdensome social and regulatory costs, discontented and disloyal work forces, a rising tide of global competition, geopolitical turmoil, unreliable currency systems, and episodic threats of inflation, recession, and general market instability. A deep knowledge of how values impel business practitioners, their workers, and their firms to do what they might do well [sic] help them not only survive present difficulties but also to ride the powerful social and technological currents transforming the world's business systems. It may just be that the values within (as well as those outside) the organization are as important to successful management as a skilled command of financial resources, marketing techniques. . . . (p. 5)

According to Frederick (1995), businesses have typically been aware of and operated within the confines of two of these value clusters: economizing, which involves concerns over sufficient profit and sustainable cooperation; and power aggrandizement, or concerns over the extent to which power is dispersed. Often overlooked is the value set related to ecologizing values—concerns over the macro environment and the microenvironment. Reflection on the interdependency of each of the three values sets can provide a foundation for understanding ethical dilemmas and values conflicts.

Adapting William Frederick's work, we discuss these value clusters as tensions or dialectics as a way to promote dialogue on ethics and organizational culture. The assumption guiding this work, in concert with dialectic theory, is that these value tensions are an inevitable part of communication in organizations (Barge, Lee, Maddux, Nabring, & Townsend, 2008; Tracy, 2004). The goal, therefore, is not to escape the tension but to learn to respond to these tensions with mindfulness or an awareness of ways to respond ethically. Jian (2007) offers one example of dealing with dialectical tensions regarding organizational change. He notes that senior management and employees, because of different interests and dialectical power relationships, develop different meaning processes about an organizational change effort. While senior management may focus on the change in terms of organizational efficiency and profitability, employees may experience the change in terms of personal losses of jobs, salaries, and customary ways of operating. Jian proposes that a solution to these value tensions is dialogue and negotiation. He states that

> dialogue and negotiation allow creation of innovative interpretations and choices that are mutually acceptable and accommodate both sides' interests. In contrast, synchronous monologues, through which one side attempts to persuade the other, will lead to negative unintended consequences because the interaction only reifies positions on both sides and escalates tensions and differences. (p. 14)

As we present each value tension, we include rehearsal questions designed to promote reflection and connections to your analysis. One implication of your analysis might involve introducing the language of the value tension to the organization. The potential for improved decision making occurs when members learn to talk about ethics in terms of value tensions. Thus, for instance, rather than seeing economizing values as a matter of selecting between making profit versus attending to sustainable cooperative values, we can learn to attend to both poles of this value tension. We end this chapter by challenging you to give thought to other value tensions. We will treat each of the three tensions in the following order: (1) economizing, (2) power distancing, and (3) ecologizing.

Economizing

The economizing continuum involves the tensions of short-term profit values and human values of sustainable cooperation. This value tension, like the others, is an essential societal dialectic. The values in this cluster support activities that cause individuals and groups to act efficiently in using resources required for survival and material prosperity. The accepted measure of economizing is monetary profit and loss. However, as we argue in the discussion of organizational effectiveness in Chapter 13, the bottom line of profits is insufficient as a measure of effectiveness. Other measures revolve around the interests of employees, customers, and other stakeholders. Indeed, as Frederick (1995) notes, "Though desired, profits appear not to be essential to a particular firm, although some minimum (varying) number of companies need to be profitable if their host economy is to grow" (p. 54).

One international company, Axciom, places honesty and open relationships with stockholders, clients, business partners, and associates at the core of their values. Their company website provides access to charters and governance documents that guide their company. Charles Morgan, the founder and former CEO, states that "integrity results in the establishment of trust, which in turn results in good business" (Morgan, 2004). An independent, external marketing report is provided that cites Axciom as an industry leader, substantiating the validity of their focus on integrity as a good business strategy. Informal interviews with employees of Axciom suggest that this core value is not merely just one espoused by leadership but one found throughout the company. Axciom has for a number of years topped state and national lists as an excellent company to work for.

Economizing, therefore, demands a degree of cooperative interactions to promote goals that do not work against other, important societal values (Gardner, 1990). Without such cooperative interactions, decisions will often fall far below an ethical "high-water" mark. For example, Enron, before the ethical scandals went public, was a strong culture, in a negative sense. A strong value set kept those at the top embedded in a value that focused on short-term profit to the detriment of employees and other stakeholders. The lack of integrity as a core value meant that the company lost its balance in its efforts to realize the economizing value (Seeger & Ulmer, 2003; Ulmer, Sellnow, & Seeger, in press). Lyon (2008) goes further to claim that the culture contributed to a self-serving value set that added to unethical practices. This same imbalance, as introduced earlier, has been linked to several U.S. organizations, instigating a worldwide economic recession (Hofstede, n.d.; see also Hofstede, Van Deusen, Mueller, Charles, & The Business Goals Network, 2002).

In short, economizing suggests that profit is one value but is not the end itself. Economizing suggests an essential role for values that promote cooperative interactions such as fairness, equality, and caring for both individual and group needs. Take time to reflect on the rehearsal questions in light of your cultural data. As you do so, give thought to the value of introducing the idea of the economizing value tension to others in your organization and/or the organization you are analyzing.

Rehearsal 11.2 Applying the Economizing
Value Tension

Purpose: Apply your cultural data to the economizing value tension to gain insight to your organization.

What rationales for decision making are dominant in the organization?

_____

_____

_____

What is said (or not said) when a team member suggests a strategy that may reduce profits in the short run?

_____

_____

_____

What examples can you find of heroes who are known for achieving productive goals while maintaining other values, such as fairness and equality?

_____

_____

_____

Power Distancing

Power distancing is the attempt to balance hierarchy values and equality values. We use this term, as opposed to Frederick's "power aggrandizing." His term captures primarily the negative aspect of this value tension. In contrast, power distancing parallels one of the deeper level metaphors that can be used to analyze and reflect on communication in organizations. Morgan (2007) and others (e.g., Bolman & Deal, 2008) introduce a political metaphor as a way to draw attention to issues of power. Viewing organizations as political realities involves an assumption that power and control are inherent parts of organizing. This perspective is shared by critical theorists who seek to decipher communication patterns that may contribute to abuses of power in the decision-making process (see Deetz, 1991). Understanding both poles of this tension places leaders in a position to meaningfully critique the way responses to this tension impact ethics.

One end of the pole, high power distances or concentrated power in a hierarchy, is found when organizations impose a rank order and coercive power on organizational resources. This pole refers to the acquisition, accumulation, and retention of coercive power among a small group of individuals for both instrumental and domineering purposes. This hierarchical focus is not necessary for a company to be profitable or successful. "Giving allegiance to such values almost invariably diverts a company from making effective use of resources" (Frederick, 1995, p. 57). Consider, for example, organization leaders who become too concerned with maintaining position and power, and in the process cease to adapt strategically to the interests of customers or employees (Kotter & Heskett, 1992). The tragic tales from the financial industry that contributed to the global recession provide an example of power imbalances that harmed the economizing value.

Equality values, or lower power distances, can be viewed as distributed power webs. This pole refers to organizations that seek to distribute decision making throughout the organization. Thus, for example, various units are understood to have a certain level of autonomy over resources and decisions. The assumption held in developing this type of structure is that decisions are often best made by individuals closer to the process or problem they are charged to address. For instance, a case analysis of the *Columbia* space shuttle incident revealed that despite an awareness of the need for changes after the *Challenger* tragedy, the same interorganizational structures were still in place. These structures meant decisions were being made in the same way as they had in the past without sufficient consultation with lower-level engineers. "NASA's interactions with members of its interorganizational network have become so routinized through the years that NASA can be controlled without necessarily being conscious of that control" (Garner, 2006, p. 380).

The need to manage the power distancing tension is clear, yet the way such alignment happens also varies by national culture. Hofstede (2003) describes national cultures with a "high power distance" versus a "low power distance." In a high power distance culture there is a tendency to accept inequality between members of that culture. A high power distance culture holds norms that value hierarchy or vertical patterns of organizing and communication (e.g., Korea, Mexico, India). In contrast, a low power distance indicates a national culture that values equality, thus it tends to be horizontal or less focused on hierarchy in relationships (e.g., New Zealand, the United States, Australia).

Organizations within a culture with a low or high power distance value set are likely to share that norm with the national culture. Weaver (2001) suggests implications for ethics initiatives based on this value set. Organizations situated in high power distance cultures, for instance, are less likely to be receptive of ethics initiatives that "focus on all organizational members" because the norm is to locate decision making and primary responsibility at the top (p. 9). However, an exception to this tendency can be seen when the failure to empower lower-level employees proves to be disastrous. For example, Gladwell (2008) reviews the case of Korean Airlines (KAL) in the context of their high power distance score. Korea is second highest in the world on Hofstede's scale, and in the context of a study with pilots, power distance tends to be higher (Helmreich & Merritt, 2000). These same authors observe that "regardless of the personality and experience of the person working in the cockpit with you, your duties and obligations have been clearly defined and should not be breached. Having an unchanging routine ensures . . . unchallenged hierarchy" (p. 9). Korean Airlines, after close scrutiny of the fatal crash of KAL 1997 and the dismal record of KAL overall, made changes that proved successful. They identified one of the issues as the reticence of first officers to take initiative even when they felt the flight was in danger. Due to a number of major changes, including training to counter the tendency toward deference, their safety record has been spotless since 1999. One major change involved empowering first officers to respond in critical situations when the captain may have missed or not understand the need for changes in a flight plan.

Again, it may be helpful to use a Rehearsal activity to reflect on a few core questions to apply this value to understanding a culture. Consider using the Hofstede link found on the Student Study Site, www.sagepub.com/driskill2estudy, to gain a country score for the organization you are studying. Regardless of the national country score that may provide insight to the culture or subcultures in the organization, recall two central realities: (1) value tensions are ongoing; thus a single structure or "solution" to manage political or power issues does not exist, and (2) whether an organization maintains a focus on hierarchy or more distributed power webs, creating systems of accountability is critical.

Rehearsal 11.3 Applying the Power Distancing Value Tension

Purpose: Apply your cultural data to the power distancing value tension to gain insight to your organization.

1. What is the power distance value reflected in the communication practices of this organization?
   - For instance, do employees tend to value close supervision?
   - Is "effective management" viewed as close supervision?
   - Is the chain of command clear and does it tend to include multiple levels?

   _____

   _____

   _____

   _____

   _____

2. What role does a newcomer or someone in a "lower position" have in decision making?

   _____

   _____

   _____

   _____

   _____

3. What communication practices, if any, empower subordinates to participate in decisions related to ethical practices?

   _____

   _____

   _____

   _____

   _____

Ecologizing

Ecologizing focuses on managing macroenvironment and microenvironment values. As the term suggests, this value set is concerned with the impact and relationship of the organization to the external environment. Ecologizing includes values, on one hand, that focus on a larger macro value for the environment, a learned survival trait of human communities. Ecological relationships interweave the life activities of groups in ways conducive to the perpetuation of an entire community, including the flora, fauna, and physical features that constitute the groups' ecosystem. On the other hand, in tension with the macro value is a concern over the microenvironment, which includes accepted allegiance to stockholders seeking profits.

The rise in the number of people in the "creative class" (Florida, 2002) parallels a trend toward greater attention to the external environment. Individuals in this class serve an economic function of creating new content, technologies, and/or ideas. Members of the creative class are part of a shift that includes great concern for environmental issues. For instance, Florida and Davison (2001) report on manufacturing plants that utilize an environmental management system that results in reduced environmental risks to communities. Such efforts reflect a larger initiative called the "creative communities leadership project." One such project in Roanoke, Virginia, boasts plans to develop a carbon neutral region (Creative Class Community Initiatives, n.d.).

This trend captured by Florida's work is also found in a wide array of organizations. In a shift from just a few decades ago, it is now popular for a company to boast of its attention to the environment, both social and physical, beyond the walls of the organization. For instance, "Interface," the world leader in modular carpet, made a major shift in their business practices in the mid-1990s. This shift grew from their chairman, Ray Anderson, who had been asked to give a speech to his sales force on the company's environmental stance. At that point in their history, Interface primarily responded to mandated emission controls. In what he describes as "pure serendipity," Mr. Anderson had been sent a copy of Paul Hawken's book *The Ecology of Commerce.* The end result was a major corporate shift with impressive results that Anderson claims have actually meant overall reductions in cost. From Interface's 1996 baseline, the company has (a) reduced waste by about 52%, which has generated $372 million of cost avoidance; (b) reduced net greenhouse gases in absolute tonnage by 88%; (c) reduced water usage by 79%; and (d) six of their 11 factories now run on 100% renewable electricity (Interface, n.d.-a). The Interface track record has resulted in community partnerships ranging from projects focused on affordable housing for the economically disadvantaged in Georgia to tree planting in Brazil (Interface, n.d.-b).

This Interface (n.d.-a) story and others like it point to the significance of counter-narratives in introducing such changes. As introduced in Chapter 4, counter-narratives suggest positive ways to frame tensions to avoid polarized management practices. It is also a story that illustrates Goodpaster's (2007) stages of development of organizational conscience, moving from compliance with external laws or standards to an understanding of interdependence between corporate success and ecological responsibility. Livesey, Hartman, Stafford, and Shearer (2009) underscore the significance of narratives in a case analysis of a successful collaboration between environmental advocates and the rice industry in one region in California. They argue that stories are generated by eco-collaboration and in turn institutionalize new understandings for improved, ethical decision making. In all, an understanding of how the ecologizing value tension interweaves with other value clusters is important to seeing intersections and conflicts and ways to manage them. A series of rehearsal questions relevant to the culture of the organization should aid you in deciphering the relevance of this value in light of the other two.

Rehearsal 11.4 Applying the
Ecologizing Value Tension

Purpose: Apply your cultural data to the ecologizing value tension to gain insight to your organization.

1. To what extent do company documents explicitly discuss environmental policies?

_____

_____

_____

_____

2. How are ecological concerns weighed when making decisions about stock profit margins?

_____

_____

_____

_____

3. To what extent is it permissible to criticize a policy or decision based on larger environmental concerns?

_____

_____

_____

_____

_____

**Connections:
Other Tensions?**

Paying close attention to these value conflicts is not an easy leadership task. Yet time spent reflecting on these value tensions provides new insights into effective ways to manage the ethical landscape. In an effort to connect these value sets with your own cultural analysis, consider instances when your data indicate an implicit or explicit tension existing across the three values: economizing, power distancing, and ecologizing. For example, are there stories that indicate concerns over management treatment of the environment or use of power? Or do any of your themes suggest a tension between profits and ecological values?

However, as we opened this chapter, we indicated that these three value tensions are not intended to be exhaustive. For example, based on Chapter 9, another value tension could be diversity versus uniformity. Or in this same context, a tension could exist between resistance versus withdrawal in response to mistreatment. In one study, minority members who perceived maltreatment faced a dilemma: Resistance might result in more mistreatment whereas reacting by disengaging might result in strengthening the power structure that kept them from being heard in the first place (Meares, Oetzel, Torres, Derkacs, & Ginossar, 2004). Rehearsal 11.5 provides a place for you to brainstorm additional tensions that you see as critical in the process of making ethical decisions.

Rehearsal 11.5 Other Value Tensions

Purpose: Apply your cultural data to other value tensions to gain insight to your organization.

1. Value tension:

   _____

   Questions to ask:

   _____

   _____

   Ethical implications:

   _____

   _____

   _____

2. Value tension:

   _____

   Questions to ask:

   _____

   _____

   Ethical implications:

   _____

   _____

   _____

Summary

Organizations with a conscience are a pressing need in our society. The statistics are alarming, as is the significance of ethical abuse in terms of fairness, safety, and our environment. However, enacting an honest portrayal involves more than being aware of these abuses. One study suggests limited progress. Pederson (2010) captures data concerning the responsibilities of business toward society from more than 1,000 managers in eight international firms. Findings indicated that these leaders focused on taking care of workers and making products and services that customers want in an environmentally friendly way. However, the company leaders failed to include responsibilities related to issues such as "social exclusion, third world development, and poverty reduction" (p. 163). These findings and the three value tensions we have introduced take us back to an application of the first step in the cultural analysis process: We all act out our ethics based on implicit frames, metaphors, or theories. Reviewing the ways we can maximize a positive influence and minimize the negative influences embedded in each of the metaphors or implicit theories is critical not only for our lives but for future generations.

In short, managing these tensions is a basic part of our job descriptions. We cannot avoid them. Our hope is that we each find inspiration in the counter-narratives of individuals and organizations, such as Feuerstein at Malden Mills or Anderson at Interface. Such narratives challenge us to respond to value tensions in ways that bring equity, empowerment, and environmentally sustainable practices. As you reflect on these value tensions, consider completing Rehearsal 11.6 to prompt further reflection on ethics and culture. This chapter captured five major ideas to aid in the process of improving our ethical performances.

1. The challenges we face in our world economy and in our daily interactions in organizations frequently grow from moral and ethical lapses.

2. Organizational maturity in ethical behavior is marked by such habits as reflectiveness, humility, anticipation, and community involvement.

3. Value tensions are an inherent part of responding to ethical issues in organizations.

4. Reflecting on three main tensions in light of cultural data provides a tool for addressing ethical concerns:

   a. Economizing: Short-term profit and cooperative human values

   b. Power distancing: Hierarchy and equality values

   c. Ecologizing: Macroenvironment and microenvironment value tensions make ethical dilemmas a reality.

5. Ethical leaders should explore these three value tensions along with others that are relevant to highly ethical performances.

Rehearsal 11.6 Ethics and Communication Leadership

Purpose: Identify leadership practices that contribute to an ethical or unethical organizational communication pattern.

Steps:

1. Review your cultural analysis, including elements, themes, and overall characterization.

2. Write down instances when your data indicate implicit or explicit examples of positive and ethical leadership behaviors. For instance, are there examples of when a cultural hero stood for a constructive, ethical principle despite the potential loss of money?

3. Write down instances when your data indicate implicit or explicit examples of negative and unethical leadership behaviors. For instance, are norms and rules in place that make disclosure of ineffective or unethical practices difficult?

4. Brainstorm another short list of implications drawn from the observations you made. For example, if you noted ethical leadership strengths, how might these be useful in introducing changes you see the need to implement? Conversely, if you noted certain unethical leadership behaviors, how might these be addressed?

12

The Director's Chair

Symbolic Leadership

Articulate the value of the culture metaphor

Define major cultural elements

Use multiple data collection methods

Synthesize and interpret cultural data

★ **Identify applications**

Step Five: Identify Applications for Organizational Diversity, Change, Ethics, Leadership, and Effectiveness

Caring for the culture cannot be delegated. It can be shared but not left for someone else to do. . . . The leader is the fountainhead. This is true whether that individual is the entrepreneur-founder who first lays out the guiding beliefs, or the current CEO who has been given the right to reinterpret the guiding beliefs and state new ones. If the leader is a great person then inspiring ideas will permeate the corporation's culture.

—Stanley M. Davis (1984),
Managing Corporate Culture, pp. 7–8

Objectives:

- Explain the role of leader as "manager of meaning"
- Explore symbolic forms through which the leader shapes meanings within the culture
- Recognize ideology and identification as forms of unobtrusive control
- Develop optimal competence as a leader through multiframe thinking
- Evaluate yourself as a cultural leader or potential cultural leader

Stage Terms:

- Framing/reframing
- Vision
- Symbolic leadership
- Contrast
- Spin
- Unobtrusive control

In theater or film the director plays a critical role in shaping the performance of actors to create a unified artistic vision. To be effective, directors must have clear interpretations of the work they wish to produce and the skill to communicate that vision to the actors who will help them realize that vision. Their skill includes the ability to communicate and to motivate the actors to call on their best efforts in realizing the vision. In the end the production is a cooperative venture between the talents of the director and actors. In earlier management literature, the role of a manager was seen as planning, control, and coordination of organizational resources and systems. However, much of current leadership theory places more emphasis on the intangible leadership functions of creating the organizational mindset and influencing how employees interpret organizational events, very similar to the way the director shapes and encourages the performance of actors.

Alvesson (2002) notes that there is a symbiotic relationship between leadership and culture. Leaders emerge because organization members see a unique fit between the leader and values of the organizational culture. The leader, once he or she emerges, becomes an embodiment of the culture and has a unique perspective for influencing culture creation, maintenance, and change. Bolman and Deal (2008) offer a relational view of leadership: "Leadership is thus a subtle process of mutual influence fusing thought, feeling, and action. It produces cooperative effort in the service of purposes embraced by both leader and the led" (p. 345). They note that an important function of leadership is interpreting and reinterpreting experience within the organization, much as President Franklin D. Roosevelt performed on a national level when he assured citizens, "The only thing we have to fear is fear itself." Fairhurst (2008) calls this approach to leadership "discursive leadership" and distinguishes it from psychological approaches to leadership studies by its focus on leader–member communication processes that exert mutual influence toward the achievement of goals. Bennis (1986) concurs that leaders exert a powerful influence on culture, writing,

> the single most important determinant of corporate culture is the behavior of the chief executive officer. He or she is the one clearly responsible for shaping the beliefs, motives, commitments and predispositions of all executives—from senior management to the operators of the organization. (p. 64)

Schein (1992) went so far as to state that the only thing of real importance that managers do is to create and manage culture. Keyton (2005) writes that leader influence on culture can be direct or indirect. Direct forms of influence may include designing systems and procedures for work, allocating resources, and giving or withholding rewards. Leaders also have discretion over what they choose to endorse as a rite or ritual. However, the greater influence of leaders on culture may be through more informal means, especially through personal modeling and communicative interactions with employees.

In previous chapters we have noted that there are limits to the influence of an organizational leader on culture. Because culture emerges from the interaction of organization members over time, organizational leaders can inspire change or shape visions, but the members of the organization must implement the vision for the culture before it becomes a reality. Our focus in this chapter will be on the direct and indirect ways that the leader can influence the creation, maintenance, and change of culture. Kouzes and Posner (2003) write that although leaders cannot create or change the culture unilaterally, they can create the conditions for cultural change by embracing and modeling new values and assumptions, interacting with and listening to employees, and responding appropriately to resistance to change.

In this chapter, we focus on the communication processes of leadership in culture. In the first section, we talk about opportunities for leaders to shape meanings in organizations, a process we call "reframing." We then follow with a section on specific symbolic processes that are helpful to leaders in reframing.

Reframing

The term *framing* or *reframing* refers to adopting a different perspective or interpretation of an event or person. When we refer to reframing as a central function of leadership, we mean that leaders often have the ability to help organizational actors change their perspective on organizational events. However, Bryman (1996) cautions that leaders are not unlimited in their ability to shape meanings in organizations. He notes that organization members are not "passive receptacles but imaginative consumers of a leader's visions and of manipulated cultural artifacts" (p. 286). Some leaders, when facing a financial crisis in their organizations, might frame the emergency as a time to seek out and eliminate weak programs, a perspective that would lead to turf protection and competition. Another leader facing the same challenge could frame the crisis as "a time for the family to pull together and make joint sacrifices for the common good." This framing might lead to stronger ties and a common commitment to making it through the financial crisis. Each of these ways of framing has constraints. The leader who uses the crisis to set organizational priorities may have relational fallout but will also avoid the democratic pitfall of weakening all programs rather than making hard decisions. The second approach will build common ties and commitments but may result in overall weakening. Each might be the appropriate response in a given organizational situation.

What kind of meanings or interpretations can leaders influence? Leaders set organizational perceptions on a number of important areas that affect every other decision within the organization. *Leaders can manipulate perceptions of external threat.* History is rife with leaders who have used perceptions of external threat to divert attention from internal problems or to create internal unity to deal with a common enemy. Sometimes employees have become complacent and need to be more aware of potential threats than they currently are. A perception of external threat gives urgency and focus to their work. *Leaders can also influence perceptions of competitors and benchmark institutions.* One university president we observed had a massive impact on his school when he influenced faculty to accept they were no longer competing against small in-state colleges but should consider larger regional universities as their "benchmark" comparisons. This changed views of faculty salaries, research expectations, student admission standards, and many other decisions within the university. *Leaders often create the internal perceptions of primary stakeholder groups to whom the organization should be accountable.* A central question for any organization is: To whom are we accountable? Who has an interest in what we do? A corporation that sees itself as accountable primarily to shareholders might focus more on short-term profits while a corporation that sees itself as equally accountable to shareholders, employees, and customers might stress balanced values of profitability, responsibility, and safety. *A leader through overt and subtle messages also shapes what is most valued.* Is it profit and efficiency? Is it service? Is it people? Is it the environment? Too often, leaders may send inadvertent messages about what is most valued by where they spend time, what they talk about, and what they reward. Shockley-Zalabak and Morley (1994), in a longitudinal organizational study of the influence of the founder on organizational values and rules, concluded that organizational founders were influential in shaping both management and worker values and rules over time.

Finally, and most important, a leader creates meaning by casting a vision for the future. Bolman and Deal (2008) write,

> One powerful way in which a leader can interpret experience is by distilling and disseminating a vision—a persuasive and hopeful image of the future. A vision needs to address both the challenges of the present and the hopes and values of followers. Vision is particularly important in times of crisis and uncertainty. When people are in pain, when they are confused and uncertain, or when they feel despair and hopelessness, they desperately seek meaning and hope. (p. 369)

Bolman and Deal (2008) make the point that leaders do not create a vision in isolation and then persuade organization members to adopt it but rather gather the vision by listening to hints throughout the organization of needs, deficiencies, dreams, and goals and synthesizing all that varied input into a compelling image of the future.

Deetz, Tracy, and Simpson (2000) contrast mission, strategic planning, and vision. They define mission as the direction the organization wants to go and the strategic plan as a roadmap for getting there but say that the vision is the compelling image of what it will be like once you arrive at that destination. They conclude,

> In short, a good vision is realistic enough to create a recognizable picture of the future, powerful enough to generate commitment to performance, coherent enough to provide coordination, and open enough that others can make it their own. If this is done the vision can inspire and motivate, provide direction and enable benchmarking progress toward the future. (p. 52)

The power of these various reframing practices should be clear. Rehearsal 12.1 provides an opportunity to reflect on your experiences with these various practices.

Rehearsal 12.1 Identifying Leader Reframing Practices

Purpose: Identify leaders or cultural heroes from your cultural analysis who have engaged in reframing practices. How did they influence meanings for other culture members?

_____

_____

_____

_____

_____

_____

Symbolic Dimensions of Leadership

Not only do leaders greatly influence the organizational culture through shaping meaning and interpretations, but they also achieve this influence by symbolic means. They shape the culture by the very cultural elements you have been studying throughout this text. Schein (1992) discusses five ways leaders embed and transmit organizational culture: (1) by what they pay attention to, measure, and control; (2) by their reactions to critical incidents and crises; (3) by deliberate role modeling, coaching, and teaching; (4) by their choice of criteria for allocation of reward and status; and (5) by their choice of criteria for recruitment, selection, promotion, retirement, and "excommunication." Schein also discussed five "secondary mechanisms" for creating, displaying, and maintaining culture: (1) the organization's design and structure; (2) organizational systems and procedures; (3) the design of physical space, façades, and buildings; (4) stories, myths, legends, and parables about important events and people; and (5) formal statements of organizational philosophy, creeds, and charters.

We offer seven communicative principles that capture how effective symbolic leaders shape and define organizational culture. For each principle, we encourage you to write down insights gleaned from your analysis. *First, symbolic leaders recognize that all their actions and statements will convey cultural significance.* If the CEO's office is much more opulent and luxurious than offices of other employees, it sends a message. If a nonprofit manager throws a fund-raiser at an expensive hotel while claiming the nonprofit is in dire need of funds, it sends a message both without and within that organization. One large organization hosts a company picnic at which all the corporate officers serve the meal to janitors, secretaries, and other employees. They are serious about servant leadership. What leaders spend time doing, what they talk about in public addresses, who they interact with, what information they ask for, what they spend money on, and a variety of other seemingly insignificant choices send clear value messages. If you want to show you value employee input, eat in the company cafeteria. If you want to emphasize customer service, serve as a role model yourself, talk about it in every message you give, and appoint the most important members of the organization to a task force you chair yourself.

What values and lessons would employees learn by observing the example of the leader of the culture you studied?

_____

_____

_____

_____

_____

_____

Second, symbolic leaders tell stories. They understand the power of the narrative structure. Bormann (1969), in his theory of symbolic convergence, states that when we participate together in telling or hearing a powerful story we share a common experience that binds and unifies us. Stories are powerful because they are memorable, multifaceted, and dramatic. We can draw multiple messages from a story; thus the storyteller should recognize that symbolic convergence will vary because some listeners may have more to gain than others in acting on the implications of the story. Furthermore, they may see cause to confront or challenge the story based on power relations (Olufowote, 2006). Nonetheless, the significance of stories remains due to their power to connect and motivate. Recall that stories, like other symbolic elements, "reflect and reproduce the culture of an organization and in the process, they provide the material from which new stories of organizational life can be created" (Barge, 2004, p. 106).

Stories can tap into a rich historical legacy to interpret the present or can paint an inspiring picture of the future in imagery to which listeners can relate. Stories can also be a force for change. Recall our discussion of counter-narratives in Chapter 4. Counter-narratives are stories that foreground outliers, individuals, or groups that have overcome the odds. Bolman and Deal (2008) write about the power and danger of stories. The symbolic leader crafts a story about our past, present, and future:

> The past is usually a golden one, a time of noble purposes, of great deeds, of legendary heroes or heroines. The present is troubled, a critical moment when we have to make fateful choices. The future is a dreamlike vision of hope and greatness, often linked to past stories. (p. 370)

Yet, as we know from history, such stories may be believed even when they lack ethical or valid support. For instance, Martin Luther King, Jr., or Gandhi, as well as Hitler, used stories for starkly different ends. As this historic contrast suggests, stories told about leaders are often as important, if not more, than the stories a leader may tell.

The power of stories told about leaders is evidenced by two stories we have heard. In one case, Angi heard a provost of a small university tell an especially poignant story about one of his predecessors. The former president had retired, and on his last workday, unknown to him, every member of the administration and staff gathered in a long line outside the building to wish him well and show their love and respect for him. The provost ended the story by saying, "That's who we are at this university. That's what makes us different." In a second example, during a cultural analysis we performed, we heard the same story about the CEO from several interviewees. The company had a regional meeting at a hotel in the Southwest. The CEO noticed when one of the regional managers did not arrive at dinner and called his room. When he did not answer, the CEO got the manager to open the door and found the regional manager barely alive after a heart attack. The CEO cancelled an international conference to stay at the hospital with the family for 4 days until the manager was out of danger. Then he paid for all medical expenses and travel expenses for the family. He became a legend, and the story did much to create and display the organizational value of caring and responsibility for others.

Stories may not be completely true and the use of history may be "deliberately selective" (Bolman & Deal, 2008, p. 371). However, as noted earlier, if employees find a story credible or even partially true, stories may be believed. Many politicians, trying to seize on the communication success of Reagan, Clinton, and Obama, have integrated storytelling into important addresses, parading the subject of the stories past national audiences. Some of the stories seem so contrived and manipulative that they not only lose their impact but also may even have a negative one in that listeners may discount the speaker altogether. A story should be ethical and, to be credible, it must be relevant and believable to the intended audience.

One way to develop stories that are credible and ethical is to engage in what Barge (2004) refers to as "systemic story" creation. Systemic stories involve a process that "values, respects, and incorporates the differing stories other members in a human system have created" (p. 111). At a pragmatic level, this means that symbolic leaders take the time to listen deeply to the voices of others in the organization. They humbly respect the fact multiple stories or representations of the culture could be told. This process means that the resultant stories reflect the inherent tensions in organizational life. For instance, a systemic story about a change would represent voices of those championing as well as those challenging the change. Rather than a story criticizing the past or those opposed to the change, leaders weave a story that respects other voices by

> valuing the contributions of others and working with them to create and sustain the collective resources available within a system as opposed to adopting a morally superior position and instructing others in what changes are needed and how to perform them. (Barge, 2004, p. 122)

Systemic story creation is one process or tool you might use. As you reflect on your analysis, consider these questions: Did the leader of the organization you studied tell stories? What did they convey relative to the culture? Did you hear stories about the leader of the organization you studied? Did you learn whether leaders' stories were deemed credible? Ethical?

_____

_____

_____

_____

_____

_____

Third, symbolic leaders capitalize on the significance of rituals. We described rituals in Chapter 4 as the "acting out of cultural values." Rituals can be everyday routines such as a daily religious observance at a parochial school or a weekly staff meeting at a camp. They can also involve organization-wide events such as family picnics, awards banquets, celebrations of achievements, or retirement rituals. Rituals are windows on a culture and demonstrate values in action. Whether an organization has traditions and the nature of those traditions tell us a great deal about its values. A company with a tradition of rowdy Friday afternoon happy hours is different from a company with an annual family picnic. An organization that has implemented a rite or ritual that includes mentoring for minority members stands in sharp contrast to one that gives lip service to valuing diversity. In short, it is very important that an organization's rituals, especially recognition rituals, line up with the values the leader wants to imbue in the culture.

For example, one of Angi's clients was in the midst of a cultural transition shifting to a team-based culture and was frustrated that employees were still emphasizing individual action over team cooperation. After a review of the culture, she noted that all their corporate awards were for individual achievement rather than team accomplishments. In another organization, a leader wanted to emphasize a performance-based culture, yet the only corporate-wide event that employees attended was an annual retirement dinner at which employees were honored for length of service rather than excellence of performance. Symbolic leaders know what you reward says more to employees than the formal mission statement. They reward employees in public ways that emphasize values the culture wants to encourage.

What rituals did the leader of the culture you studied participate in and/or promote? What rewards did he or she present to employees? What does he or she do to imbue rituals with meaning? What did these rites and rituals indicate about the culture?

_____

_____

_____

_____

_____

_____

Fourth, symbolic leaders understand the value of historical continuity. Our first clue to a weak or fragmented culture is when employees in interviews know nothing of an organization's history. Cultural values and vision are rooted in history. Even if an organization had a dismal history and has reacted by changing core values and practices, it is essential to remember that history in order to ground and understand the current values. For instance, an effective community organization identified the power of surfacing historic values for unity and working together. References to these values helped engage previously divided groups to serve the community (Driskill & Camp, 2006).

In a medical care context, one large university hospital had lost its focus on caring for the most fragile and underserved populations through an emphasis on managed care, Medicare reimbursement formulas, funded research, and the bottom line. Few employees knew that the hospital had once been a private charity hospital formed as a health care safety net for the poor. Leaders became intentional in including that history in employee orientations, in posting pictures of the first hospital throughout the current facility, and in telling stories about the early heroes. In a similar situation, another organization hit an impasse on a major decision. Several hours of group meetings and debate over the best route to take proved to be of no avail. Then, one senior member recalled an event early in the life of the organization. He said something like: "We would not even have this decision to make if we had not originally placed our customers and needs above profit or convenience. We have to make this change if we are going to keep our core values what they have always been." His statement prompted a discussion that made it easy to develop consensus.

Did the cultural leader you studied make reference to organizational history? To what purpose? Were members aware of history passed on by leaders? What role did this knowledge play in the culture?

_____

_____

_____

_____

_____

_____

Fifth, symbolic leaders use language as a tacit way of shaping meanings and values. Fairhurst and Sarr (1996), in their book *The Art of Framing: Managing the Language of Leadership,* discuss language tools for leaders. They include metaphors, jargon or catchphrases, contrast, spin, and stories. Metaphors a leader uses consciously or unconsciously will shape employee perceptions and meanings. One university president assumed leadership of a university that was second in the state to the "flagship" research campus. In his inaugural address he said, "I don't care that we're not the flagship. Flagships are an anachronism in today's military. They're large, unwieldy, and difficult to turn. Let's be a starship." That imagery and metaphor started to overcome a "second-best" mentality among the faculty, staff, and students and probably served as a basis for a number of initiatives during his presidency to create a modern, flexible, and technologically sophisticated university. Some metaphors are unconscious and emerge through language patterns. A leader, for example, who talks continually in athletic terms may create an athletic metaphor for the organization that has both positive and negative implications. It may foster team commitments but may also encourage competitiveness and exclude employees with less experience with team sports.

Fairhurst and Sarr (1996) define *jargon* as "language that is peculiar to a particular profession, an organizational culture, or a well-developed vision or program" (p. 108). Our university defines itself as a "metropolitan" university. That had the internal connotation for organization members when it was first used to refer to the responsiveness of the university to the community, consisting of a diverse group of nontraditional students, and an emphasis on applied scholarship. Over the years, however, the concept of a metropolitan university has been difficult to translate to the community and has taken on less positive connotations internally. To some, "metropolitan" has come to mean second-class education, open admission of unqualified students, and a lack of support for academic research. In a strategic planning process we are struggling with new terminology to capture the intent of the old term without also carrying its baggage.

Contrast is the opposite of metaphor. Rather than explaining the common elements of two unlike things through comparison, the leader highlights an essential trait by placing one object, person, or idea in opposition or contrast to another. Just as we talked about the power of a leader to define competitors for an organization, or to suggest similar benchmark institutions, contrast can define an organization by what it is not. In one church organization that Gerald has researched, leadership used contrast to call the church to a new vision. The church was no longer to be a country club but a bridge. The contrast was intended to help the members move away from a focus on taking care of themselves to being a bridge to segments of the community not being served.

Spin is a term that has come from politics, as political handlers compete to place their own interpretations on speeches, debates, or political contests. Is finishing third a good or bad thing? Spin is also an important tool of symbolic leaders. Is a 10% drop in revenues a crushing blow, or an opportunity to evaluate which functions are most efficient and essential to the organizational mission? Are layoffs a betrayal of employee trust or the chance to create a leaner, more competitive organizational structure? Spin has its limits. Most organization members are sophisticated enough to see through an obviously self-serving interpretation. Yet many events can be seen in both positive and negative ways, and the leader can help organization members see events in different perspectives by "spin."

What types of language behavior did you notice in the leader you studied? Can you give examples of metaphor, contrast, stories, spin, or jargon?

_____

_____

_____

_____

_____

_____

Sixth, symbolic leaders recognize identification with organizational values as a form of unobtrusive control of employee behavior. Tompkins and Cheney (1985) write of unobtrusive control as a "third generation" of organizational control systems. In earlier eras, employees were controlled directly by a supervisor watching every action and correcting errors. In the second generation, bureaucratic rules replaced direct supervision. If we could make rules for every possible situation, then employees would be controlled by rules rather than direct supervision, making possible larger spans of supervision. We suspect we are now in an era of technological control in which software can count and trace every action in a way that monitors performance. Tompkins and Cheney's argument still applies: Leaders can influence employee behavior more powerfully through identification with values than with any control mechanism. If you control by supervision, then I will comply only when I am in your line of sight. If you control by rules, you are successful only to the extent I believe you will enforce the rules and know if I have broken them. If you control by technology, I may find ways to modify the technology or to manipulate counting systems. However, if I understand and believe in an organizational value like service, and that value is strong and unequivocal, then I will know what to do in any situation. Many credit Johnson & Johnson's ability to survive an incident of product tampering with strong and consistent organizational values that placed patient safety first. Thus there was no question that all products would be pulled from the shelves and new product packaging developed. It is ironic that as we write this second edition that Johnson & Johnson is in the midst of another controversy about product safety and has been charged with failing to recall drugs they knew could have safety risks. Whether the charges will prove true or false, the story underscores the importance of continually reinforcing key values of the culture over time. The significance of control via shared values in responding effectively and ethically to crisis has been documented in numerous case studies (Ulmer, Sellnow, & Seeger, 2011).

One of Angi's hospital clients has an employee policy that employees must call in the day before to be eligible for a sick day. Otherwise, if they are absent, they must count the day as a vacation day. The rationale for such a policy is valid because it is critical to public health that hospitals maintain sufficient staffing levels on any given day. However, the effect of the policy is that employees come to work sick and view the sick days as an entitlement that they take when they want to have a day off. How much more effective would it be if leaders would truly inculcate a value of how important each and every employee is to the hospital's mission, and employees really believed that? They would come to work because they felt their work was important and would take responsibility for making arrangements if they could not come to work.

The power of unobtrusive control should, however, give leaders and members cause for pause. Recent applications of this construct suggest reasons or causes for resistance to this type of control (Bisel, Ford, & Keyton, 2007). Unobtrusive control, as indicated in the hospital example, depends on members having a strong sense of identification with the mission of the organization. Yet, individuals typically carry multiple and complex identifications. Thus, certain values of organizational life may be salient to one member but not another. An employee may seek, for instance, to work extra for an ill coworker due to an internalized value of being a team player but may refuse extra work if sensing it is requested only for profitability goals. In short, as we have stressed at various junctures, the leader–follower relationship is complex. Individuals select the types of values that create the level of identification needed for unobtrusive control. Thus, reflecting on core organizational values and aiding members in making informed choices about the importance of these values is an essential leadership task.

Did the culture you studied use rules or values to influence employee behavior? What was the effect?

_____

_____

_____

_____

_____

_____

Seventh, symbolic leaders demonstrate optimal competence by demonstrating the ability to take multiple points of view on the organizational culture. We discussed levels of competence in Chapter 7. An individual with minimal competence may demonstrate culturally competent behavior without being able to articulate the underlying logic or rule. An individual with satisfactory competence can explain the rationale but will not be able to see the situation from multiple points of view. A leader with optimal competence can see the culture from multiple points of view and thus be in a position to help others understand the culture in multiple ways. Leaders can be competent in being aware of, and being able to take the point of view of, various subcultures within the organization. Because they understand the power of the metaphor or story, they also know its limits and how such symbolic forms could be "read" or understood in multiple ways.

One approach to helping leaders adopt multiframe thinking is in the excellent book by Lee Bolman and Terry Deal (2008), *Reframing Organizations*. They explain how organizations can be seen through structural, human resource, political, and symbolic frames. *Structural leaders* are architects and analysts who are skilled in restructuring the organization to perform more efficiently. They do their homework, are skilled at analysis, and see the connections among structure, function, and environment. They pay attention to the details of implementation and are not hesitant to reorganize if their data and analysis indicate another structure might be more efficient. A downside of this style is that they may lose sight of the human consequences of continual structural changes, they can be micromanagers, and they may not be as adept at seeing the synergy between human and system elements in performance.

A leader who operates primarily from the *human resource frame* is a facilitator and catalyst who motivates and "empowers through participation and inclusion insuring that people have the autonomy and support needed to do their job"

(Bolman & Deal, 2008, p. 331). Leaders who excel in this way of seeing the organization often adopt a servant leader model and see their role as supporting organization members to achieve goals. Strengths of human resource leaders are communication abilities, accessibility, serving as visible role models, and anticipating impacts of change and motivation on people. Weaknesses can include oversensitivity to how they are viewed by others, insufficient decisiveness, and failure to see that many problems have both human and system components.

Political leaders are pragmatic and realistic. They are adept at analyzing power and in determining whose interests are being served by any particular initiative. They are good at developing coalitions to support change, and in gaining the support of opinion leaders within the organization and key external stakeholders. Bolman and Deal (2008) point out that political leaders "persuade first, negotiate second, and coerce only if necessary" (p. 366). Political leaders are effective in getting things done, but they can fall prey to pragmatism over idealism, and can be seen as divisive and manipulative.

Symbolic leaders as defined by Bolman and Deal (2008) are master image weavers. Organizations are represented as both theaters and temples in this frame.

> As theater, an organization creates a stage on which actors play their roles and hope to communicate the right impression to their audience. As temple, an organization is a community of faith, bonded by shared beliefs, traditions, myths, rituals, and ceremonies. (p. 367)

Symbolic leaders exemplify many of the skills we have described throughout this text of framing meaning, considering the importance of symbols, and recognizing the durable fabric of organizational culture. The downside is that without substance, the focus on forms can feel empty and meaningless.

When leaders are able to see the organization through multiple points of view, they are better equipped to understand the implications of various cultural choices and to interpret the culture to others, recognizing their different perceptions. In short, an optimally competent leader is not only able to reframe situations but is adept at interpreting events and casting vision in ways that transcend the diverse national and subcultures within an organization.

What frame seemed to be the strength of the leader you studied? What were his or her deficiencies?

_____

_____

_____

_____

_____

_____

Summary

Too many organizations leave culture to chance and haphazard development. Leaders who understand the importance of culture are better equipped to use symbolic forms to create organizational vision and strategies to achieve their vision, to embody organizational values, and to use a variety of symbolic tools for transmitting those values to others. To be effective, leaders must be sure that cultural elements are consistent in conveying values. Of course, as we have stated throughout this text, there are limits to manipulating culture. While the leader has an important role to play in establishing, modifying, and protecting culture, organizational meaning is an interactive process between leaders and organizational members. Members must identify with values and vision for the culture to penetrate and guide the organization to desired outcomes.

In this chapter you should have learned the following:

- The most important job of a cultural leader is shaping meaning.
- The leader can shape many types of meanings
  1. Perceptions of external threats
  2. Perceptions of competitors and benchmark organizations
  3. Accountability to stakeholders
  4. What is valued in the organization
- The leader is influential in synthesizing a vision and communicating it to organization members.
- Leaders use several types of symbolic means to reflect and shape the organizational culture:
  1. Personal modeling
  2. Telling stories
  3. Using rites and rituals
  4. Understanding the impact of history
- Leaders can use language to influence meaning
  1. Metaphors
  2. Jargon
  3. Contrast
  4. Spin
- Identification with organizational values can exert unobtrusive control over employee behavior.

Rehearsal 12.2 Assessing Yourself as a Leader

Purpose: Assess yourself as a cultural leader or potential cultural leader.

Consider each of the leadership qualities below, and rate yourself on a 1–10 scale with 10 highest if your leadership style reflects this quality. On items on which you rate yourself less than 7, consider an action plan for how you can cultivate this cultural leadership behavior in yourself.

1. Use personal examples to convey values or norms.

   Culture members can watch what I do and get a sense of what the organization values.

   Rating on a 1–10 scale:_____

(Continued)

(Continued)

Action plan if score is less than 7:

_____

_____

_____

_____

_____

_____

_____

2. Tell stories to convey culture.

I make points dramatic and memorable by telling stories in speeches and remarks that reinforce organizational values and expectations.

Rating on a 1–10 scale:_____

Action plan if score is less than 7:

_____

_____

_____

_____

_____

_____

_____

3. Use rituals to reinforce values.

I participate in rituals and give employees rewards that are consistent with organizational values and priorities.

Rating on a 1–10 scale:_____

Action plan if score is less than 7:

_____

_____

_____

_____

_____

_____

_____

4. Use language elements of metaphor, jargon, or spin to shape organizational meanings.

Rating on a 1–10 scale:_____

Action plan if score is less than 7:

_____

_____

_____

_____

_____

_____

_____

5. Use shared values rather than rules to guide employee behavior.

Rating on a 1–10 scale:_____

Action plan if score is less than 7:

_____

_____

_____

_____

_____

_____

_____

6. I have a clear vision for the organization, developed with input from employees, and I have clearly communicated that vision to the members of my organization.

Rating on a 1–10 scale:_____

Action plan if score is less than 7:

_____

_____

_____

_____

_____

_____

_____

(Continued)

(Continued)

7. I use at least three of the four leadership frames described by Bolman and Deal (structural, human resources, political, symbolic).

Rating on a 1–10 scale:_____

Action plan if score is less than 7:

_____

_____

_____

_____

_____

_____

_____

Rehearsal 12.3 Case Study of Cultural Leadership

Purpose: Apply principles of effective cultural leadership to a case.

David Tate is dean of a College of Arts and Sciences at a Midwestern university. He guides his college according to two clear values: excellence and community. He stresses the value of excellence in a number of ways. He maintains his own professional scholarship at a high level even with his heavy administrative demands. He participates personally in the hiring of every faculty member in the college of almost 200 faculty members. In the interview process he stresses the expectations of the university. He has been known to veto the hiring of a candidate if he feels the department is settling, and he has been known to extend searches if the right candidate cannot be found. In his 10 years in the position, he has fired three department chairs because they did not meet the standards he set for college leaders. In each case this was done after extensive counseling, and in each case he met with each member of the affected department to explain his actions and solicit their views on a new departmental leader. He encourages faculty members and chairs to compete for university-wide awards, and faculty and students in the college are represented disproportionately each year in university-wide awards.

He also reinforces the value of community in a number of ways. He knows each faculty member in the college and is aware of their activities and accomplishments. He often drops by faculty members' offices to hear about their classes and professional activities. He personally hosts a first-year orientation program for all new faculty members in the college to get to know them and to socialize them to expectations and practices within the college. These orientation sessions include a couple of Friday afternoon happy hours in his home. He hosts a dinner and tent theater performance each summer for all faculty and staff members and their families. He states that he makes the college calendar his own and is almost always present at concerts, performances, readings, and other college events. His collegiality and sense of community extends to other deans in the university. Although he is assertive about the needs of his college, he is seen as a cooperative and knowledgeable colleague who is a trusted team player. He recently developed a strategic plan for the college with extensive input from every member of the college. He also allocates all discretionary funding in the college through a democratic process in which all of the department chairs in the college explain their needs to one another, and then as a group the chairs vote on spending priorities. The norm is very clear in the group that competitive behavior is not expected or valued.

Questions:

1. In what ways does David Tate demonstrate symbolic leadership?

2. How do his actions create cultural values and expectations?

3. Which of Bolman and Deal's four frames seem especially strong in his leadership style?
4. Are there any drawbacks to the culture in David Tate's leadership style?

13 Reading Reviews

Organizational Effectiveness

Articulate the value of the culture metaphor

Define major cultural elements

Use multiple data collection methods

Synthesize and interpret cultural data

★ **Identify applications**

Step Five: Identify Applications for Organizational Diversity, Change, Ethics, Leadership, and Effectiveness

We forget that the primary function of language, if we have something to say and are not merely babbling, is to uncover something within the world, to bring it into the open.

—Barrett, *The Illusion of Technique*, 1979, p. 158

Objectives:

- Describe three major perspectives on the relationship between culture and effectiveness
- Explain the dimensions of an effective organizational culture

Stage Terms:

- Strong versus weak cultures
- Strategically appropriate cultures
- Adaptive cultures

Full Circle

We began our work by examining expected payoffs or benefits of conducting a cultural analysis. We noted that our five phase or step process of analyzing a culture aids an organization in such areas as hiring and socialization practices, managing change, and planning. We also noted how understanding culture is an essential aspect of being an effective and ethical leader. We have provided tools for you to link your cultural analysis findings to relevant aspects of organizational cultural performances: diversity, change, ethics, and leadership. Each of these areas contributes to overall organizational effectiveness, and thus our final application of organizational culture to effectiveness will draw together leadership, ethics, diversity, and change.

With this final application chapter on effectiveness we have come full circle. Performance reviews in the workplace, like reviews of dramatic performances, are not always productive and useful. Sometimes managers veer off on tangents; sometimes a reviewer has a personal bias against an actor. Yet a review of overall organizational effectiveness in light of cultural data should not be discarded or discounted because the process is sometimes flawed. In fact, we would argue that effective organizational performances always involve review. Like a thorough review of a play, a review of organizational effectiveness should provide a perspective on the organization that is convincing, enlightening, and empowering. The hope is that this review process will inspire new insights into ways to improve communication within the organization. We also believe that you should leave this process with a clearer sense of how you can improve your own effectiveness by being an observer of your own thinking (Singe, 1990). Such improvements should provide a greater sense of direction, meaning, and value for your organizational experiences. As one CEO, writing about the process of leadership and organizational success suggests,

> *Listen*
>
> *In every office*
>
> *you hear the threads*
>
> *of love and joy and fear and guilt,*
>
> *the cries of celebration and reassurance,*
>
> *and somehow you know that connecting those threads*
>
> *is what you are supposed to do and business will take care of itself.*
>
> —Autry, 1991, p. 26

You may have noted important aspects of your own communication that contribute to or distract from certain organizational cultural values. For example, you may realize that you tend to discourage innovation by focusing on failed projects. You may also have noticed cultural themes that are consistent or inconsistent with ethical values that are espoused. For instance, a webpage may have included value statements about community and environmental engagement. However, your analysis of organizational rituals and employee talk reveals the opposite. Or you may have observed how an organization marginalizes minority populations in decision making. Such insights, whether personal or organization-wide, are major payoffs in the analysis process.

Regardless of your organizational role, you may be in a position to provide specific recommendations as a trainer, "internal performance consultant," or external consultant. Furthermore, even if your analysis is never to be formally presented to the organization, this chapter will encourage applications of value for your development as a leader. We begin by reflecting on the concept of organizational effectiveness. In particular we focus on three different takes on the relationship between culture and effectiveness. We encourage you to use the Rehearsals in this chapter to reflect on your experiences and your cultural data in light of their relationship to effectiveness.

Organizational Effectiveness

Concepts like *the bottom line*, *productivity/profit*, and *return on investment* are perhaps the most commonly used rationales for making changes or justifying the existence of an organization. You may have said or heard the phrase, "If we don't make a profit, what are we here for?" ROI, or return on investment, continues to be a hot topic in the training industry as human resource professionals seek to justify the expense of training and other organizational development (OD) efforts. Definitions of productivity and effectiveness vary, but the approaches of short- versus long-term productivity (Crandall & Wooton, 1978; Huselid, 1995), the attainment of organizational goals (Steers, 1977), and/or the highest level of performance with the least expenditure of resources (Mali, 1978) share a common emphasis. Not surprisingly, the concern over maximizing profits and increasing efficiency is either implicit or explicit in most discussions about productivity and performance. Leaders in organizations, like directors bringing a play to the stage, seek a payoff—they want their work to have some sort of success beyond opening night.

We accept the importance of the bottom line; however, there are three problems with making the bottom line the primary rationale to drive changes in culture. First, organization *members typically react to and resist efforts at change that they view as manipulative for management gain.* Employees may actually counter such efforts and resist changes. In fact, it is critical to realize that the cultural analysis process may reveal information that the organization or individuals in the organization are not ready to hear (Deetz, Tracy, & Simpson, 2000). Thus, even if your analysis is a convincing one, grounded in careful consideration of multiple elements gathered over time, how you make sense of the analysis and present it to others is a challenging process that merits planning and preparation. Your preparation should take into consideration one particular fact: Culture change grounded in a profit motive alone is likely to backfire.

A second consideration in linking culture to effectiveness is the fact that *effectiveness is defined in different ways by organizations.* In fact, three different logics have emerged concerning effectiveness. Baker and Branch (2002 present these logics and argue that the third logic best represents current trends. Example adjectives in *Logic III* (Table 13.1) reflect ideas in earlier chapters: collaboration, partnerships, alliances, positioning in external environment. This logic has "given rise to the identification of new performance functions, such as change management, organizational learning, knowledge management, organizational partnerships and network formation, innovation and creativity" (p. 10).

Table 13.1   The Changing Logic of Organizations

Logic I	*Logic II*	*Logic III*
Bureaucratic control	Engagement	Networking and collaboration
Internal orientation	External awareness and adaptation	External positioning orientation
Internally oriented hierarchical relationships and processes	Internally oriented lateral relationships and processes	Externally oriented relationships, partnerships, and alliances
Generic organizational design	Contingent organizational design	Flexible and fluid network design
Organization designed around internal functions	Organization designed around externally oriented products and customers	Organization designed to effect positioning in external environment
Primary value-added is management	Value-added of all employees	Value-added of partnerships and alliances
Management focus	Leadership focus	Facilitation focus

This shift in logic reflects the need to challenge the notion of the single bottom line of profit. One could ask: Was Enron an effective organization? It certainly was profitable over the short run. Yet because of unethical practices and lack of concern for employees and stockholders, its house of cards eventually collapsed. Organizations are realizing that environmental impact, community citizenship, financial stewardship, global development, and corporate responsibility are as important to evaluate as profitability in determining an organization's effectiveness. For instance, the idea of a "triple bottom line" (people, profit, planet), introduced by Elkington (1998), resonates with the two mission statements (Tom's Shoes & Nike) that were part of the linguistic analysis exercise in Chapter 5 (Rehearsal 5.3). If you completed this activity, did you observe that the latest generation of corporate mission statements has as much to say about ethics and values as about profitability?

Consider again the case of Interface. The first line in their mission statement reads: "Interface will become the first name in commercial and institutional interiors worldwide through its commitment to **people, process, product, place and profits**" (Interface, n.d.-a). Furthermore, nonprofits now account for approximately 5% of the national GNP, which contributes more than $660 billion to the economy (Nonprofits, n.d.). As such, they represent a significant sector of the U.S. economy. Nonprofits do not exist to make a profit, but they can be examined by a number of other outcome measures.

REHEARSAL

Rehearsal 13.1 How Do You Measure Effectiveness?

Purpose: Reflect on how your organization defines effectiveness.

Steps:

1. Select an organization you have worked in or participated in (from business, to nonprofit, to faith based).

2. Write down the statements you can recall from members, memos, and so on, that best capture how effectiveness is/was measured.

   _____

   _____

   _____

   _____

   _____

3. Do you agree with those measures? If so, why? If not, what would you measure?

   _____

   _____

   _____

   _____

   _____

A third issue with trying to manipulate culture to improve performance is that research paints a complex picture concerning the relationship between culture and performance. A review of this research provides a backdrop for the model of organizational effectiveness we find useful in the application of cultural data. Research in this area can be captured in terms of three major perspectives on the link between culture and performance.

Perspective 1: Strong Cultures Are Good

Early discussions of the link between culture and performance argued for the notion of "strong cultures" being associated with excellent performances. Deal and Kennedy (1982) popularized this argument by defining strong cultures as possessing the following themes: (a) shared vision and values, (b) supportive business environment, (c) recognized corporate heroes, (d) effective rites and rituals, and (e) effective formal and informal communication networks. These authors highlighted organizations like IBM and Tandem Computers for their strong cultures. Peters and Waterman (1982) also popularized certain characteristics of strong cultures based on their study of 62 successful companies. For instance, they noted things like a "bias for action," "close relations to the customer," "simple form, lean staff," and "hands-on value driven or strong core values."

Though dated, the work of Deal and Kennedy (1982) and Peters and Waterman (1982) still resonates. Who can argue against strong core values or effective networks? Still, further exploration of the strong culture concept has shown that some of the organizations identified in these studies have not been strong performers over the long haul. Strong cultures, paradoxically, may honor certain values or communication patterns that are actually detrimental to the organization (Kunda, 1993). In the worst case, unethical practices may become embedded in the culture. As Kotter and Heskett (1992) point out, "the strong culture theory" fails to account for the success of weak cultures. Such organizations as McGraw-Hill and Pitney Bowes, for example, received "weak corporate culture" scores but had impressive performance records.

Perspective 2: Strategically Appropriate Cultures Are Good

A second perspective argues for the notion of "strategically appropriate cultures"—the contents of the culture "fit" the context (conditions of the industry, degree of competitiveness, amount of change, degree of government regulation, degree of uncertainty). This "contingency" notion, like the strong culture, has appeal in the logic presented. It makes sense that an effective organization would somehow adapt its strategies to fit specific economic conditions. However, research has shown that while short- and medium-term performance can be predicted by the notion of "fit," prediction of long-term effectiveness remains as elusive with this theory as the "strong-cultures" perspective (Kotter & Heskett, 1992, p. 43). In fact, Collins (2001) based his theory of effective organizations on distinguishing companies that perform well in the short run versus those that have moved from "good to great" over a longer period of time. His analysis indicates that strategic fit is not the key to being a great organization.

Rehearsal 13.2 Finding the Drawbacks of the Best Fit

Purpose: Reflect on the limits of the concept of strategically appropriate to measuring effectiveness.

Steps:

1. Reflect on the discussion of strategically appropriate cultures.

2. Identify an instance in your experience or that you have read or heard about when an organization worked to adapt to its environment yet did not prove to be an effective organization over time.

_____

_____

_____

_____

3. Review the facets of the culture that may have contributed to this lower-than-expected performance.

_____

_____

_____

_____

Perspective 3: Adaptive Cultures Are Good

A third and final perspective, "adaptive cultures," presents arguments for cultures that can "help organizations anticipate and adapt to environmental change" (Kotter & Heskett, 1992, p. 44). Organizations like Apple Inc., 3M, and Procter & Gamble Company have been successful in finding ways to reinvent themselves with products like the iPhone, Post-it notes, and "green" cleaning products. Leadership is the key to maintaining and passing on a value set focused on making the changes needed to satisfy the legitimate interests of stockholders, customers, and employees. In contrast, less adaptive cultures tended to have leadership that was absorbed in self-advancement or protection of position and status.

Collins (2001) documented 11 organizations that made the move from "good to great." He argues that leadership is at the core of this "leap." These organizations, according to Collins's careful market analysis, stood out from competitors in their markets over a 15-year time period. His research team, despite instructions to downplay the role of top executives, found each of these organizations had a type of leadership that blended "personal humility and professional will" (p. 20). In short, their ambition was for the institution, not for themselves. They tended to leave behind an organization that could be great without them. For instance, 75% of the comparison companies, those that did not make the leap from good to great, had executives who set their successors up for failure or chose weak successors (or both).

In summary, an organization is likely to be effective because of its ability to adapt. Although certain traits of strong cultures, such as effective communication practices, make sense, they do not provide sufficient direction. Furthermore, the ability to "fit" current market conditions, while a critical component, fails to account for long-term effectiveness. So a core question remains. What is it about adaptive cultures that we need to pay attention to in relation to the data found in a cultural analysis? Leadership has been mentioned, but what other characteristics might be used to guide the analysis of organizational culture data? What are the themes likely to surface that encourage an organization to be adaptive?

Adaptive cultures do tend to share certain characteristics. Table 13.2 highlights a model of organizational effectiveness that captures themes and qualities that

Table 13.2   Linking Effectiveness With Culture

The organization adopts strategies and tactics for:

Employees

- High value on developing vision based on facts/truth
- Leading with questions—using informal networks to develop vision
- Consensus building rather then coercion
- Open forum for discussing differences, disagreements
- Learn from failed efforts without assigning blame
- Understanding and sharing a vision of what the organization does best
- Selecting and keeping the best
- Merit-based (rather than political) rewards and advancement
- Tapping into strengths of cultural diversity

Customers

- Communicating a clear vision to customers of what the organization does best
- Channels for receiving customer input and feedback
- Always listening and changing based on feedback

Stakeholders

- Balancing demands of stockholders for profits with concerns for the physical environment
- Balancing demands of stockholders for profits with concerns for employees and customers

Leadership

- Empowering and shared leadership functions
- Based on principle and values rather than personal charisma
- Focus on leadership identification and development
- Plans for leadership succession

Organizational Structure

- Flexible and dynamic structure
- Permeability to allow environmental input and scanning

should be considered in determining implications of your organizational analysis. These themes grow from the review presented above but focus on communication "habits" of organizations that have proven track records in the marketplace for great long-term performance. Remember, however, that any insight or potential recommendation for change needs to be sifted through the lenses of diversity, ethics, and change management. For instance, it would be a mistake to assume that national cultures do not have an influence on taken-for-granted values such as a relationship versus a results focus. In the United States, a value is placed on the management of objectives (e.g., working toward clearly established goals). Thus, success is determined and measured by time-efficient goal achievement. In contrast, in other cultures, such as Mexico, business is not conducted until partners have a chance to get to know one another (Varner & Beamer, 1995). Effective organizations find ways to adapt to and manage these cultural differences when engaged in the global environment.

As you review this model, think about the extent to which your cultural analysis contains themes and values that encourage or discourage moves toward being effective through being adaptive. The themes you interpreted in your analysis as well as the overall definition of culture often give hints as to the extent to which an organization is enacting the cultural themes and communication practices indicated in Table 13.1. Embedded in the themes you identified, for example, may be value statements about how stakeholders are to be treated, or about communication rules regarding customer communication. For instance, if you identified a theme related to conflict ("Customers are heard only when they file formal complaints"), you might generate a list of possible applications because this theme has such clear ties to important organizational performance issues. You might note as a strength that this theme makes it clear that customer complaints are important. Yet, in contrast, other important information from customers may be downplayed. Any number of insights and potential interventions might be suggested by such an analysis. Yet, before jumping to recommendations, reflect on aspects of the organization's history that contribute to this theme. Furthermore, exploration of socialization and/or training practices related to customer service merit attention. This process of cultural analysis should be about a willingness to hear themes that contribute to effectiveness as well as those that are detrimental.

Summary

Research on organizational culture and effectiveness has prompted a revision of earlier, overly simplistic ideas. We agree that profitability is essential, yet we concur with others that it "should not be maximized at the expense of other equally important social needs, including living wages, sustainable development, quality of work/life, and self-determination" (Eisenberg, Goodall, & Trethewey, 2010, p. 140). We covered two major approaches to defining an effective culture before introducing the one that is best supported by research. We also encouraged your own review process. The following summary points capture the main ideas presented.

- Problems may arise if profits become the driving rationale in making changes to culture. Employees may resist such efforts if they are seen as solely for management's gain.

- In the wake of corporate scandals, top corporations now realize that corporate responsibility and values must be evaluated as well as profitability in determining long-term organizational effectiveness.

- The first approach to defining an effective culture is the notion that "strong is good." Reviews of long-term strong performers show they do not always fit this model and, in some cases, unethical practices can be embedded in a strong culture.

- A second approach suggests that a "contingency" or strategically appropriate culture is a good one. Again, the long-term high-performance companies that were reviewed do not fit this approach.

- The final approach, and the one argued for in this workbook, is that efficiently adaptive cultures are the most effective. This perspective finds support for long-term, high-performing organizational cultures maintaining and passing on a value set focused on changing as needed.

- We encourage you to review your themes and overall definition of culture to gain clues about the extent to which the culture you studied is efficiently adaptive.

Rehearsal 13.3 Gauging Effectiveness

Purpose: Identify cultural themes that contribute to effective organizational communication patterns.

Steps:

1. Review your cultural interpretation, including elements, themes, and an overall definition(s).

2. Write down instances when your data indicate implicit or explicit examples of *in*effective communication practices based on Table 13.1.

3. Write down instances when your data indicate implicit or explicit examples of effective communication practices based on Table 13.1.

4. Brainstorm a list of two or more implications of the observations you made in your data. For example, if you noted effective communication patterns, how might the values inherent in these patterns be further strengthened? Conversely, if you noted ineffective behaviors, how might these be addressed?

14 Opening Night

Conclusion

The kind of concentration necessary for acting demands the ability to recreate something which is not there. It leads not only to the workings of the imagination, but also the presence of that kind of belief or faith which has often been characterized as the essential element in acting.

—Strasberg, *A Dream of Passion*, 1987, p. 131

Objectives:

- Apply your cultural analysis to professional communication goals
- Apply your cultural analysis for organizational development

---

Comments from students in cultural analysis classes:

- *I cannot believe all that I am seeing here. I really have a better sense of how to make it in this organization. I realize now why things seem to be going faster than the speed of light. I am not as stressed as I once was and I am far less critical of management. I began my analysis as I began my second week here and now I feel like an insider after just a few months. In fact, I was able to make some suggestions on how to manage our recent transitions to a new facility.*

- *I think it was a mistake doing this study. Well, I knew before I started that I held some strong biases, but now I have to face them. The truth is that I would rather not address these issues at this time. It is hard to admit, but it really is easier not changing my communication habits even when I see from my study that they need changing.*

- *I actually went to my boss and said: "Do you know how my new cultural and communication skill sets can help us?" He listened and I have been given new and exciting opportunities.*

- *This analysis has pretty much convinced me that I do not belong in this organization.*

Back to Change

Change often begins with one single, solitary insight. The challenge of enhancing your own performance or that of an organization is to act on that insight. Opening night is that moment when an insight, an interpretation of a role, is put into action. After much thought, planning, and rehearsal, a role is enacted, a script is brought to life. As the statements on the previous page suggest, the outcomes of paying close attention to culture vary greatly—from aiding in a transition to a new organization to an awareness of a lack of self-motivation in the change process. If these insights are to have value, it is essential to remember that regardless of the insight, significant organizational and professional communication developments come only from developing and enacting a plan. As the following quote indicates, the challenge of taking responsibility for such action is both significant and meaningful.

> [A] lasting organizational community requires more than commitment and communication. It requires discipline and mastery. This mastery is achieved as each person makes his or her contributions and assumes responsibility for them. Instead of a solitary leader responsible for performance, each member becomes a leader depending on the skills, knowledge, and experience needed in each situation. (Eisenberg, Andrews, Murphy, & Laine-Timmerman, 1999, pp. 145–146)

Your newly gained knowledge of how to conduct a cultural analysis as well as the applications you have identified place you in the position to make a contribution to an organization. The contribution should begin by changes you make in your communication. Your credibility as a leader or future leader requires such intentional efforts. In fact, the definition of cultural analysis presented early in the book included personal development as a goal. *A cultural analysis is a process of capturing the unique qualities of an organization as revealed in values, history, stories, and other elements created through interactions that have significance for organizational effectiveness and personal development of members.*

In short, the analysis process, as reviewed in Figure 14.1, is intended to move from reflection on elements, through an interpretation process that results in application. In turn, your application will influence the culture. Put differently, we hope you will have stories to tell others about the minor and/or major transformations that occurred in your communication behavior. We envision some of you hearing stories about the changes others see in you! What is the basis for such high hopes? Such hope has grown from several decades of hearing from students. We are confident that paying careful attention to culture, to a wide array of cultural elements, prompts reflection on your role on the stage. Such reflection results in an array of responses, as indicated in the statements above. While not all students leave with major insights and/or a willingness to improve their communication, the majority gain practical tools of value to organizational or personal and professional development.

Regardless of the insight or application, we encourage you to share your experiences and be enriched through interactions with students and colleagues.

We trust you will see your role as a leader and change agent in paying attention to culture, to giving shape to cultures that improve life for others. Pearce (2007) challenges us to realize that our diverse world requires that effective leaders become champions of attending to how we communicate—the processes we create to tap into diversity and manage value tensions. The cultural analysis process enhances this focus on communication. Thus, even if you are not formally presenting results to your own organization or to the organization you analyzed, you have gained insights that merit further reflection and application. After discussing an analogy aimed at keeping the planning and change process in perspective, activities designed to aid you in professional and organizational development are outlined.

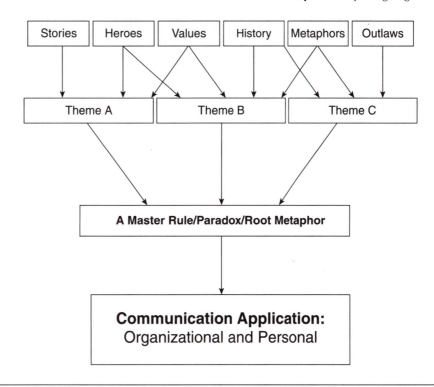

Figure 14.1   Moving From Interpretation to Application

A Compass, Not a Map

Goal setting and the process of developing an action plan can give the illusion that we can know exactly where our plans will take us. The tendency is to think that an action plan is like a map to be followed; for instance, take I-30 west from Little Rock, Arkansas, to Dallas, Texas. Using this map analogy, we might think to ourselves: *I know where I am going, and I am not lost.* In contrast, we view action plans as more in keeping with the statement: *I don't know where I am going, but I am not lost.* Action plans are more like a compass than a map. A compass gives you the confidence that you are not lost; you know the general direction you are going, but you may not know exactly where that direction will lead you. You cannot predict all the consequences of all the plans you put in place. You may, still, gain confidence in moving in the best possible direction with the information you have garnered.

In the business of culture change, and more particularly making changes in professional or organizational communication, usually the best that can be done is gaining an awareness of where you are through an analysis and then using an action plan to point you in the direction of desired change. In fact, there is value in learning to maintain a level of uncertainty about decisions that may flow from plans. Langer (1989) summarizes a study that assessed the level of certainty managers had about decisions they made every day. She and her colleagues also evaluated the work relationship of these managers with their subordinates. They found that "those managers who were confident but relatively uncertain were evaluated by their employees as more likely to allow independent judgment and a general freedom of action" (p. 144). Put differently, there is value in using a compass rather than a map.

The need for both confidence and uncertainty is due in part to the fact that the process of implementing changes involves continual readjustment. For example, you may identify a goal for professional development that involves setting up a conflict management ritual in the workplace. Once initiated, this change may make you aware that you have not adequately addressed the issue of motivating coworkers or employees to engage in productive conflict. Thus, new goals relevant to creating support for effective conflict management may need to be developed. Nonetheless, the process you engage in, a process of awareness, action, and adjustment, is at the heart of enhancing your organizational culture performances.

The compass illustration suggests that we have a sense of a desired direction (i.e., a goal to implement an organizational change), and we have an awareness of where we are now (i.e., as a result of the cultural analysis), but even the best action plans cannot predict the future (e.g., what will the actual result of the change be?). Students and practitioners have shared with us the variety of outcomes that have come through their cultural analysis process: promotions and transfers; business as usual; others speak of personal insights or being more effective in adapting to the culture; still others have left their organizations for various reasons.

In short, action plans do not guarantee certain outcomes, but they should be developed to make certain desired changes possible. We provide Rehearsals 14.1 and 14.2 as means for reviewing your cultural analysis experience with the intent of helping you visualize personal and organizational application. These Rehearsals involve you in the familiar process of writing action plans. The final product will be of your making; still, the checklists include reminders on writing an effective action plan. The first rehearsal focuses on professional communication development goals and the second rehearsal on organizational development. Each section includes space for writing a rough draft of your goals. You can also find example student papers that include organizational communication development recommendations on the book's Student Study Site, www.sagepub.com/driskill2estudy.

Summary

You made it! Regardless of whether you engaged in completing a small-scale analysis involving a few weeks of data collection or a more ambitious one spanning several months, you have improved your grasp of the process. The stage is now set for you to use your analysis in ways that make the most sense to you. Remember, as you engage in discussing your analysis and informal and/or formal recommendations, you are involved in a process of shaping communication patterns and thereby the culture in an organization. In this process, you have an ethical responsibility to act on your awareness of your culture, and to act in ways that improve and enhance organizational life.

Our desire is that both the process and the outcome of cultural analysis will surprise you. The uncertainty you had at the start of the process may be reduced, but the insights and possibilities for future application should provide a sense of curiosity and wonder. We began this workbook by reflecting on the span of experiences we have in organizations, from the cradle to the grave, with tragic and comic stories. Given the significant time we spend in organizations, our passion is for each of us to be able to describe our organizational stories with a sense of hope, joy, love, and purpose. Both the training tools of method actors and the process of cultural analysis encourage you to keep awareness of communication in the foreground. We have found the outcome of this foregrounding process to be no less than greater participation in the meaning-creation process. We concur with Barrett (1979): "Life is many days, day after day. But it is not, we hope, a mere succession of days. We long that these days will somehow add up to a meaning or a drama that we can call a life" (p. 154).

> A compass gives you the confidence that you are not lost; you know the general direction you are going, but you may not know exactly where that direction will lead you.

Rehearsal 14.1 Action Plan for Professional Communication Development

Purpose: Develop an action plan for at least two communication goals important to your leadership development.

Step 1: Identify two communication goals that have the following characteristics.

Specific communication behavior, rather than general attitudes or values. For example, a theme may have made you aware of the types of tensions and value dilemmas existing in the organization. If your first draft of the goal is something like, "Gain a better perspective on the problems faced by the organization," revise this goal to focus on a communication behavior. For example, you might revise it to be, "Tell my immediate supervisor of my awareness of certain organizational challenges/dilemmas. Ask what role I can have in managing these challenges."

Contextualized communication behavior (appropriate setting, purpose, etc.), rather than general statements of what you plan to do. The above example does not provide a sense of reflection on the most competent way to approach this topic with a supervisor. For instance, consider the different interpretations and impact of a statement about your awareness of a specific organizational challenge made to a supervisor informally spoken over a morning cup of coffee versus a formal discussion during a performance review. Thus, a revised version should contextualize your plan and might read like this: "I will connect the cultural theme of conflict over values with my own performance goals to improve communication with my coworkers. I will plan on having this discussion during my next review."

Your communication behavior, rather than something that requires a change in someone else. We have found that a common tendency is for us to quickly see ways a supervisor or coworker needs to improve. We might say: "If I could just get them to change or if we could just get a decent boss life would get better around here!" However, this focus is ultimately defeating in that it places the hope for a more productive and meaningful life in the organization on everyone else. Thus, for example, the goal, "To get my supervisor to provide clearer feedback" would be better worded as, "To provide paraphrases of my supervisor's feedback to ensure understanding."

Inspiring or motivating—remember these are your goals. Go for what is most important to you—something you know will be good for you to do, something you believe the data indicate would be right for you to do, something you will be glad you did or at least glad you attempted. We find it valuable to reflect on deeper values and passions that you carry that transcend and yet also encompass daily interactions. For instance, a former student moved into the role of CEO of a homeless shelter. If you had asked

(Continued)

(Continued)

her if the issue of homelessness had been a top priority or passion, she would have said *no*. However, she does hold a passion for empowering individuals and addressing injustices. Thus, her daily communication is imbued with meaning as she serves in this context.

Step 2: Identify a time frame with action steps.

For example, one *goal* might be: "During my upcoming review this June, discuss my professional development goals in light of specific cultural themes." We provide an example set of dates and steps. Such details create a level of commitment. Note that in the second step (b), the encouragement is to include a review with a trusted peer or mentor. Change in communication behaviors happen best in the context of support.

Dates	Steps
May 15	a. Summarize data on theme one as it relates to my ability to negotiate differences between work groups.
June 1	b. Review my ideas and goals with a colleague and mentor.
June 15	c. Make revisions in goals and gather resources (books, training, etc., that may be needed).
July 7	d. Present my goals at my performance review.

Step 3: Set a time frame to review results
of your action plan and evaluate appropriate next steps.

An evaluation step is a way to encourage you to picture desired results and then determine ways to revise and develop a plan. Drafts of this step may actually prompt revisions of the earlier steps. The following example illustrates elements that might be included in this step.

Follow up by October 1.

a. Discuss with key parties the effectiveness of recent meetings that depended on my negotiation skills.

b. Keep a journal of meetings—review impact of integrating alternative negotiation tactics based on each of the four frames.

c. Revise goals as needed.

Write a brief follow-up plan that relates to the steps you wrote earlier. Again, remember that a compass allows you to adjust your plan as you gain more information. The adjustments should be considered part of your ongoing commitment to acting on your awareness of ways to enhance your communication in the context of the overall performance of the organization.

Step 1: Communication goals that identify specific and contextualized communication behavior and focus on your own rather than others' behavior.

Goal A: _____

_____

_____

_____

_____

Goal B: _____

_____

_____

_____

_____

Step 2: Identify a time frame with action steps.

Goal A: _____

Date	**Steps**
_____	_____
_____	_____
_____	_____
_____	_____
_____	_____

Goal B: _____

Date	**Steps**
_____	_____
_____	_____
_____	_____
_____	_____
_____	_____

Step 3: Time frame for reviewing action plan results; evaluate appropriate next steps.

Date	**Evaluation Comments**
_____	_____
_____	_____
_____	_____
_____	_____
_____	_____

Rehearsal 14.2 Organizational Communication
Development Action Plan

Purpose: Identify two organizational communication development goals important for the effectiveness of your organization.

Imagine the sense of loss if you have information that is pertinent and important for organizational effectiveness but you are not able to find the appropriate channel for introducing that information. Further imagine the sense of wrong or misdirection if you are aware that a failure to translate your insights into action may not only cost the organization money but may also mean unethical practices continue unchecked. However, introducing ideas based on your own detective work, your own artistry in action, is not an easy task. This section will guide you through a set of steps intended to make the process comprehensible and more likely to succeed. Remember, however, that this process should not be treated separately from the first section. Recall that formal and informal recommendations are more likely to be received if you have already demonstrated meaningful changes in your communication behaviors. If, for example, you see the need for improved meeting management skills among all supervisors, and if you have already begun to improve your own skills in this area, recommendations are much more likely to be heard. Because of the breadth of questions reviewed in the next section, space is not provided for all of your responses. We encourage you to draft your ideas, review them, and check them against your cultural analysis before deciding on a final plan of action.

Steps for Developing Recommendations

1. Reflect on insights gained from the application chapters (Chapters 9–13). Write down specific themes that relate to issues in each of these chapters.

Chapter 9: Diversity _____

_____

_____

_____

_____

_____

Chapter 10: Change _____

_____

_____

_____

_____

_____

Chapter 11: Ethics _____

_____

_____

_____

_____

Chapter 12: Leadership _____

_____

_____

_____

_____

Chapter 13: Effectiveness _____

_____

_____

_____

_____

2. Select no more than two issues that you see as most important and most likely to be accepted if presented as organizational development (OD) goals. Such focus will increase the likelihood of application. Develop these issues into OD goals. The intent here is for you to brainstorm and envision an OD initiative that would enhance or develop a cultural theme that supports effective communication in your organization. For example, you might have concluded from several elements of culture that the organization culture is inconsistent in supporting diversity initiatives. However, you did learn that one cultural hero encouraged diversity initiatives and that a diversity strategy was in place. Thus, you might brainstorm a next step that would include additional rituals and communication training in the area of diversity.

Possible Areas of Focus:

_____

_____

_____

_____

_____

_____

_____

_____

_____

_____

(Continued)

(Continued)

3. Decide whether these OD (organizational development) goals would be best presented in a formal manner or introduced informally. (Note: You might have aspects that you present formally and others that are best introduced informally.) A few criteria to check to determine if you are in position to make formal recommendations:

- Your organization knows of your study and expects you to present your findings.
- Your position allows you such freedom.
- Your relationship with management makes it possible.

If you are not able to answer yes to at least one of the above, then develop your action plan for this section according to the guides provided in the informal recommendation section. If you were able to answer yes to one or more of these criteria, then create your action plan based on the suggestions in the formal recommendations section.

Informal Recommendations

Informal recommendations take on numerous forms. These recommendations, the process you engage in, challenge you to be more than an observer. Wearing the "hat" of a change agent, a leader willing to find ways to bring meaningful changes is invigorating and challenging. The following set of questions, if thoroughly considered, will guide you in dealing with this challenge. You should answer these questions in conjunction with each of the two applications you selected for organizational communication development.

Questions for Analysis: Informal Recommendations

What are you presenting?

- What has been the content of past attempts (your own as well as those of colleagues) at making informal recommendations?
- In what ways, if any, does the content of your current recommendation relate to past recommendations?
- Is your recommendation positively worded? Restate one of your recommendations in positive language.

Who are you presenting your ideas to?

- Is there more than one person who would be receptive?
- What aspects of diversity or national culture should be considered?
- Who can you rely on to champion your ideas?
- Who in your organization is known for implementing change? Who is listened to/respected?
- Who will be reluctant to accept or is against this idea?
- What can you learn about their reluctance to accept it?
- How can you deal effectively with the reasons for resistance?

Why should they listen?

- Why are these changes of value to the organization?
- Are the changes connected with employee, stockholder, and/or customer satisfaction data/issues? Explain.

When will you present?

- What time of day will you be best received?
- Is there a time in the week or year that you are most likely to be heard fully?
- Is there a time in the day when the person you present ideas to is most receptive?

How will you present?

- What are the expectations of those to whom you will present your ideas?
- Do they expect detailed, written support of the ideas?
- Do they prefer to be involved in shaping the idea?

Action Plan:

1. Review your responses to each of the above questions.

2. Write/rewrite at least two of your *informal* organization-wide applications, in single-sentence, positively worded statements.

3. Write down the date(s), place(s), and person(s) important to implementing these goals.

Formal Recommendations

Writing and presenting a formal recommendation requires an analysis of your audience, setting, purposes, and so on, in a way much like that of preparing for informal recommendations. The following set of questions mirrors the informal recommendation development exercise with only minor differences. If thoroughly considered, it will guide you in preparing effective recommendations. Each question encourages you to examine not only your own recommendation but the history of past recommendations. The reason for doing this additional history step is so you will be able to determine what was effective or ineffective. You should answer these questions in conjunction with each of the two applications you selected for organizational communication development.

What are you presenting?

- What has been the content of past OD recommendations (your own as well as those of colleagues)?
- In what ways, if any, does the content of your current recommendation relate to past recommendations?
- Is your recommendation positively worded? Restate your recommendations in positive language.

(Continued)

(Continued)

Who are you presenting your ideas to?

- Is there more than one person who would be receptive?
- What aspects of diversity or national culture should be considered?
- Who can you rely on to champion your ideas?
- Who in your organization is known for implementing change?
- Who is listened to/respected?
- Who will be reluctant to accept this idea?
- What can you learn about their reluctance to accept it?
- How can you deal effectively with the reasons for resistance?

Why should they listen?

- Why are these changes of value to the organization?
- Are the changes connected with employee, stockholder, and/or customer satisfaction data/issues? Explain.

Where will you present?

- Where will you be presenting your recommendations?
- Will media equipment be expected in this setting?

When are you most likely to be best received?

- Is there a time in the week or year that you are most likely to be heard fully?
- Is there a time in the day when the person(s) you present your ideas to is most receptive?

How does this organization define an effective presentation?

- How have successful recommendations been presented?
- Formats used? Audiences? Time length?
- Other audience expectations?

Action Plan:

1. Review your responses to each of the above questions.
2. Write/rewrite at least two of your formal organization-wide applications, in single-sentence, positively worded statements.

_____

_____

_____

_____

_____

_____

3. Write down the date(s), place(s), and person(s) important to implementing
   these goals.

   Date: Place: Contact Names:

   _____   _____   _____

   _____   _____   _____

   _____   _____   _____

   _____   _____   _____

   _____   _____   _____

   _____   _____   _____

   _____   _____   _____

   _____   _____   _____

References

Adams, S. (1996). *The Dilbert principle*. New York: HarperCollins.

Allen, B. J. (1995). Diversity and organizational communication. *Journal of Applied Communication Research, 23,* 143–155. doi:10.1080/00909889509365420

Alvesson, M. (2002). *Understanding organizational culture*. Thousand Oaks, CA: Sage.

Amason, P., Allen, M., & Holmes, S. (1999). Social support and acculturation stress in the multicultural workplace. *Journal of Applied Communication Research, 27,* 310–334. doi:10.1080/00909889909365543

Anderson, S., Cavanagh, J., Collins, C., Pizzigati, S., & Laptham, M. (2008, August 25). *Executive excess 2008: How average taxpayers subsidize runaway pay—15th Annual CEO Compensation Survey*. Retrieved December 21, 2009, from http://faireconomy.org/executive_excess_reports

Auer-Rizzi, W., & Berry, M. (2000). Business vs. cultural frames of reference in group decision making: Interactions among Austrian, Finnish, and Swedish business students. *Journal of Business Communication, 37,* 264–288. doi:10.1177/002194360003700304

Autry, J. (1991). *Love and profit: The art of caring leadership*. New York: Avon.

Axley, S. (1984). Managerial and organizational communication in terms of the conduit metaphor. *Academy of Management Review, 9,* 428–437. doi:10.2307/258283

Babbie, E. (2001). *The practice of social research* (9th ed.). Belmont, CA: Wadsworth.

Baker, K. A., & Branch, K. M. (2002). Concepts underlying organizational effectiveness: Trends in the organization and management science literature. In E. L. Malone, K. M. Branch, & K. A. Baker (Eds.), *Managing science as a public good: Overseeing publicly-funded science*. Unpublished manuscript.

Barge, J. K. (2004). Antenarrative and managerial practice. *Communication Studies, 55*(1), 106–127.

Barge, J. K., Lee, M., Maddux, K., Nabring, R., & Townsend, B. (2008). Managing dualities in planned change initiatives. *Journal of Applied Communication Research, 36,* 364–390. doi:10.1080/00909880802129996

Barrett, W. (1979). *The illusion of technique*. Garden City, NY: Anchor.

Bennis, W. (1986). *Leaders and culture: Orchestrating the organizational culture*. New York: The Conference Board.

Benoit, W. L. (1995). *Accounts, excuses and apologies: A theory of image restoration strategies*. Albany: State University of New York Press.

Benoit-Barné, C. (2007). Socio-technical deliberation about free and open source software: Accounting for the status of artifacts in public life. *Quarterly Journal of Speech, 93*(2), 211–235. doi:10.1080/00335630701426751

Berger, P. L., & Luckmann, T. (1966). *The social construction of reality: A treatise in the sociology of knowledge*. Garden City, NY: Anchor Books.

Bisel, R. S., Ford, D., & Keyton, J. (2007). Unobtrusive control in a leadership organization: Integrating control and resistance. *Western Journal of Communication, 71,* 136–158. doi:10.1080/10570310701368039

Boje, D. M., Luhman, J. T., & Cunliffe, A. L. (2003). A dialectical perspective on the organization theatre metaphor. *American Communication Journal, 6*. Retrieved from http://www.acjournal.org/holdings/v016/iss2/articles/boje.pdf

Bolman, L., & Deal, T. (2008). *Reframing organizations* (4th ed.). San Francisco: Jossey-Bass.

Bormann, E. (1969). *Interpersonal communication in the modern organization*. Englewood Cliffs, NJ: Prentice Hall.

Bostdorff, D. (2009). Judgment, experience, and leadership: Candidate debates on the Iraq War in the 2008 presidential primaries. *Rhetoric & Public Affairs, 12*(2), 223–277. Retrieved from Academic Search Complete database.

Brenton, A. (1993). Demystifying the magic of language: Critical linguistic case analysis of legitimization of authority. *Journal of Applied Communication Research, 21,* 227–244. doi:10.1080/00909889309365369

Bridges, W. (1991). *Managing transitions: Making the most of change*. Reading, MA: Perseus.

Brown, M. H. (1990). Defining stories in organizations: Characteristics and functions. In J. A. Anderson (Ed.), *Communication yearbook, 13* (pp. 162–190). Newbury Park, CA: Sage.

Bryman, A. (1996). Leadership in organizations. In S. R. Clegg, C. Hardy, & W. R. Nord (Eds.), *Handbook of organization studies* (pp. 276–292). Thousand Oaks, CA: Sage.

Burke, K. (1972). *Dramatism and development*. Barre, MA: Clark University Press.

Chao, J. T., Waltz, P. M., & Gardner, P. H. (1992). Formal and informal mentorships: A comparison of mentoring functions and contrast with nonmentored counterparts. *Personnel Psychology, 45*, 619–636.

China rights. (2010, January 25). China rights groups hit by cyberattacks, activists say. Retrieved from http://www.totaltele.com/view.aspx?ID=452382

Clair, R. P. (1993). The use of framing devices to sequester organizational narratives: Hegemony and harassment. *Communication Monographs, 60*, 113–136. doi:10.1080/03637759309376304

Clair, R. P. (1998). *Organizing silence: A world of possibilities*. Albany: State University of New York Press.

Cleveland, J. N., Stockdale, M., & Murphy, K. R. (2000). *Women and men in organizations*. Mahwah, NJ: Lawrence Erlbaum.

Collins, J. (2001). *Good to great: Why some companies make the leap and others don't*. New York: HarperCollins.

Columbia Business School. (n.d.). *Aaron Feuerstein and Washington SyCip (MS '43) Receive 1996 Botwinick Prizes for Ethics*. Retrieved January 23, 2010, from http://www.columbia.edu/cu/record/archives/vol22/vol22_iss3/Feuerstein_SyCip_Botwinick.html

Condon, J. (1997). *Good neighbors: Communicating with the Mexicans* (2nd ed.). Yarmouth, ME: Intercultural Press.

Conquergood, D. (1991). Rethinking ethnography: Towards a critical cultural politics. *Communication Monographs, 58*, 179–194. doi:10.1080/03637759109376222

Conrad, C., & Poole, S. M. (1998). *Strategic organizational communication: Into the twenty-first century* (4th ed.). Fort Worth, TX: Harcourt Brace College.

Cotton, J. L. (1995, May). *Protegee outcomes from formal and informal mentoring*. Paper presented at the annual meeting of the Society for Industrial and Organizational Psychology, Orlando, FL.

Cox, T. H., Jr. (1993). Becoming a multi-cultural organization. In *Cultural diversity in organizations: Theory, research and practice*. San Francisco: Berrett-Koehler.

Crandall, N., & Wooton, L. (1978). Development strategies of organizational productivity. *California Management Review, 21*, 37–46.

Creative Class Community Initiatives. (n.d.). Retrieved from http://www.creativeclass.com/creative_class_communities

Croucher, S., Long, B., Meredith, M., Oommen, D., & Steele, E. (2009). Factors predicting organizational identification with intercollegiate forensics teams. *Communication Education, 58*, 74–91. doi:10.1080/0363452080245052

Culture Strategy Fit. (2010). *Culture by design, not default: Changing corporate organizational culture*. Retrieved from http://www.culturestrategyfit.com

Davis, S. M. (1984). *Managing corporate culture*. Cambridge, MA: Ballinger.

Deal, T., & Kennedy, A. (1982). *Corporate cultures*. New York: Addison-Wesley.

Deal, T., & Kennedy, A. (2000). *Corporate culture: The rites and rituals of organizational life* (Reissued). Cambridge, MA: Perseus.

Deetz, S. (1991). *Democracy in an age of corporate colonization*. Albany: State University of New York Press.

Deetz, S., Tracy, S., & Simpson, J. (2000). *Leading organizations through transition: Communication and cultural change*. Thousand Oaks, CA: Sage.

Denison Consulting. (n.d.). Retrieved from http://www.denisonconsulting.com

DeYmaz, M. (2007). *Building a healthy multi-ethnic church*. San Francisco: Jossey-Bass.

Dodd, C. (1998). *Intercultural communication*. Dubuque, IA: McGraw-Hill.

Downs, C., & Adrian, A. (2004). *Assessing organizational communication*. New York: Guilford.

Driskill, G. (1995). Managing cultural differences: A rules analysis in a bi-cultural organization. *Howard Journal of Communications, 5*, 353–379.

Driskill, G., Arjanakova, S., & Schneider, T. (2010). Assessing intercultural communication: Models and methods. In P. Backlund & G. Whitfield (Eds.), *An assessment primer: The role of assessment in the life of a communication department*. Washington, DC: National Communication Association.

Driskill, G., & Camp, J. (2006). The Nehemiah Project: A case study of the unity movement among Christian church organizations in Central Arkansas. *Journal of Communication and Religion, 29*, 445–483.

Driskill, G., & Downs, C. (1995). Hidden differences in competent communication: A case study of Asian Indians in a bi-national organization. *International Journal of Intercultural Relations, 19*, 505–522. doi:10.1016/0147-1767(95)00031-3

Driskill, G., & Meyer, J. (1994, November). *Communication theory and action research in the daycare organization.* Presented to the Speech Communication Association, New Orleans, LA.

Driskill, G., & Meyer, J. (1996a, November). *Communication patterns in the day care organization: An application of the coordinated management of meaning.* Paper presented to the Speech Communication Association, San Diego, CA.

Driskill, G., & Meyer, J. (1996b, November). *Participant observation methods for communication consultation with day care workers: A case study.* Paper presented to the Speech Communication Association, San Diego, CA.

Eblen, A., & Eblen, J. (1987). *A sense of place: Setting as symbol in an organizational culture.* Paper presented at the annual meeting of the Speech Communication Association, Boston.

Edwards, A. P., & Shepherd, G. J. (2004). Theories of communication, human nature, and the world: Associations and implications. *Communication Studies, 55,* pp. 197–208.

Eisenberg, E. (1984). Ambiguity as strategy in organizational communication. *Communication Monographs, 51,* 227–242. doi:10.1080/03637758409390197

Eisenberg, E., Andrews, L., Murphy, A., & Laine-Timmerman, L. (1999). Transforming organizations through communication. In P. Salem (Ed.), *Organizational communication and change* (pp. 125–147). Cresskill, NJ: Hampton Press.

Eisenberg, E., Goodall, H., & Trethewey, A. (2010). *Organizational communication: Balancing creativity and constraint* (6th ed.). New York: St. Martin's.

Eisenberg, E., & Riley, P. (2001). Organizational culture. In F. M. Jablin & L. L. Putnam (Eds.), *The new handbook of organizational communication* (pp. 291–322). Thousand Oaks, CA: Sage.

Elkington, J. (1998). *Cannibals with forks.* Gabriola Island, BC, Canada: New Society Publishers.

Emerson, M. (2006). *People of the dream: Multiracial congregations in the United States.* Princeton, NJ: Princeton University Press.

Fairhurst, G. T. (2008). Discursive leadership: A communication alternative to leadership psychology. *Management Communication Quarterly, 21,* 510–521. doi:10.1177/0893318907313714

Fairhurst, G. T., & Sarr, R. (1996). *The art of framing: Managing the language of leadership.* San Francisco: Jossey-Bass.

Fisher, W. (1987). *Human communication as narration: Toward a philosophy of reason, value, and action.* Columbia: University of South Carolina Press.

Florida, R. (2002). *The rise of the creative class and how it's transforming work, leisure, community, and everyday life.* New York: Basic Books.

Florida, R., & Davison, D. (2001). Gaining from green management: Environmental management systems inside and outside the factory. *Harvard Business Review, 43*(3), 64–84.

Forbes, D. A. (2002). Internalized masculinity and women's discourse: A critical analysis of the (re)production of masculinity in organizations. *Communication Quarterly, 50,* 269–291.

Ford, J. D., & Ford, L. W. (1995). The role of conversations in producing intentional change in organizations. *Academy of Management Review, 20,* 541–570. doi:10.2307/258787

Fowler, R. (1986). *Linguistic criticism.* Oxford, UK: Oxford University Press.

Frederick, W. (1995). *Values, nature, and culture in the American corporation.* New York: Oxford University Press.

Friedman, T. (2005). *The world is flat: A brief history of the 21st century.* New York: Farrar, Straus & Giroux.

Frost, P., Moore, L., Louis, M., Lundberg, C., & Martin, J. (1985). *Organizational culture.* Beverly Hills, CA: Sage.

Gardner, J. (1990). *On leadership.* New York: Free Press.

Garner, J. (2006). Masters of the universe? Resource dependency and interorganizational power relationships at NASA. *Journal of Applied Communication Research, 34,* 368–385. doi:10.1080/00909880600911249

Geertz, C. (1973). *The interpretation of cultures.* New York: Basic Books.

Giddens, A. (1979). *Central problems in social theory.* London: Macmillan.

Gladwell, M. (2008). *Outliers: The story of success.* New York: Little, Brown.

Glaser, S. R., Zamanou, S., & Hacker, K. F. (1987). Measuring and interpreting organizational culture. *Management Communication Quarterly, 1,* 173–198. doi:10.1177/0893318987001002003

Goffman, E. (1959). *The presentation of self in everyday life.* Hammondsworth, UK: Penguin Books.

Goffman, E. (1974). *Frame analysis.* New York: Harper Books.

Goodall, H. L. (1989). *Casing a promised land.* Carbondale: Southern Illinois University Press.

Goodpaster, K. E. (2007). *Conscience and corporate culture.* Malden, MA: Blackwell.

Grimes, D. S., & Richard, O. C. (2003). Could communication form impact organizations' experience with diversity? *Journal of Business Communication, 40,* 7–27. doi:10.1177/002194360304000102

Harre, H., & Secord, P. F. (1973). *The explanation of social behavior.* Totowa, NJ: Littlefield, Adams.

Harris, L. (1979). *Communication competence: Empirical tests of a systematic model.* Unpublished doctoral dissertation, University of Massachusetts, Amherst.

Hart, R. (2000). *Diction 5.0* [Computer software]. Thousand Oaks, CA: Sage.

Harter, L. M. (2009). Narratives as dialogic, contested, and aesthetic performances. *Journal of Applied Communication Research, 37*(2), 140–150. doi:10.1080/00909880902792255

Harter, L. M., Scott, J., Novak, D., Leeman, M., & Morris, J. (2006). Freedom through flight: Performing a counter-narrative of disability. *Journal of Applied Communication Research, 34,* 3–29. doi:10.1080/00909880500420192

Harter, L. M., Stephens, R. J., & Japp, P. M. (2000). President Clinton's apology for the Tuskegee syphilis experiment: A narrative of remembrance, redefinition, and reconciliation. *Howard Journal of Communications, 11,* 19–35.

Hays-Thomas, R. (2004). Why now? The contemporary focus on managing diversity. In M. S. Stockdale & F. J. Crosby (Eds.), *The psychology and management of workplace diversity*. Malden, MA: Blackwell.

Helmreich, R., & Merritt, A. (2000). Culture in the cockpit: Do Hofstede's dimensions replicate? *Journal of Cross Cultural Psychology, 31,* 283–301. doi:10.1177/0022022100031003001

Hofstede, G. (2003). *Culture's consequences: Comparing values, behaviors, institutions and organizations across nations*. Thousand Oaks, CA: Sage.

Hofstede, G. (2009). American culture and the 2008 financial crisis. *European Business Review, 21,* 307–312. doi:10.1108/09555340910970418

Hofstede, G. (n.d.). *Cultural dimensions*. Retrieved from http://www.geert-hofstede.com/hofstede_dimensions.php

Hofstede, G., & Hofstede, G.-J. (2004). *Cultures and organizations: Software of the mind*. New York: McGraw-Hill.

Hofstede, G., Van Deusen, C., Mueller, C., Charles, T., & The Business Goals Network. (2002). What goals do business leaders pursue? A study in fifteen countries. *Journal of International Business Studies, 33,* 785–803, doi:10.1057/palgrave.jibs.8491044

Holger, R., Gross, M., Hartman, J., & Cunliffe, A. (2008). Meaning in organizational communication: Why metaphor is the cake, not the icing. *Management Communication Quarterly, 21,* 393–412. doi:10.1177/0893318907309929

Holmes, M. (1988, November). *Depth-interpretation of organizational memorandum*. Paper presented at the annual meeting of the Speech Communication Association, Boston.

Holvino, E. (1998). *The multicultural organizational development model* [Unpublished training materials]. Brattleboro, VT: Chaos Management.

Holvino, E., Ferdman, B. M., & Merrill-Sands, D. (2004). Creating and sustaining diversity and inclusion in organizations: Strategies and approaches. In M. S. Stockdale & F. J. Crosby (Eds.), *The psychology and management of workplace diversity*. Malden, MA: Blackwell.

Huselid, M. A. (1995). The impact of human resource management practices on turnover, productivity, and corporate financial performance. *Academy of Management Journal, 38,* 635–672.

Interface. (n.d.-a). *Interface's values are our guiding principles*. Retrieved from http://www.interfaceglobal.com/Company/Mission-Vision.aspx

Interface. (n.d.-b). *Philanthropy and community partnerships*. Retrieved from http://www.interfaceglobal.com/Sustainability/Social-Responsibility/Philanthropy—Community-Partnerships.aspx

Islam, G., & Zyphur, M. (2009). Rituals in organizations: A review and expansion of current theory. *Group & Organization Management, 34,* 114–139. doi:10.1177/1059601108329717

Jabs, L. B. (2005). Communication rules and organizational decision-making. *Journal of Business Communication, 42,* 265–288. doi:10.1177/0021943605277008

Jameson, D. A. (2001). Narrative discourse and management action. *Journal of Business Communication, 38,* 476–511. doi:10.1177/002194360103800404

Jameson, D. A. (2007). Reconceptualizing cultural identity and its role in intercultural business communication. *Journal of Business Communication, 44,* 199–235. doi:10.1177/0021943607301346

Jian, G. (2007). "Omega is a four-letter word": Toward a tension-centered model of resistance to information and communication technologies. *Communication Monographs, 74,* 5–28. doi:10.1080/03637750701716602

Jung, C. (1964). *Man and his symbols*. London: Aldus Books.

Kanter, R. M. (1977). *Men and women of the corporation*. New York: Basic Books.

Keyton, J. (2005). *Communication and organizational culture*. Thousand Oaks, CA: Sage.

Keyton, J., & Menzie, K. (2007). Sexually harassing messages: Decoding workplace conversation. *Communication Studies, 58,* 87–103.

Kimoto, D. (2007). Giving voice to culture: Stories of change. *International Journal of Diversity, 6*(5), 37–45.

Kirby, E., & Krone, K. (2002). "The policy exists but you can't really use it": Communication and the structuration of work-family policies. *Journal of Applied Communication Research, 30,* 50–77. doi:10.1080/00909880216577

Kirkwood, W. (1983). Story-telling and self-confrontation: Parables as communication strategies. *Quarterly Journal of Speech, 69,* 56–74. doi:10.1080/00335638309383635

Kirkwood, W. (1985). Parables as metaphors and examples. *Quarterly Journal of Speech, 71,* 422–440. doi:10.1080/00335638509383746

Kirkwood, W. (1992). Narrative and the rhetoric of possibility. *Communication Monographs, 59,* 30–47. doi:10.1080/03637759209376247

Kirschbaum, K. (2009, October 10). Germany criticizes Google for copyright infringement. *Reuters.* Retrieved from http://www.reuters.com/article/idUSTRE5991L120091010

Knoten, T. (1999). The Foreign Corrupt Practices Act: Practicable considerations for U.S. corporations. *Journal of the Missouri Bar, 55*(1). Retrieved January 21, 2004, from http://mobar.org/journal/1999/janfeb/knoten.htm

Kotter, J. P. (1995, March–April). Leading change: Why transformation efforts fail. *Harvard Business Review,* pp. 59–67.

Kotter, J. P. (2002). *The heart of change.* Boston: Harvard Business School Press.

Kotter, J. P., & Heskett, J. (1992). *Corporate culture and performance.* New York: Macmillan.

Kouzes, J. M., & Posner, B. Z. (2003). *Academic administrators guide to exemplary leadership.* San Francisco: Jossey-Bass.

Kramer, M., & Noland, T. (1999). Communication during job promotions: A case of ongoing assimilation. *Journal of Applied Communication Research, 27*(4), 335–355. doi:10.1080/00909889909365544

Kreps, G. I. (1983). Using interpretive research: Development of a socialization program at RCA. In L. Putnam & M. Pacanowsky (Eds.), *Communication and organizations: An interpretive approach* (pp. 243–254). Beverly Hills, CA: Sage.

Kuhn, T., & Corman, S. R. (2003). The emergence of homogeneity and heterogeneity in knowledge structures during a planned organizational change. *Communication Monographs, 70,* 198–229. doi:10.1080/0363775032000167406

Kunda, G. (1993). *Engineering culture: Control and commitment in a high-tech corporation.* Philadelphia: Temple University Press.

Laird, A. (1982). *An investigation of communication rules and productivity in three organizations.* Unpublished doctoral dissertation, University of Kansas.

Langer, E. (1989). *Mindfulness.* Cambridge, MA: Perseus Books.

Lauring, J. (2007). Obstacles to innovative interaction: Communication management in culturally diverse organizations. *Journal of Intercultural Communication, 15.* Retrieved from http://www.immi.se/intercultural/nr15/lauring.htm

Levi-Strauss, C. (1967). *The scope of anthropology.* New York: Jonathan Cape.

Livesey, S., Hartman, C., Stafford, E., & Shearer, M. (2009). Performing sustainable development through eco-collaboration. *Journal of Business Communication, 46,* 423–454. doi:10.1177/0021943609338664

Louis, M. R. (1985). Perspectives on organizational culture. In P. J. Frost, L. F. Moore, M. R. Louis, C. C. Lundbert, & J. Martin (Eds.), *Organizational culture.* Newbury Park, CA: Sage.

Lyon, A. (2007). "Putting patients first": Systematically distorted communication and Merck's marketing of Vioxx. *Journal of Applied Communication Research, 35,* 376–398. doi:10.1080/00909880701611052

Lyon, A. (2008). The mis/recognition of Enron executives' competence as cultural and social capital. *Communication Studies, 59,* 371–387.

Lyon, A., & Ulmer, R. R. (2010). Ethics in "Big Pharma": Communicating the risks of medicine. In J. Keyton & P. Shockley-Zalabak (Eds.), *Case studies for organizational communication* (3rd ed.). Los Angeles: Roxbury.

Mali, P. (1978). *Improving total productivity.* New York: John Wiley.

Marris, P. (1974). *Loss and change.* New York: Pantheon.

Martin, J. (1992). *Cultures in organizations: Three perspectives.* New York: Oxford University Press.

Martin, J. (2002). *Organizational culture: Mapping the terrain.* Thousand Oaks, CA: Sage.

McKinley, W., & Scherer, A. G. (2000). Some unanticipated consequences of organizational restructuring. *Academy of Management Review, 25,* 735–753. doi:10.2307/259202

Meares, M., Oetzel, J., Torres, A., Derkacs, D., & Ginossar, T. (2004). Employee mistreatment and muted voices in the culturally diverse workplace. *Journal of Applied Communication Research, 32,* 4–27. doi:10.1080/0090988042000178121

Meyer, J. (1995). Tell me a story: Eliciting organizational values from narratives. *Communication Quarterly, 43,* 210–224.

Meyer, J. (1997). Humor in member narratives: Uniting and dividing at work. *Western Journal of Communication, 61,* 188–208.

Meyer, J. (2000). Humor as a double-edged sword: Four functions of humor in communication. *Communication Theory, 10*(3), 310–331. doi:10.1111/j.1468-2885.2000.tb00194.x

Meyer, J. (2009). Unity in response to mystery: Uniting diverse views to plan worship. *Journal of Communication & Religion, 32,* 62–92.

Meyerson, D., & Martin, J. (1987). Cultural change: An integration of three different views. *Journal of Management Studies, 24,* 625–647. doi:10.1111/j.1467-6486.1987.tb00466.x

Miles, M., & Huberman, A. (1984). *Qualitative data analysis: A sourcebook of new methods.* Beverly Hills, CA: Sage.

Miller, V., & Jablin, F. (1991). Information seeking during organizational entry. *Academy of Management Review, 16,* 92–120. doi:10.2307/258608

Mirivel, J., & Tracy, K. (2005). Premeeting talk: An organizationally crucial form of talk. *Research on Language & Social Interaction, 38*(1), 1–34. doi:10.1207/s15327973rlsi3801_1

Moran, R., Harris, P., & Moran, S. (2007). *Managing cultural differences: Global leadership strategies for the 21st century* (7th ed.). Houston, TX: Gulf Professional.

Morgan, C. (2004). *Corporate governance.* Retrieved January 19, 2004, from http://www.acxiom.com/default.aspx?ID=2192&Country_Code=USA

Morgan, G. (1986). *Images of organization.* Newbury Park, CA: Sage.

Morgan, G. (1997). *Images of organization* (2nd ed.). Thousand Oaks, CA: Sage.

Morgan, G. (2007). *Images of organization* (Updated ed.). Thousand Oaks, CA: Sage.

Mumby, D. (1993). *Narrative and social control.* Newbury Park, CA: Sage.

Mumby, D. (1997). The problem of hegemony: Rereading Gramsci for organizational studies. *Western Journal of Communication, 61,* 343–375.

National Pan-Hellenic Council. (2004). Retrieved January 22, 2004, from http://www.nphchq.org/about.htm

National Whistleblowers Center. (n.d.). *Meet the whistleblowers.* Retrieved December 22, 2009, from http://www.whistleblowers.org

Nicotera, A., & Cushman, D. (1992). Organizational ethics: A within-organization view. *Journal of Applied Communication Research, 20,* 437–462. doi:10.1080/00909889209365348

Nonprofits. (n.d.). Retrieved January 22, 2010, from http://www.urban.org/nonprofits/index.cfm

O'Brien, C. (1980). *A rule-based approach to communication within a formal organization: Theory and case study.* Unpublished doctoral dissertation, University of Massachusetts, Amherst.

Office for Human Research Protections. (n.d.). *Belmont report of ethical principles and guidelines for the protection of human subjects of research.* Retrieved from http://www.hhs.gov/ohrp/belmontArchive.html

Olufowote, J. (2006). Rousing and redirecting a sleeping giant: Symbolic convergence theory and complexities in the communicative constitution of collective action. *Management Communication Quarterly, 19,* 451–492. doi:10.1177/0893318905280326

Ouchi, W. (1981). *Theory Z.* Reading, MA: Addison-Wesley.

Pacanowsky, M., & O'Donnell-Trujillo, N. (1982). Communication and organizational cultures. *Western Journal of Speech Communication, 46,* 115–130.

Pacanowsky, M., & O'Donnell-Trujillo, N. (1983). Organizational communication as cultural performance. *Communication Monographs, 50,* 126–147. doi:10.1080/03637758309390158

Papa, M., Singhal, A., & Papa, W. (2006). *Organizing for social change: Dialectic journey of theory and praxis.* New Delhi, India: Sage.

Patel, A., & Reinsch, L. (2003). Companies can apologize: Corporate apologies and legal liability. *Business Communication Quarterly, 66,* 9–25. doi:10.1177/108056990306600103

Pearce, W. (1989). *Communication and the human condition.* Carbondale: Southern Illinois University Press.

Pearce, W. (2007). *Making social worlds: A communication perspective.* Malden, MA: Blackwell.

Pearce, W., & Pearce, K. (2000). Combining passions and abilities: Toward dialogic virtuosity. *Southern Communication Journal, 65*(2), 160–175.

Pearce, W., & Pearce, K. (2004). Taking a communication perspective on dialogue. In R. Anderson, L. Baxter, & K. Cissna (Eds.), *Dialogue: Theorizing difference in communication studies* (pp. 39–56). Thousand Oaks, CA: Sage.

Pedersen, E. (2010). Modelling CSR: How managers understand the responsibilities of business towards society. *Journal of Business Ethics, 91,* 155–166. doi:10.1007/s10551-009-0078-0

Pepper, G. (2008). The physical organization as equivocal message. *Journal of Applied Communication Research, 36,* 318–338. doi:10.1080/00909880802104882

Pepper, G., & Larson, G. (2006). Cultural identity tensions in a post-acquisition organization. *Journal of Applied Communication Research, 34,* 49–71. doi:10.1080/00909880500420267

Peters, T., & Waterman, R. (1982). *In search of excellence.* New York: Harper & Row.

Piaget, J. (1932). *The moral judgment of the child.* London: Routledge & Kegan Paul.

Poole, M. S. (1992). Structuration and the group communication process. In L. Samovar & R. Cathcart (Eds.), *Small group communication: A reader* (6th ed.). Dubuque, IA: William C. Brown.

Poole, M. S., Seibold, D., & McPhee, R. (1986). A structurational approach to theory-building in group decision-making research. In R. Hirokawa & M. Poole (Eds.), *Communication and group decision making.* Newbury Park, CA: Sage.

Prato, L. (2000). Asking the tough questions: Debate over a controversial interview with Pete Rose puts the spotlight on sports journalism. *American Journalism Review, 22,* 78.

Richardson, B., & Taylor, J. (2008). Sexual harassment at the intersection of race and gender: A theoretical model of the sexual harassment experiences of women of color. *Western Journal of Communication, 73,* 248–272.

Rosenfeld, L. B., Richman, J. M., & May, S. K. (2004). Information adequacy, job satisfaction, and organizational culture in a dispersed-network organization. *Journal of Applied Communication Research, 32,* 28–54. doi:10.1080/0090988042000178112

Saffold, G. (1998). Culture traits, strength, and organizational performance: Moving beyond "strong" culture. *Academy of Management Review, 13,* 546–558. doi:10.2307/258374

Saltmarsh, M. (2009, December 18). Google loses in French copyright case. *New York Times.* Retrieved from http://www.nytimes.com/2009/12/19/technology/companies/19google.html?_r=1

Schall, M. (1983). A communication-rules approach to organizational culture. *Administrative Science Quarterly, 28,* 557–581. doi:10.2307/2393009

Schein, E. (1992). *Organizational culture and leadership* (2nd ed.). San Francisco: Jossey-Bass.

Schein, E. H. (1996). Culture: The missing concept in organizational studies. *Administrative Science Quarterly, 41,* 229–240.

Scher, S. J., & Darley, J. M. (1997). How effective are things people say to apologize? Effects of the realization of the apology speech act. *Journal of Psycholinguistic Research, 26,* 127–141. doi:10.1023/A:1025068306386

Scott, C. R., Corman, S. R., & Cheney, G. (1998). Development of a structurational model of identification in the organization. *Communication Theory, 8*(3), 298–336.

Scott, C. W., & Trethewey, A. (2008). Organizational discourse and the appraisal of occupational hazards: Interpretive repertoires, heedful interrelating, and identity at work. *Journal of Applied Communication Research, 36,* 298–317. doi:10.1080/00909880802172137

Seeger, M. W., & Ulmer, R. R. (2001). Virtuous responses to organizational crisis: Aaron Feuerstein and Milt Cole. *Journal of Business Ethics, 31,* 369–376. doi:10.1023/A:1010759319845

Seeger, M. W., & Ulmer, R. (2003). Explaining Enron: Communication and responsible leadership. *Management Communication Quarterly, 17*(1), 58–84. doi:10.1177/0893318903253436

Shafron, A. (2002). *Aaron Feuerstein: Bankrupt and wealthy.* Retrieved January 30, 2010, from http://www.aish.com/ci/be/48881397.html

Shakespeare, W. (1954). *As you like it* (S. Burchell, Ed.). New Haven, CT: Yale University Press.

Shockley-Zalabak, P., & Morley, D. (1994). Creating a culture: A longitudinal examination of the influence on management and employee values on communication rule stability and emergence. *Human Communication Research, 20,* 334–355. doi:10.1111/j.1468-2958.1994.tb00326.x

Sigman, S. J. (1980). On communication rules from a social perspective. *Human Communication Research, 7,* 37–51. doi:10.1111/j.1468-2958.1980.tb00549.x

Singe, P. (1990). *The fifth discipline: The art and practice of the learning organization.* Garden City, NY: Doubleday.

Smircich, L. (1983). Concepts of culture and organizational analysis. *Administrative Science Quarterly, 28,* 339–358. doi:10.2307/2392246

Smith, F., & Keyton, J. (2001). Organizational storytelling: Metaphors for relational power and identity struggles. *Management Communication Quarterly, 15,* 149–183. doi:10.1177/0893318901152001

Smith, R., & Eisenberg, E. (1987). Conflict at Disneyland: A root-metaphor analysis. *Communication Monographs, 54,* 365–380. doi:10.1080/03637758709390239

Stablien, R., & Nord, W. (1985). Practical and emancipatory interests in organizational symbolism: A review and evaluation. *Journal of Management, 11,* 13–28. doi:10.1177/014920638501100203

Steers, R. (1977). *Organizational effectiveness: A behavioral view.* Santa Monica, CA: Goodyear.

Stephens, K., & Davis, J. (2009). The social influences on electronic multitasking in organizational meetings. *Management Communication Quarterly, 23,* 63–83. doi:10.1177/0893318909335417

Stohl, C. (2001). Globalizing organizational communication. In F. Jablin & L. Putnam (Eds.), *The new handbook of organizational communication* (pp. 323–375). Thousand Oaks, CA: Sage.

Strasberg, L. (1987). *A dream of passion: The development of the method.* Boston: Little, Brown.

Strauss, A., & Corbin, J. (1990). *Basics of qualitative research: Grounded theory procedures and techniques.* Thousand Oaks, CA: Sage.

Sugimoto, N. (1997). A Japan–U.S. comparison of apology styles. *Communication Research, 24,* 349–370.

Tapscott, D. (2009). *Grown up digital: How the net generation is changing your world.* New York: McGraw-Hill.

Thomas, R. R. (1996). *Redefining diversity.* New York: American Management Association.

Tompkins, P. K., & Cheney, G. (1985). Communication and unobtrusive control in contemporary organizations. In R. D. McPhee & P. K. Tompkins (Eds.), *Organizational communication: Traditional themes and new directions.* Newbury Park, CA: Sage.

Toor, S. R., & Ofori, G. (2009). Ethical leadership: Examining the relationships with full range leadership model, employee outcomes, and organizational culture. *Journal of Business Ethics, 90*(4), 533–547. doi:10.1007/s10551-009-0059-3

Tracy, S. (2004). Dialectic, contradiction, or double bind? Analyzing and theorizing employee reactions to organizational tension. *Journal of Applied Communication Research, 32,* 119–146. doi:10.1080/0090988042000210025

Tracy, S., Lutgen-Sandvik, P., & Alberts, J. (2006). Nightmares, demons, and slaves: Exploring the painful metaphors of workplace bullying. *Management Communication Quarterly, 20,* 148–185. doi:10.1177/0893318906291980

Trice, H. M., & Beyer, J. (1984). Studying organizational cultures through rites and ceremonials. *Academy of Management Review, 9,* 653–669. doi:10.2307/258488

Trice, H. M., & Beyer, J. (1985). Using six organizational rites to change cultures. In R. H. Kilmann, M. J. Saxton, & R. Serpa (Eds.), *Gaining control of the corporate culture* (pp. 370–399). San Francisco: Jossey-Bass.

Trice, H. M., & Beyer, J. (1993). *The cultures of work organizations.* Englewood Cliffs, NJ: Prentice Hall.

Ulmer, R. R. (2001). Effective crises management through established stakeholder relationships. *Management Communication Quarterly, 14*(4), 590–615. doi:10.1177/0893318901144003

Ulmer, R. R., & Sellnow, T. L. (1997). Strategic ambiguity and the ethic of significant choice in the tobacco industry's crisis communication. *Communication Studies, 48,* 215–233.

Ulmer, R. R., & Sellnow, T. L. (2000). Consistent questions of ambiguity in organizational crisis communication: Jack in the Box as a case study. *Journal of Business Ethics, 25,* 143–155. doi:10.1023/A:1006183805499

Ulmer, R. R., Sellnow, T. L., & Seeger, M. W. (2009). Post-crisis communication and renewal: Understanding the potential for positive outcomes in crisis communication. In R. Heath & D. O'Hair (Eds.), *Handbook of risk and crisis communication.* New York: Routledge.

Ulmer, R. R., Sellnow, T. L., & Seeger, M. W. (2011). *Effective crisis communication: Moving from crisis to opportunity* (2nd ed.). Thousand Oaks, CA: Sage.

U.S. Census Bureau. (n.d.). *Population profile of the United States.* Retrieved from http://www.census.gov/population/www/pop-profile/natproj.html

Van Maanan, J. (1979). Reclaiming qualitative methods for organizational research. *Administrative Science Quarterly, 24,* 520–526.

Varner, I., & Beamer, L. (1995). *Intercultural communication in the global workplace.* Chicago: Irwin.

Vineberg, S. (1991). *Method actors: Three generations of an American acting style.* New York: Schirmer Books.

Wasson, C. (2004). The paradoxical language of enterprise. *Critical Discourse Studies, 1*(2), 175–199. doi:10.1080/1740590042000302067

Weaver, G. (2001). Ethics programs in global businesses: Culture's role in managing ethics. *Journal of Business Ethics, 30*(1), 3–15. doi:10.1023/A:1006475223493

Weick, K. E. (1979). *The social psychology of organizing* (2nd ed.). Reading, MA: Addison-Wesley.

Weick, K. E. (1995). *Sensemaking in organizations.* Thousand Oaks, CA: Sage.

West, M., & Carey, C. (2006). (Re)enacting frontier justice: The Bush administration's tactical narration of the Old West fantasy after September 11. *Quarterly Journal of Speech, 92,* 379–412. doi:10.1080/00335630601076326

Whyte, D. (1994). *The heart aroused: Poetry and the preservation of the soul in corporate America.* New York: Doubleday.

Zak, M. W. (1994). It's like a prison in there. *Journal of Business and Technical Communication, 8,* 282–298.

Index

About the Authors

Gerald W. Driskill is Professor of Speech Communication and Graduate Program Coordinator at the University of Arkansas at Little Rock. He has taught graduate classes in Organizational Culture, Intercultural Communication, Organizational Development, and Communication Theory at UALR since 1990. He previously taught Managerial Communication in Bangkok, Thailand, and has published a number of organizational communication articles, including ethnographic research in a multinational engineering firm and in a day care organization. He has served as president of the local chapter of ASTD (American Society for Training and Development). This workbook grew from a framework for cultural analysis created by Angela Brenton. They both received positive feedback from midlevel managers and others in the ASTD network who used the course material in their organizations.

He continues to teach in the areas of organizational and intercultural communication. On campus he takes a lead role in internationalizing the curriculum. His work in this arena led to an invitation from Heifer International to develop intercultural training. He has also conducted intercultural training for students from Pakistan as part of a USAID grant. His current participant–observer research focuses on communication and unity among religious, nonprofit, and government organizations engaged in community building. This research provides a window into issues relevant to leaders creating a culture of community mindedness within their organizations.

Gerald has been married to his wife, Angela, for 18 years, and they have two children, Eli, 11, and Abigail, 9.

Angela Laird Brenton is Dean of the College of Professional Studies at the University of Arkansas at Little Rock. She has taught graduate classes in Organizational Culture since 1982 at UALR, Pepperdine University, Abilene Christian University, and Missouri State University. She has published a number of articles about using qualitative research methods to study organizational communication—from critical linguistic analysis of organizational texts to analysis of organizational identification. She collaborated on the workbook with Gerald Driskill using materials she has developed over the years of teaching and consulting in the areas of organizational culture.

With her current administrative duties as dean of a seven-department college, she teaches primarily in the area of conflict analysis and mediation and plans future writing projects in that field. She is particularly interested in conflict analysis in religious and nonprofit organizations, as well as developing consensus in public policy disputes. She was a founding faculty member of the Clinton School of Public Service, associated with the Clinton Presidential Library in Little Rock. She is also an adjunct faculty member at the Straus Institute for Dispute Resolution at Pepperdine University School of Law and in the Dispute Resolution program at Southern Methodist University. She recently taught a class for SMU in Dublin, Ireland, focusing on dispute resolution in Northern Ireland. Her recent consulting work has focused on facilitating large multiparty disputes, facilitating strategic planning for juvenile justice reform in Arkansas, and training on influence strategies in organizations.

Angi has been married to her husband, Keith, for 20 years, and they have two children, Matt, 17, and Laura, 14.

Supporting researchers for more than 40 years

Research methods have always been at the core of SAGE's publishing program. Founder Sara Miller McCune published SAGE's first methods book, *Public Policy Evaluation*, in 1970. Soon after, she launched the *Quantitative Applications in the Social Sciences* series—affectionately known as the "little green books."

Always at the forefront of developing and supporting new approaches in methods, SAGE published early groundbreaking texts and journals in the fields of qualitative methods and evaluation.

Today, more than 40 years and two million little green books later, SAGE continues to push the boundaries with a growing list of more than 1,200 research methods books, journals, and reference works across the social, behavioral, and health sciences. Its imprints—Pine Forge Press, home of innovative textbooks in sociology, and Corwin, publisher of PreK–12 resources for teachers and administrators—broaden SAGE's range of offerings in methods. SAGE further extended its impact in 2008 when it acquired CQ Press and its best-selling and highly respected political science research methods list.

From qualitative, quantitative, and mixed methods to evaluation, SAGE is the essential resource for academics and practitioners looking for the latest methods by leading scholars.

For more information, visit **www.sagepub.com**.